KARL POPPER

The Arguments of
the Philosophers

EDITOR: TED HONDERICH

Reader in Philosophy, University College London

The group of books of which this is one will include an essentially analytic and critical account of each of the considerable number of the great and the influential philosophers. The group of books taken together will comprise a contemporary assessment and history of the entire course of philosophical thought.

Already published in the series

Plato J. C. B. Gosling

Meinong Reinhardt Grossman

Santayana Timothy L. S. Sprigge

Wittgenstein R. J. Fogelin

Hume B. Stroud

Descartes Margaret Dauler Wilson

Berkeley George Pitcher

Kant Ralph Walker

The Presocratic Philosophers (2 vols) Jonathan Barnes

Russell Mark Sainsbury

Socrates Gerasimos Xenophon Santas

KARL POPPER

Anthony O'Hear

Department of Philosophy
University of Surrey

Routledge & Kegan Paul
London, Boston and Henley

For Tricia

First published in 1980
by Routledge & Kegan Paul Ltd
39 Store Street London WC1E 7DD,
9 Park Street Boston Mass. 02108 USA and
Broadway House Newtown Road
Henley-on-Thames Oxon RG9 1EN
Set in Monotype Garamond 11 on 12 pt by
Ronset Ltd Darwen Lancs.
and printed in Great Britain by
Unwin Brothers Ltd
Old Woking Surrey
© *Anthony O'Hear 1980*

British Library Cataloguing in Publication Data

O'Hear, Anthony
Karl Popper. – (The arguments of the philosophers).
1. Popper, Sir Karl Raimund
I. Series
192   B1649.P64   79 41631
ISBN 0 7100 0359 5

Contents

Introduction

In this book, I attempt to give a critical account of the main philosophical positions taken up by Sir Karl Popper in his published
writings.

In chapters I to V, I consider his views on the nature of knowledge,
how it relates to experience and how it is developed in science in a
systematic way. What he says here forms the basis from which he moves
both into more specialized questions in science and into general questions relating to society and human nature. For Popper, the Socrates
of ignorance is the prime example of a man imbued with the scientific
spirit. Popper's epistemology is deeply sceptical, involving rejection
of any claim to certainty or authoritative knowledge. The scientific
attitude for Popper comes to terms with the rejection of certainty, as it
consists above all in criticism and self-criticism. I consider in some
detail Popper's attempt to construct a philosophy of science which,
while avoiding any claim to be able to justify theories, nevertheless
provides an account of science as progressing towards the truth. This
is despite arguing that even observations are theory-laden and so open
to possible refutation in the future. My general strategy in considering
Popper's epistemological views is to question whether his or any other
account of knowledge can do without at least provisionally accepted
and partially justified certainties. I conclude that Popper is in fact
unable to erect a system on a complete rejection of justification in any
form. It may indeed be questioned whether knowing the extent of
one's ignorance is equivalent to adopting thoroughgoing scepticism.

In chapter VI, I consider and reject Popper's attempt to demarcate
science from other activities in terms of falsifiability. At the same time,
I question whether Popper's supposedly realistic account of science is
much different from instrumentalism or whether his fallibilism leaves
him with enough ammunition to launch an effective attack on relativistic

philosophies of science. I suggest how relativism may be avoided on the basis of positions I adopted in criticizing Popper's epistemology.

In chapter VII, Popper's analysis of probability and his adherence to indeterminism are considered. In both these areas, his views are supported by philosophical arguments, although, as I show, these arguments do have a bearing on controversies in physics. However, I do not consider either Popper's technical work on the probability calculus or his views on time and entropy, as what he says on these matters is largely concerned with issues in mathematics and physics respectively, and so is outside the scope of this book.

Chapter VIII deals with Popper's views on rationality and society. He argues that the acceptance of a rational attitude to knowledge and experience is not itself rationally defensible, but requires an irrational choice, possibly an ethical one. His account of society explores the desirability of a critical and rationalistic approach to social policy and is a strong attack on totalitarian attempts to impose uncriticized blueprints on society. Popper appears to regard a desirable society as one in which the members are like members of a scientific community working towards common ends through the criticism and improvement of policies adopted. I criticize his claim that there is no essential difference between a science of the physical world and one of society and indicate consequent shortcomings in the analogy between society as a whole and a community of working scientists.

Chapter IX is a survey of Popper's later siting of his epistemology in a full-blooded theory of nature. He sees his epistemology as showing the operation of the Darwinian biological process of trial-and-error elimination in the realm of conscious knowledge. Human knowledge is nevertheless radically discontinuous from lower evolutionary stages, because our minds are seen as working in a Platonic world of abstractly existing ideas and theories, which is not reducible to the world of physical nature or even to the world of conscious mental states. I question the need for such a world to explain human knowledge, and conclude by speculating that, through his Platonism, Popper may be trying to reconcile the radical scepticism of his epistemological views with his commitment to objective knowledge and truth by seeing in their Platonic reality just the sort of transcendent justification for our theories that is so emphatically rejected in his earlier epistemology.

Editions and Abbreviations of Popper's Works

CR   *Conjectures and Refutations*, Routledge & Kegan Paul, London, 1963 (quoted here in the 3rd ed., 1969).

'EP'   'Is There an Epistemological Problem of Perception?', in I. Lakatos and A. Musgrave (eds), *Problems in the Philosophy of Science*, North Holland, Amsterdam, 1968, pp. 163–4.

'IA'   'Intellectual Autobiography', in P. Schilpp (ed.), *The Philosophy of Karl Popper*, 2 vols, Open Court, La Salle, Illinois, 1974, pp. 1–181.

'IQP'   'Indeterminism in Quantum Physics and in Classical Physics', *BJPS*, 1 (1950), pp. 117–33, 173–95.

'LA'   'Logic without Assumptions', *Proceedings of the Aristotelian Society*, 67 (1947), pp. 251–92.

LSD   *The Logic of Scientific Discovery* (German edition, 1934), Hutchinson, London, 1959 (quoted here in the 2nd ed., 1968).

'NSD'   'Normal Science and Its Dangers', I. Lakatos and A. Musgrave (eds), *Criticism and the Growth of Knowledge*, Cambridge University Press, 1970, pp. 51–8.

'NV'   'A Note on Verisimilitude', *BJPS*, 27 (1976), pp. 147–59.

OK   *Objective Knowledge*, Clarendon Press, Oxford, 1972.

OS   *The Open Society and its Enemies*, Routledge & Kegan Paul, London, 1945 (quoted here in the 5th ed., 1966).

'PDR'   'Remarks on the Problems of Demarcation and of Rationality', in I. Lakatos and A. Musgrave (eds), *Problems in the Philosophy of Science*, North Holland, Amsterdam, 1968, pp. 88–102.

PH   *The Poverty of Historicism*, Routledge & Kegan Paul, London, 1957.

'PICP' 'The Propensity Interpretation of the Calculus of Probability, and the Quantum Theory', in S. Körner (ed.), *Observation and Interpretation*, Butterworth Scientific, London, 1957, pp. 65–70.

'PIP' 'The Propensity Interpretation of Probability', *BJPS*, 10 (1959), pp. 25–42.

'PM' 'Probability Magic or Knowledge out of Ignorance', *Dialectica*, 11 (1957), pp. 354–74.

'QM' 'Quantum Mechanics without "The Observer" ', in M. Bunge (ed.), *Quantum Theory and Reality*, Springer, Berlin, 1967, pp. 7–44.

'RC' 'Replies to my Critics', in P. Schilpp (ed.), *The Philosophy of Karl Popper*, 2 vols, Open Court, La Salle, Illinois, 1974, pp. 959–1197.

'RSR' 'The Rationality of Scientific Revolutions', in R. Harré (ed.), *Problems of Scientific Revolution*, Clarendon Press, Oxford, 1975, pp. 72–101.

SB (with J. Eccles), *The Self and Its Brain*, Springer International, Berlin, 1977.

'SR' 'Scientific Reduction and the Essential Incompleteness of All Science', in F. Ayala and T. Dobzhansky (eds), *Studies in the Philosophy of Biology*, Macmillan, London, 1974, pp. 259–84.

'Supp. R' 'Supplementary Remarks (1978)', appendix 2 to the revised edition of *OK*, Clarendon Press, Oxford, 1979.

UQ *Unended Quest*, Fontana Collins, London (this is a reprint, with some changes, of the 'Intellectual Autobiography', 'IA', above).

Acknowledgments

First and foremost, I am deeply grateful to David E. Cooper and Paul Gilbert, both of whom read several drafts of this book, and whose help and advice has been invaluable.

I should also like to thank William Donaldson, Ted Honderich, David Miller and Richard Swinburne for their advice on specific topics, and my colleagues and students at Hull and Surrey for helping me to think about many of the topics tackled in the book.

Finally, I am grateful to Sir Karl Popper and the publishers of his books for permission to reproduce copyright material from *Conjectures and Refutations* (Routledge & Kegan Paul), *The Logic of Scientific Discovery* (Hutchinson), *Objective Knowledge* (Oxford University Press), *The Open Society and its Enemies* (Routledge & Kegan Paul and Princeton University Press), *The Philosophy of Karl Popper*, ed. P. A. Schilpp (Open Court), *The Poverty of Historicism* (Routledge & Kegan Paul) and *Unended Quest* (Fontana Collins). Sir Karl was also good enough to let me see the new edition of *Objective Knowledge* before publication, and I much appreciate this piece of generosity.

A. O'H.

Not the truth in whose possession any man is, or thinks he is, but the honest effort he has made to find out the truth, is what constitutes the worth of a man. For it is not through the possession but through the inquiry after truth that his powers expand, and in this alone consists his ever growing perfection. Possession makes calm, lazy, proud.

Lessing (*Eine Duplik*)

Lessing, the most honest theoretical man, dared to announce that he cared more for the search after truth, than for truth itself, and thus revealed the fundamental secret of science – to the astonishment, and indeed the anger, of the scientific community.

Nietzsche (*Birth of Tragedy*)

He remembered that Goethe had written in an essay on art: 'Man is not a didactic being, but one that lives and acts and influences'. Respectfully he shrugged his shoulders. 'At the most,' he thought, 'only in so far as an actor loses his awareness of the scenery and his make-up and believes acting is really action, is it permissible for man to-day to forget the uncertain background of knowledge on which all his activities depend.'

Musil (*The Man Without Qualities*)

I

Popper's Conception of Epistemology

1 *The central problem of epistemology*

Over the years Popper has given various characterizations of the main problem to be tackled by anyone undertaking a philosophical investigation into knowledge. Thus we read in the text of *The Logic of Scientific Discovery* that 'the main problem of philosophy is the critical analysis of the appeal to the authority of experience' (pp. 51–2), while in the Preface to it (p. 15) we read that 'the central problem of epistemology has always been and still is the problem of the growth of knowledge. And the growth of knowledge can be studied best by studying the growth of scientific knowledge.' Following on from this, in *Conjectures and Refutations* (p. 42) we read that the solution of the problem of demarcation between scientific statements and other types of statement 'is the key to most of the fundamental problems of the philosophy of science', while in *The Philosophy of Karl Popper* ('RC', p. 1061), Popper writes that 'the main task of the theory of human knowledge is to understand it as continuous with animal knowledge; and to understand also its discontinuity – if any – from animal knowledge'. That the tension between these statements is really only one of emphasis is a striking example of the unity of Popper's thought and of its comprehensiveness. This unity emerges if we regard the growth of knowledge as the key. For scientific knowledge is the clearest example we have of knowledge growing. Unlike common sense, which appears static and somewhat conservative except when pushed by science, scientific knowledge makes impressive progress with successions of better theories and new discoveries. If we can understand what is happening here through clearly demarcating science from other activities in order to make clear what is peculiar to science, we shall understand not only how knowledge grows, but, in a curious sense, what knowledge actually is. For, as we shall see, Popper holds that knowledge never starts from firm foundations (this is the *critical* analysis of the appeal to experience) but exists only in so far as one progresses from necessarily uncertain starting points. As in evolution, progress is achieved by weeding out the weakest elements (species or theories) through pressure from the environment. Not only is evolution the best analogy we have of knowledge, but human knowledge is itself a part of the overall process of evolution. Some of its properties are shared by animal knowledge (e.g., the primacy of theories or expectations over observations), but in important respects, particularly in the ability to formulate theories in language and to criticize them, it transcends animal knowledge. In analysing this transcendence, Popper is eventually led to elaborate a theory of an abstract world of theories and problems, and an immaterial human self which interacts with it. The formulation and criticism of theories is, of course, primarily manifested in science. So examining human knowledge in an evolutionary context takes us back to the philosophy of science and the problem of demarcation, to examine the way in which science, as opposed to other disciplines, is tested by and tests experience. Doing this will in turn lead us to a general characterization of rationality, 'because there is nothing more "rational" than the method of critical discussion, which is the method of science' (*OK*, p. 27); this point is made again (*CR*, p. 248) as the thesis that it is 'the *growth* of our knowledge, our way of choosing between theories, in a certain problem situation, which makes science rational'. Having understood the role of the critical method in science, through examining the way knowledge grows in science, we can apply what we have learned to moral and social problems, which brings us to the doctrine of the open society itself, another of Popper's major concerns.

In taking the growth of scientific knowledge as a basic datum we are, in Popper's view, led to far-reaching conclusions about knowledge generally, and about language, evolution and society. These conclusions will not be open to those whose epistemology is confined to the study of common-sense knowledge (or its expression in ordinary language) or to the formalization of scientific language, because they will miss the element of growth which is so striking a feature of scientific knowledge, and from which the conclusions about criticism and rationality follow. An assumption underlying Popper's whole philosophy, then, is that in science we do have a prime example of the growth of knowledge. This must be an assumption on his part because, as his criteria for the growth of knowledge derive *from* his study of science, they cannot be used to justify any claim that in science knowledge grows. I imagine that Popper would hardly be prepared to argue seriously with anyone who denied outright that scientific knowledge has grown over the centuries, because in a perfectly obvious sense it has; one pointer to this growth is the growth in the technology connected with science, though Popper would not necessarily want to rest his claim that science grows on technological achievement, for such a defence would smack of an instrumentalist attitude to knowledge. Clearly, though, scientific knowledge has grown in the sense that the number and diversity of phenomena that have been brought under scientific explanations have constantly increased. However, there might be more difficulty for the view that this obvious growth of scientific knowledge in the western tradition represents any real growth of knowledge. A cultural relativist might be sceptical that our science was in any identifiable sense an improvement on the theories of pre-scientific cultures. At this point we will simply note this possibility, which will be further examined in chapter VI.

Connected with the cultural relativism just alluded to is scepticism as to the ultimate desirability of growth of scientific knowledge. Not only might someone feel that many scientific advances have been misused, and that it would have been better for these not to have been made at all, but epistemological stability might appear preferable to the constant revolutions envisaged by Popper. Epistemological stability would not, however, appear to be an ideal for Popper for two types of reason. The first is epistemological and derives from what we shall see is his deep scepticism (or, as he might prefer, fallibilism). That is, all our theories are uncertain, and so any stability obtained is going to be illusory. Whether Popper's own dash for growth can on his sceptical view be ultimately any less illusory will, however, be open to question. Nevertheless, even given the lack of certainty admitted by Popper to obtain in his epistemology, there remains a moral reason for plumping for growth in knowledge, and that is that it is anti-dogmatic and ultimately leads to a more humane attitude to life and society (*LSD*, p. 38):

> I freely admit that in arriving at my proposals I have been
> guided, in the last analysis, by value judgments and predilections.
> But I hope that my proposals may be acceptable to those who
> value not only logical rigour but also freedom from dogmatism;
> who seek practical applicability, but are even more attracted by
> the adventure of science and by discoveries which again and
> again confront us with new and unexpected questions,
> challenging us to try out new and hitherto undreamed-of
> answers.

This freedom from dogmatism naturally is beneficial not only in the quest for knowledge but equally in society generally. The implications of this and of the opposed dogmatic attitudes to social policy are worked out in *The Open Society and its Eenemies*. Stability of thought in either pure science or social policy would require the acceptance of authorities, and, after rejecting the idea that we have any means of reaching certainty, Popper denies authoritative status either to any particular means of attaining knowledge (such as sensory experience) or to any particular social theorists (such as Plato or Marx).

In saying that we must study science in order to understand the growth of knowledge, Popper immediately comes face to face with a difficulty confronting any philosopher of science, but in a particularly acute way. For, although science does provide us with examples of knowledge growing, not everything scientists do in their scientific work meets with Popper's approval. To put this another way, the criteria for the growth of knowledge which Popper arrives at from the study of science are not always satisfied by scientists, who may break the rules Popper has gleaned from science generally. Popper thus has to say that the scientists concerned either misunderstand what they are really doing or even that they are acting unscientifically, that they are 'bad' scientists. Popper's account of science, then, is prescriptive rather than descriptive. It derives from an idealized account of science, which itself is intended to account for and is based in an examination of just those moments in science when growth has indisputably occurred. Although there can be no quarrel with the idea of a prescriptive account of science, which attempts to show the principles underlying the progressive moments of science, it will be particularly embarrassing for such an account if, as we shall see, growth equally clearly occurs on some occasions when Popper's prescriptions for growth are actually broken. What will be embarrassing here is not that scientists are seen to break the prescriptions, but that they can break them without ceasing to be 'good' scientists, particularly if we can also show the reasons why growth can still occur in these cases.

2 *Initial opposition to justificationism*

That Popper based his prescriptive account of the logic of science on an examination of an important incident in the history of science (to which other important moments were then seen to conform) is made very clear in his own introduction to his work, which forms the first chapter of *Conjectures and Refutations*. Popper argues there in effect that the opposition to justificationism which so characterizes his philosophy stems from the contrast he was thereby enabled to draw between scientific and non-scientific attitudes. For the problem that interested him as a young man in 1919 was that of deciding when a theory should be classed as scientific. From the start, this problem was distinguished from that of discovering the truth, for while science

4

often errs, pseudo-science 'may happen to stumble on the truth'. But what was important about science was that its method was not haphazard in the way pseudo-science was. Science seemed to provide a systematic way of developing and testing theories which, even if untrue, promised real explanations of phenomena. The insight of 1919 was to see that a genuinely scientific explanation differed in a crucial way from the theory and practice of pseudo-science, and it derived from a comparison of the methods of Einstein and his followers with those of Freud, Adler and Marx and their followers.

The Freudians, Adlerians and Marxists who flourished in the Vienna of 1919 were constantly pointing to 'the incessant stream of confirmations, of observations which "verified" the theories in question', while purported counter-evidence was easily explained away by additional theories showing how it really supported rather than told against the doctrines. As a last resort it could be dismissed as deriving from the class bias or psychological repression of its proponent, so even the fact that people were prepared to argue against the theories could be turned to advantage. In fact, reflected Popper, despite the disagreements between the viewpoints of Freud and Adler, it was impossible to think of any human behaviour which could not be interpreted in terms of either theory (CR, p. 35):

> It was precisely this fact – that they always fitted, that they were always confirmed – which in the eyes of their admirers constituted the strongest argument in favour of these theories. It began to dawn on me that this apparent strength was in fact their weakness.

In contrast, Einstein's theory of relativity made a startling and unexpected prediction (that light would be attracted by a heavy body such as the sun, just as material bodies were), and Eddington's expedition of 1919 to South America had been undertaken to see whether the predicted effect could be observed during the total eclipse of the sun (CR, p. 36):

> Now the impressive thing about this case is the *risk* involved in a prediction of this kind. If observation shows that the predicted effect is definitely absent, then the theory is simply refuted. The theory is *incompatible with certain possible results of observation* – in fact with results which everybody before Einstein would have expected. This is quite different from the situation (with the theories of Freud and Adler), when it turned out that the theories in question were compatible with the most divergent human behaviour, so that it was practically impossible to describe any human behaviour that might not be claimed to be a verification of these theories.

It should be mentioned here that Popper's hostile attitude to psycho-analysis has itself been vigorously attacked by Grünbaum (1979). Grünbaum points out, not unfairly, that Popper nowhere shows any places in which Freud or Adler themselves claim the same behaviour as verifications of their competing theories. More importantly, Freud, at least, repeatedly modified, altered and even abandoned theories when they were confronted with counter-evidence. An example is his rejection in 1897 of his earlier view that hysteria was due to seduction in infancy. He also on occasion rejected what might have seemed strong confirming evidence for theories when that evidence was itself suspect (such as the 'memories' of patients) and which, if true, would have had highly implausible consequences. Grünbaum finally shows that there are places where Freud's theories on such central matters as repression, dreaming and even reaction formation are refutable and, in part, actually refuted. However, even if Grünbaum is right about Freud himself, it remains true that many people (including no doubt some followers of Freud) do treat their pet theories in the way Popper is objecting to. From the point of view of an analysis of Popper's philosophy, what will concern us is not so much the correctness of his historical remarks as the distinction he is trying to draw between seeing theories as all-enveloping structures to be 'confirmed' by all possible events and seeing them as open to critical testing in experience, and the success or otherwise Popper has in attempting to account for good scientific practice in terms of the latter viewpoint.

Science has been accused by Wittgenstein (1969, p. 18) of leading us to an obsessive craving for generality, in order to reduce all phenomena in any field to the smallest possible number of natural laws. Popper does not share Wittgenstein's hostility to science or to its methods and he would undoubtedly contest Wittgenstein's assumption that it is an untrammelled craving for generality which is dominant in science. An uncritical tendency to generalize in the shape of a search for parallels, comparisons and proofs to confirm one's theories is for Popper characteristic of pseudo-science rather than of science. Genuine science will never ignore or explain away the particular case. On the contrary, attention to the particular case is of the utmost significance to science, for when science compares what a theory says about a particular case with how the case actually is, it submits to the discipline of experience and it is this submission which, in Popper's view, makes a scientific theory genuinely explanatory.

The contrast between Einstein's theory and the others lies for Popper in the fact that Einstein specifies in advance what will count against it. The irrefutability of the others is, scientifically speaking, a vice not a virtue. The mass of confirming evidence that is taken to be supporting them is of no epistemological significance because the support it offers is quite illusory. If a picture is such that any possible event whatever can be fitted into it, the fact that some actual events 'confirm' it is hardly to be wondered at. Only when a theory excludes some possibilities does it have real explanatory power, for then the mechanisms it sees at work in the world are actually making an impact on the way things are – making them happen this way rather than that. For this reason Popper insists that genuine explanations of natural phenomena should be *independently* testable, that they should make predictions about events other than those that they have been invoked to explain. The contrast is between on the one hand saying that the sea is rough today because Neptune is angry and then that we know Neptune is angry because we see that the sea is rough, and on the other hand that saying the sea is rough today because in certain conditions (such as the force and direction of the wind) the sea is always rough. In the latter case, not only are the conditions themselves independently observable but the connection between the conditions and the result can be independently checked by seeing if the conditions produce on other occasions the effect they are supposed to be causing on this occasion. Contrast this with the situation in popular psychiatry where inferiority complexes can be held just as easily to cause either aggressive or pusillanimous behaviour.

Scientific method is seen by Popper in terms of explanatory theories from which the data to be explained and other as-yet-unknown data can, in certain circumstances, be deduced. Provided that our theories permit deduction of consequences in this way, the terms in which they are framed are unimportant. Precision in a theory does not result from clearly defining the terms of the theory, but from seeing clearly how it can be tested. Popper inveighs constantly against the tendency to move from problems and their attempted solutions through testable theories to what he sees as the trivializing and self-defeating attempt to define the words we use.

This latter tendency (which he calls essentialism) is perhaps more common outside than within science (where workers have a better grasp of what amounts to the solution of a problem), but is harmful wherever it operates. It is trivial because it leads away from the real problem (e.g., how can we best maximize opportunities for under-privileged pupils?) to merely verbal discussion (e.g., what is equality of opportunity?). It is self-defeating because the process of definition can never be brought to an end, so we must always have some un-defined terms. It is harmful because it suggests that by some process of intellectual intuition we can perceive the ultimate essences of things, whereas, as we shall see, Popper admits the finality of no explanation in science or elsewhere. No theories can be verified: all policies have unforeseeable consequences. Moreover, we never reach a point at which we cannot ask for explanations of the solutions we have so far produced. Fruitful theories solve some problems but, characteristically, bring others in their train.

Unfortunately Popper's hostility to essentialism has led him to dismiss all philosophies which he sees as concerned with problems arising from the concepts we use, whether these problems are purely definitional or not. Definitional problems are trivial because defining a term, such as 'length', can neither explain nor lead to any reasonable assessment of the theory of relativity, nor can stipulating what 'equality' means bring about any consensus on social policies. But it does not follow from this that reminding ourselves of what we have forgotten about the use of concepts such as solidity or voluntary action may not be a necessary preparation for considering philosophical theories of matter or freedom. Further, as I shall argue in chapter VIII, our very understanding of, say, maximizing opportunity as a problem and a goal of social policy is not independent of our conceptual framework. Nevertheless, it is clear that providing definitions of terms has little to do with producing explanatory theories in Popper's sense. The essentialism Popper attacks can be seen, along with the desire to frame untestable theories, as a means of avoiding the hard work involved in producing testable theories and testing them.

Popper's initial insight – that genuine explanations prohibit – can be seen as an extension of the familiar doctrine that a genuine empirical assertion is one that excludes some possibilities; the important twist Popper gives is to show the epistemological irrelevance of confirming evidence where a theory fails to forbid any possible state of affairs. So a genuine explanation must have falsifiable consequences. This certainly emerges from the contrast between Einstein's and the other theories. Popper, however, draws two other conclusions from the contrast, which do not follow so obviously, but which take the connection between the falsifiable and the scientific a good deal further. The first is that, if a good theory forbids, a better theory forbids more (CR, p. 36). It is not clear why the fact that a theory has to submit itself to testing means that we should strive for greater and greater falsifiability in our theories, particularly when this is interpreted, as it is by Popper, as implying that we should aim at theories which though consistent with our background knowledge are still highly improbable relative to the evidence we already have (CR, p. 219). The argument from explanatory power does not demand from our theories a reckless outstripping of evidence, nor that we work on the most unlikely theories. There is, however, a reason for working on the most unlikely theories connected with Popper's views on how science grows. That is, he thinks that we are unable ever positively to confirm theories, but only to refute them, and clearly those theories with the highest degree of falsifiability are the most likely to be quickly falsified and disposed of. Also, the more unlikely theories, being the ones which go further beyond what we already know, give us greater opportunities for extending our knowledge in as-yet-unknown areas. The second conclusion which Popper draws erroneously from examination of the Einstein story about Eddington, but which also follows from his views on the confirmation of theories, is that confirming evidence is significant only in so far as it is the result of a sincere, but unsuccessful, attempt at falsification: and it is then significant in a negative rather than a positive way. Popper ('RC', p. 991) says:

> Only negative instances . . . are of interest . . . and such
> 'positive' instances which are, in fact, negative instances, of a
> competing theory: but these derive their interest from being
> crucial experiments or crucial cases, rather than from being
> positive instances.

The Einstein story on its own does not sanction the negative attitude to confirmation or the demand for ever-higher falsifiability embodied in those two conclusions Popper draws from the story. The story as presented by Popper does naturally lead to the conclusion that a scientific theory is to be demarcated from a non-scientific theory in terms of falsifiability but no further. Although it justifies criticism of the uncontrolled and uncritical piling up of justifications which Popper found in his meetings with Freudian and Adlerian psychology, it does not in itself lead to the conclusion that the quest for justification is altogether unscientific, despite Popper's tendency to link the demarcation criterion with such a total rejection of any attempt to justify a theory (as, for example, in OK, p. 29). To understand Popper's absolute hostility to justificationism, we must turn to his examination of induction.

II

Inductive Method

In *The Logic of Scientific Discovery*, Popper writes (p. 420):

> The fundamental doctrine which underlines all theories of induction is *the doctrine of the primacy of repetitions*. Keeping Hume's attitude in mind, we may distinguish two variants of this doctrine. The first (which Hume criticized) may be called the doctrine of the logical primacy of repetitions. According to this doctrine, repeated instances furnish a kind of *justification* for the acceptance of a universal law. (The idea of repetition is linked, as a rule, with that of probability.) The second, which Hume upheld, may be called the doctrine of the temporal (and psychological) primacy of repetitions. According to this second doctrine, repetitions, even though they should fail to furnish any kind of *justification* for a universal law . . . nevertheless induce and *arouse* . . . expectations and beliefs in us. . . .

Bacon, who is usually held to be the originator of the modern theory of induction and whom Popper uses as its characteristic representative, is taken by Popper as advocating that scientists base their theories on the presuppositionless observation of repetitions in order to attain the truth about the world. Bacon thought that the observation of repetitions was not psychologically primary in Hume's sense because observation was often interfered with by mental anticipations and prejudice, but that the good scientist attempted to empty his mind of any prior beliefs or expectations in order that he might be led to unprejudiced observation and hence to correct theories. In this chapter I shall examine Popper's argument against the idea that the observation of repetitions is or should be primary in the arousal of theories, while I shall leave examination of Popper's rejection of the logical primacy of repetitions (and his claim that inductivists are straightforwardly committed to it) to the following chapter.

According to Bacon (and Mill, who later systematized the method of induction), the scientist, when investigating a certain phenomenon, should begin by collecting a large number of examples of what he is interested in. By noting at the same time all the other features of the environment which are present in each case of the phenomenon, he is able to discover which ones are constantly present, as opposed to those which are only sometimes present. Suppose, for example, we are trying to discover the cause of cancer. We examine a large number of cases and notice that they are all heavy smokers, but that they seem to have nothing else in common. We would then naturally formulate a hypothesis to the effect that it was the smoking that caused cancer. This hypothesis could then be tested by seeing if no non-smokers got cancer and if some of those that did smoke heavily did not get it. If some non-smokers got cancer we would conclude at least that smoking was not the only possible cause, while, more disastrously for our original theory, if some heavy smokers remained immune, we would have to conclude not only that smoking was not the only cause of cancer, but also that it did not cause it except in conjunction with some further factor that had escaped our notice.

As a description of scientific method, this account of induction bears some relation to what actually happens in the testing of a hypothesis once one has been formulated. But as a description of the processes leading to the formulation of scientific hypotheses, not only is it not even apparently true of the framing of many major theoretical insights (which did not follow on painstaking collation of data), but, for theoretical reasons, it cannot be adequate even in cases where a hypothesis does seem to follow a process of repeated and systematic observation like that here described. One supposed advantage of the inductive method is that it is bound to come up with the cause in the end, because the cause of a phenomenon must be among the features of its immediate environment, but this turns out to be no advantage at all, because we can never in practice enumerate all the features surrounding anything.

What is envisaged by the inductivist is that the researcher will simply compile lists of all the features accompanying his examples of the phenomenon he is interested in, and that success in isolating the constantly present and hence constantly related elements is guaranteed because his investigation can proceed in a mechanical and objective fashion without any possible cause being overlooked owing to the researcher's own subjective estimate of what is or is not relevant. The incursion of subjectivity here can be seen in retrospect as responsible for much blindness on the part of scientists of earlier generations, whose preformed ideas as to what might be relevant led them to overlook features of a situation which stare us in the face. The removal of such blindness through a presuppositionless approach appeared to Bacon to be a main advantage of the method of induction.

In fact, however, this presuppositionlessness turns out to be impossible to attain either in practice or in principle. In practice, we cannot observe all the features surrounding even one example of a phenomenon. Not only do we not have any clear idea of how close in space and time a 'surrounding' feature has to be to what it surrounds, but even within the limits of a room, say, an infinity of things is happening at any given moment. It is impossible to enumerate them all, as readers of James Joyce will appreciate. In any case, 'pure' presuppositionless observation is in principle unattainable, as Popper brings home forcibly (CR, pp. 46–7):

> The belief that we can start with pure observations alone, without anything in the nature of a theory, is absurd ... I tried to bring home the ... point to a group of physics students in Vienna by beginning a lecture with the following instructions: 'Take pencil and paper; carefully observe, and write down what you have observed!' They asked, of course, *what* I wanted them to observe. Clearly the instruction 'Observe!' is absurd ... Observation is always selective. It needs a chosen object, a definite task, an interest, a point of view, a problem. And its description presupposes a descriptive language, with property words; it presupposes similarity and classification, which in its turn presupposes interests, points of view and problems. 'A hungry animal', writes Katz (1953, p. 105), 'divides the environment into edible and inedible things. An animal in flight sees roads to escape and hiding places ... Generally speaking, objects change ... according to the needs of the animal.'

Actually, Katz says not that objects change according to the needs of the animal, but that objects change their value, but what he says still supports the general point Popper is making. Popper continues (CR, p. 47):

> We may add that objects can be classified, and can become similar or dissimilar, *only* in this way – by being related to needs and interests ... For the scientist (a point of view is provided) by his theoretical interests, the special problem under investigation, his conjectures and anticipations, and the theories which he accepts as a kind of background: his frame of reference, his 'horizon of expectations'.

So in picking out some of the limitless number of features of the environment when investigating a phenomenon, the scientist is already operating with a half-formed theory as to what type of thing is likely to be causally related to what he is investigating. Theory of a sort is also embodied in the classificatory schemes involved in his observations of the features he looks at.

This last point can be emphasized here in the light of what Popper calls the psychological primacy of repetitions. The method of induction requires that we observe repeated instances of the phenomenon we are interested in, as well as repeated instances of the various features surrounding the examples of our phenomenon. But, argues Popper, we can see on logical grounds that there is no such thing as a perfect repetition of any event. Similarity in all respects would mean that the two events were really identical, and so there would actually be only one event. So the repetitions we experience are only approximate. But this means that some features of repetition B of event A will be different from some features of A. Thus B is to be seen as a repetition of A only to the extent that we discount those features in which B differs from A. (A farmer may see his ploughing his field on two days as a repeated task; a mouse whose nest is ploughed up on the second day will be more impressed by the distinguishing features of the two days' activity.) So similarity between events is perceived only relative to a point of view: the point of view which leads us to emphasize the similarities at the expense of the dissimilarities (*LSD*, pp. 421–2):

> Similarity, and with it repetition, always presuppose the adoption of *a point of view*: some similarities or repetitions will strike us if we are interested in one problem, and others if we are interested in another problem. But if similarity and repetition presuppose the adoption of a point of view, or an interest, or an expectation, it is logically necessary that points of view, or interests, or expectations, are logically prior, as well as temporally (or causally or psychologically) prior, to repetition.

So the observation of repetition, central to the inductive method, cannot be achieved in the presuppositionless way required by induction. As with the selection and categorizing of what to observe, the observation of repetition involves a background, made up of our interests, expectations and schemes of classification. Whether it is right to lump all these background features together as hypotheses or theories will be examined in chapter V, but Popper's arguments here do convincingly demolish the idea that science (or even pre-scientific beliefs and observation) could proceed by a purely passive reception of repetitive evidence, let alone that it should proceed in this way. (Whether Bacon's advocacy of observation freed from mental anticipation meant that he was himself unable to see the scientific sterility of

13

merely passive fact-collecting has been questioned by Grünbaum (1976a, p. 250). Even so, Bacon did want to rule out mental anticipation in scientific observation, and Popper's argument shows that this is not possible.) Popper shows (*OK*, p. 358 n, pp. 204–5 n) by appeal to examples that successful scientific theories, far from always being 'induced' from evidence, often contradict the evidence on which, according to inductivist historians, they are based. Lakatos (1970, pp. 130–1) gives the interesting example of the theorist Newton (correctly) telling the observer Flamsteed to correct his observations in the light of his (Newton's) theories.

Popper's rejection on logical grounds of the psychological primacy of repetitions led him, he says to the following view (*CR*, p. 46):

> Without waiting, passively, for repetitions to impress or impose regularities upon us, we actively try to impose regularities upon the world. We try to discover similarities in it, and to interpret it in terms of laws invented by us. Without waiting for premises, we jump to conclusions. These may have to be discarded later, should observation show that they are wrong.

He goes on to say that what obtains in ordinary life would apply in science too, that science is not a digest of observations, but a field in which observations are usually made with a view to testing bold and imaginative conjectures. (The role played by imagination in Popper's account of science, in distinction to that of Bacon and Mill, has often been favourably commented on by working scientists.)

Nevertheless, against Popper and in favour of Hume, the rejection of the psychological primacy of repetitions does not mean that the observation of repetitions has no part to play in the formulation of theories, and that it is all a matter of jumping to conclusions. Popper's logical arguments do show that any observation presupposes in the observer what Quine (1960, p. 83) has called 'a prior tendency to weight qualitative differences unequally' but, given such prior tendencies, hypotheses surely often are quasi-mechanically based on registering repetitions. What Hume says about the impact of repetition is psychologically plausible once the prior tendency is granted. On the point of prior tendencies, Hume himself, or some latter-day follower of Hume, might in fact distinguish between our observation of the enduring objects with which our everyday world is populated and our observation of the primary sensory data from which they are, according to him, constructed. Only the latter, it would be said, presuppose no point of view. Against this, Popper would still urge that the noticing and classification even of sense data presuppose a direction of interest: his argument applies there, as much as to enduring objects. Some empirical confirmation of this is provided by the fact that colour and shape classifications are not culturally independent. Moreover, as I show in chapter V, identification of sensory data actually depends on the existence of enduring objects. Hume is also right in thinking that the confidence we have in many beliefs is due to the fact that they are confirmed by repeated instances. But he – like Popper – thinks that this confidence is misplaced. Popper's desire to remove repetition from the epistemological picture altogether (he says in 'RC', p. 1015, that neither animals nor men use any procedure like induction or any argument based on the repetition of instances) is perhaps due to his conviction that the observation of repeated instances not merely requires some sort of framework of expectation in the observer, but further that it can in no sense confirm any theory or hypothesis.

III

Inductive Argument and Popper's Alternative

1 *Inductive justification*

Popper holds that for inductivists the primacy of repetitions is important not merely as a method for the discovery of theories but as a method for the discovery of theories which are true, for repeated instances justify the acceptance of universal laws. An inductive proof is one which assumes that, because certain regularities have occurred in the past, we are justified in assuming that they will continue in the future. Inductive reasoning of this sort should be clearly distinguished from inductive method, even though Popper does reject both and sees both as centering on a misguided primacy of repetitions. From now on, in speaking without further qualification of 'induction', I shall be referring to induction in the sense of inductive proof.

Popper actually gives an oversimplified view of the theories of Bacon and Mill in suggesting that inductivism necessarily entails that repeated favourable instances will count in favour of a theory and that inductivism is as justificationary in spirit as astrology and the pseudo-sciences. He says (*CR*, p. 256):

> Astrologers . . . have always claimed that their 'science' was based upon a great wealth of inductive material. This claim is, perhaps, unfounded; but I have never heard of any attempt to discredit astrology by a critical examination of its alleged inductive material.

Even so, if such an attempt were made, it would be, as Grünbaum (1976a, pp. 215–22) has shown, entirely in accord with the methodologies of Bacon and Mill. Bacon emphasized that negative instances were worth more evidentially than affirmative ones because theories were proved only when their rivals had been falsified. In other words, an observation provides true support for a theory only when it is at the same time a negative result for a rival. Mill (1887, p. 313) makes a similar point, explicitly contrasting the small value of a vast mass of repetitive experience with the true probative value of an observation which speaks for one hypothesis at the same time as it speaks against an alternative. There is no need to stress the similarity between these views and Popper speaking of evidential support arising only from falsifications of rival theories. Unfortunately for Bacon and Mill, however, positive support through eliminative induction will be given not only to the one hypothesis we are interested in but, as Popper points out (LSD, p. 419), equally to the countless other possible hypotheses also consistent with the evidence; but this is a difficulty which we shall see arises with Popper's views as well.

Even if Bacon and Mill do not hold quite the view of proof by repetition which Popper attributes to inductivists, there are philosophers, such as Carnap (1962, p. 573), who have produced systems of inductive logic in which every positive instance contributes something to the support of a hypothesis. Clearly, too, in everyday life we seem continually to use inductive arguments. Having noticed that all the men who have ever lived have died eventually, we tend to conclude that all men are mortal. Of course, once we have established the general principle that all men are mortal, we can go on to deduce validly that each individual man will die, but how can we ever establish the original premise? How do we know that, just because all the men that there have so far been have died within a certain span of years, all or most (or even any) men now living or to be born will die either within, say, 200 years of their birth, or even within some unspecified yet finite time? We make assumptions of this sort all the time – indeed the very possibility of learning from experience seems based on the acceptability of induction – yet what is their justification? Unlike the process of deduction from premises to a conclusion, in which the truth of the conclusion is guaranteed by the truth of the premises, inductive reasoning seems to move to a conclusion that is necessarily beyond what is given in the premises – moving from the observation that all the men we know about in the past have died to the conclusion that all men, or even, less ambitiously, some men who are not yet dead, will die in the future.

Popper's view about induction is very simple. There is no justification in empirical matters for reasoning from phenomena of which we have had experience to other phenomena (even supposedly of the same type, though that is just the point at issue) of which we have as yet no experience. Any attempt to justify such reasoning in general by pointing to previous occasions on which we have successfully generalized from cases we had experienced to those we had not experienced at the time of the generalization simply raises once more the question we are trying to solve, because in the proposed justification we are assuming that what we have experienced is a good guide to what we have not, which is just what has to be justified. Both the principle and the argument, Popper derives from Hume (see *LSD*, pp. 29, 369-70; *CR*, p. 42; *OK*, p. 96). So Popper accepts Hume's belief in the irrationality of induction, while rejecting Hume's account of how we (irrationally on Hume's view) come to believe in natural regularities through the observation of repetitions. There are various formulations and versions of a so-called principle of induction which is assumed to underlie our everyday empirical reasonings. Some refer only to generalizations from the past to the future, while others state that nature is uniform, but they all assume the acceptability of a jump from what we have experienced to what we have not, so any argument that can show that such a jump is not justifiable will dispose of them all, and this is what Popper intends by his argument. It should be stressed that Popper is here offering a logical argument against the possibility of justifying any principle of induction, so no empirical evidence of actual regularities in the world is sufficient to refute his argument. Also his argument would apply as much to Mill's more sophisticated attempt to prove theories through negative instances as to simple induction through repetition. In both cases there is a jump from what we have experienced to what we have not, which stands in need of justification.

Hume and Popper, then, agree that inductive proof is necessarily irrational, or, alternatively, no proof at all. A strong point in their favour is that actual examples of inductive successes cannot count in favour of induction because to appeal to them in this way is either dogmatic or opening the way to an infinite regress. We either assume that induction is justified in *this* case or we need to justify this assumption, and so on *ad infinitum*. At the same time, however, empirical 'disproofs' of induction are equally beside the point. If we find that an inductively based expectation fails us, the inductivist will not conclude that his principle of induction is false, but simply that the inductive principle has been misapplied because some relevant differences between the new situation and the previous ones have been overlooked. This is why when something unexpected happens in circumstances that appear otherwise normal – as in the Comet air crashes of the 1950s – we look carefully at the differences between those situations and the ones which did not turn out unexpectedly. We feel that the reason for the unexpected turn must lie in the differences. Popper (*OK*, pp. 10-11) himself gives examples of failures of inductively based expectations to support his criticism of induction, but the inductivist would simply not agree that the midnight sun or cases of ergotism (two of Popper's examples) count against the inductively formed beliefs that the sun rises and sets every 24 hours, or that bread nourishes, even less that the principle of induction itself was to be rejected. What the inductivist would seek to show was that beliefs about the sun rising and bread nourishing were still correct, as far as they went, but that in these examples they were in conflict with other interfering factors, the nature of which he would then seek to establish and confirm inductively.

Scepticism about induction can seem curiously perverse. It says that we have no grounds for thinking that the future will be like the past, but it actually gives no reason for thinking that the future will be different in any given respect. Of course, it could hardly do that because such reasons themselves will in all probability be inductive (bread baked in a certain way being poisonous), as well as presupposing an inductive framework of reasoning (the need to specify a relevant difference in expecting the future to be unlike the past).

In order to bring out further the strange nature of scepticism about induction some philosophers have asked what it is that the sceptic is looking for. Having rejected an inductive justification of induction and having shown that inductive inference has no logical or deductive necessity, what would the sceptic count as an answer to the sceptical doubt here? In the absence of an answer to *this* question, isn't the scepticism necessarily otiose? After all, if a problem is a genuine one, we must at least have some idea of what would count as its solution. In this case, it is said to be senseless to ask whether the use of inductive standards is justified until we can say to what other standards we are appealing for this justification, just as it makes no sense to inquire in general whether the law of the land as a whole is or is not legal since there are no other legal standards to which we can appeal. Another connected attempt to show that the 'problem' of induction is a non-problem consists in pointing out that it is senseless to ask whether it is reasonable to rely on inductively based expectations, because such reliance is just what 'being reasonable' means in such circumstances. (This is sometimes referred to as the 'analytic' justification of induction because it seeks to show that in our thinking about the world we learn and understand the use of terms like 'reasonable', 'good grounds' and 'good evidence' only in cases where essentially inductive procedures are involved.) Stephen Barker sums up the analytic justification as follows (1965, p. 273):

> Already built into the normal sense of the word 'rational' is a reference to inductive standards; in the normal sense of the word 'rational', a rational man is necessarily one who, among other things, reasons inductively rather than anti-inductively.

Ayer (1956, p. 75) argues along similar lines, claiming that inductive

reasoning 'could be irrational only if there were a standard of rationality which it failed to meet; whereas in fact it goes to set the
standard: arguments are judged to be rational or irrational by reference
to it'.

However, the sceptic need not be worried by the analytical justification either in its purely linguistic form (pointing to the meaning of
'reasonable' in the context) or in Ayer's more sophisticated version
(claiming that inductive reasoning is what sets standards of rationality
in empirical matters). Ayer's point can be met by saying that it begs the
question. Ayer is arguing that there is something unintelligible in
scepticism about induction, because inductive reasoning sets the
standards for reasoning about empirical matters. Similarly, Barker
suggests that we have no way of formulating a question as to the
rationality of induction because the practice of induction is constitutive
of our understanding of what it is to be rational. But part of Popper's
point is to question whether induction is part of our practice of
rationality. Indeed, he attempts to analyse rationality in such a way
that induction is not part of it. Is Popper's question unintelligible? In
order to show (against Ayer and Barker) that it is not, we can ask
whether inductive inferences are bound to be reliable in practice,
implying that ultimately it would be reasonable only to act on reliable
inferences. A reliable inference would be one that worked in practice,
and clearly there is no guarantee that our present inductive practices –
what we think of as reasonable – are going to be reliable on that score.
This points to another problem with the analytic justification; because
it is based on our standards of rationality, it presumably implies that
our inductive methods (whatever they are) are part of what is meant by
being reasonable, but it is not unimaginable that different people in
different circumstances might judge empirical probability in quite
different ways. Would we fail necessarily to understand what they meant
when they said that they found it reasonable to believe that such and
such was going to happen or that their standards were in competition
with ours? Taking the analytic justification literally would result in an
inability to do any more than to write them off as irrational, because
we would have no grounds for judging the competition. But surely
their methods could be compared with ours for reliability, possibly to
the detriment of ours if their world was very different from ours. Such
a conclusion would in a sense involve induction at a second level,
because it would be based on showing that attention to some quite
different regularities in experience (e.g., reading tea-leaves or basing
future predictions on what has not happened before) has been reliable
in the past, and that, supposedly, this will continue. But the point still
serves to show that the analytic justification cannot be used to justify
any particular empirical methods merely on the grounds that they are

what we mean by 'reasonable', and that it is, for that reason, an empty manoeuvre.

I do not in fact think that any argument can establish the rationality of induction through showing that it is bound to be reliable. Nevertheless, the analytic justification is too quick in its attempt to dismiss any discussion of the rationality of induction by dismissing Popperian questioning out of hand. What has to be done is to show (and not simply to state) that induction is rational, even though it cannot be shown to be reliable. At the same time, in favour of the analytic justification, there is something about scepticism about induction which precludes any answer which is likely to satisfy the sceptic. No one thinks that what we have experienced in the past is simply going to be repeated in the future. There will always be some differences, merely because any new situation is bound to differ in some ways from any past situation. What we cannot be absolutely sure of is whether the differences are going to matter or not – that is, whether they are going to be such as to falsify the expectations we have based on our past experience. If the sceptic's demand is interpreted in a simplistic way, it is bound to ask for, and hence any reply will attempt to prove, too much. It would be asking for an *a priori* guarantee that the differences will not matter. Thus, as Popper (*OK*, p. 98) rightly says, any attempt to show simply that the future must be like the past and that our conclusions are bound to be correct if we simply generalize from the past to the future will inevitably prove far too much.

The discussion of induction has so far been quite general: neither the sceptic's attacks nor the counter-moves have centered on any particular form of using our past experience to form expectations about the future. Indeed, it would appear to be an empirical matter to decide just how we should attempt to make use of our experience, which particular policy would be appropriate in a given type of situation. It could, for example, be a wise inductive move on the part of a general to expect his opponent to mount his new attack in a different way from the previous one. But despite a certain concentration on cases of simple resemblance, what the Humean sceptic seems to be ultimately attacking, and therefore his opponent to be defending, is *any* form of 'inference concerning any object beyond those of which we have had experience' (Hume, 1888, p. 139). Perhaps, following Ayer (1968, p. 96), we could characterize induction as 'the policy of trusting hypotheses so long as our experience confirms them'. Does scepticism about induction imply that we should follow a non-inductive policy instead?

The first difficulty with following a non-inductive policy is that it is hard to see how to formulate such a policy. Although induction based on experience may tell us what to expect in the sense that we have an idea of which objects and properties will accompany one another, once we abandon this procedure we know only what not to expect, without having any idea which of the countless possibilities of new combinations of things to look for. (Of course, as Ayer points out, to speak of us having a policy at all presupposes a certain degree of inductive success, for we ourselves are combinations of properties and our continued existence depends on these combinations continuing. Possibly an anti-inductivist need not be worried by this, because he is not committed to saying that we will have to be around to judge the success of our policies, but this observation once again illustrates how deeply inductive assumptions enter our lives.) Let us assume, however, for the sake of argument, that the counter-inductivist decides on a way of picking out which new combinations of things to expect, and that his way of doing this runs systematically counter to his past experience. In such a case he might well get correct results quicker than the inductivist who simply and wrongly expects continuance of what he has experienced, but the counter-inductivist is going to have to pay a high price for his success. For what he has done by systematic-ally relating his expectations to this past experience is to construct a new hypothesis which has successfully revealed some pattern to a number of events. The rationality of his sticking to his policy depends upon the expected continuance of the pattern his hypothesis has revealed, but this is itself clearly an inductive move. He might, of course, apply a policy of varying his policies; in so far as this meta-policy is systematically applied to future events, it too would become inductive in the sense objected to by Hume. So even though the pattern relating later happenings to earlier ones is very complicated, this will not count against induction in a wide sense, for, as Ayer puts it (1968, p. 100), 'any successful *policy* must become an inductive policy, since in order to be successful it must correspond to some pattern in the events with which it deals; and the pattern must be projectible if the policy is to continue to succeed'. In other words, any systematic counter-inductivist policy presupposes some projectible pattern to events and is thus covertly inductivist and open to the objection that we are predicting what will happen on the basis – albeit in a complicated way – of what has happened. It is precisely reasoning of this sort that Hume's objections to induction are designed to show we have no warrant for, and so a counter-inductivist *policy* would be ruled out on the same grounds as an inductive policy.

Scepticism about induction, then, must ultimately rule out a counter-inductive policy as much as a straight inductive one. But this is no counter to the scepticism. Perhaps it is irrational to rely on *any* policy. Perhaps the whole of human life is based on a gigantic and unjustifiable act of faith. In reply to Reichenbach, who argued that induction is accepted by the whole of science and in everyday life, Popper replies (*LSD*, p. 29) that, even if that were so, it is possible that the whole of science could be in error. Popper quotes approvingly Russell's extreme view that, unless we can find an answer to the problem of induction, there is no intellectual difference between sanity and insanity, but he also agrees with Hume that scepticism about induction is inescapable for an empiricist. He is able to hold these apparently conflicting positions because his solution to the problem of induction is to show that we can do without any inductive assumptions. Popper's non-justificationist epistemology is an epistemology lacking a principle of induction; in this way, Popper is able to maintain his position on the total invalidity of induction from a rational point of view, while arguing that science is (or can be) rational.

It is worth adding here that many of the scientists who admire Popper's work as embodying a good account of their practice do so largely because of the emphasis Popper gives to the formulation and criticism of bold, imaginative hypotheses. They see this as much nearer the truth and more challenging than the view of the scientist as a collector and collator of data. So they agree with Popper's rejection of the inductive method of theory discovery. But it is another question as to whether they would subscribe to Popper's outright rejection of any way in which experience and testing can confirm theories in the sense of giving us good reasons for believing in their future reliability.

2 *Popper's 'solution' to the problem of induction*

'Solution' has a Pickwickian sense here, because Popper does not answer scepticism about induction. He embraces it, arguing instead that we can gain empirical knowledge without using inductive steps. In this section, I shall follow Popper in examining how, without induction, he thinks we are able to choose between competing scientific theories. Criticism of his proposals will occupy us in later sections. The problem for a non-inductivist is to show how he can make such choices without arguing inductively from the past successes of a theory to its soundness in the future. Popper attempts to do this by making refutation rather than justification the central tool of theory comparison, by exploiting what he calls the asymmetry between verification and falsification.

For Popper a scientific theory should take the form of a universal law applying to particular types of phenomena. The requirement of universality or exceptionlessness stems primarily from the requirement of independent testability we have already noticed, although it is clear that a fully universal law will be more useful than a theory hedged about with qualifications concerning its application. Popper writes (*OK*, p. 193):

> Only if we require that explanations shall make use of universal statements or laws of nature (supplemented by initial conditions) can we make progress towards realizing the idea of independent, or non *ad-hoc*, explanations. For universal laws of nature *may* be statements with a rich content, so that *they may be independently tested* everywhere, and at all times. Thus if they are used as explanations, they *may* not be *ad hoc* because they *may* allow us to interpret the *explicandum* as an instance of a reproducible effect.

That we want these reproducible effects to be reproducible all through space and time, not only in our cosmological area or period, also stems from what we want of a scientific explanation. As Popper explains (*PH*, p. 103), to restrict the spatio-temporal realm of validity of a scientific law is to admit laws that are themselves subject to changes, i.e., are not seen as part of a law-governed process, which amounts to an admission of miraculous or inexplicable change.

Together with initial conditions, then, we can deduce from universal laws predictions as to the future behaviour of the phenomena concerned. These predictions, being deductively related to the laws, are tests or potential falsifiers of the law. However, owing to its universality, together with the indefinite extent of the physical universe in space and time, from any given law an indefinitely large number of potential falsifiers will be derivable. We will never be in a position to examine them all and so, no matter how many tests turn out favourable, we will never be in a position to say absolutely that any theory is true. Even the most dogmatic inductivist would be wary of claiming too much here. The adoption of an inductive principle which allowed us to deduce *a priori* that a theory was true without qualification after a given amount of favourable evidence would not only be open to countless falsifications (from examples like the discovery of the midnight sun and the cases of ergotism where people died from eating bread), but it would be foolhardy in the extreme. Verification of scientific theories, in the sense of guaranteeing their truth on the basis of however much favourable evidence, is thus generally agreed to be impossible.

It might be felt that, even if a large amount of favourable evidence is insufficient to verify a law, it could still allow us to assign some degree of probability to it. Popper rejects this proposal on two counts. In the first place he argues that all mathematical attempts to assign probabilities to laws in this way lead to counter-intuitive conclusions. These arguments will be examined later, because the more fundamental argument, which is quite independent of any logico-mathematical considerations, is that this type of probabilification is just as much an inductive step as verification. Even to say that past evidence renders some future happening probable is to go beyond what is warranted by the premises. That this is part of what is involved in Hume's argument is made clear by Popper (*LSD*, p. 369), when he quotes Hume as saying that probable arguments from the past to the future assume what has to be proved just as much as demonstrations do: that there is conformity between the future and the past. In other words, the initial probabilities of statements referring to the future cannot be increased by evidence from the past.

So Hume's argument rules out attempts to verify or probabilify universal laws. Such laws, on Popper's view, having an infinite number of consequences in a world like ours, will all have zero logical probability, and no evidence will be able to increase this probability. This is because, as well as running counter to Humean scepticism, assessing the probability of a universal theory by comparing the ratio of tests passed to conceivable tests, in a universe such as ours, which is either infinite or very large, will always give the theory zero probability (or something very close to it). This means that false theories and well-confirmed theories will be equal in probability. However, we can sometimes show that a theory has failed to survive a test. In that case we can rule the theory out. At this point, Popper's dual rejection of the inductive method and the principle of induction come together to support his methodological proposals. Without an automatic method for constructing sound theories from presuppositionless premises or a means of justifying the theories we do construct, scientific method has to exploit the one resource it has: the elimination of false theories. From this it follows that science should concentrate on theories which have a high degree of falsifiability, which are therefore most likely to be eliminated if they are false and which hold out some promise of being true if they survive their tests. At the same time, a high degree of falsifiability in a theory means that it potentially clashes at many places with experience. In contrast to vague or tautological statements, such theories will have high empirical content and high explanatory power in that from them, together with initial conditions, a large range of states of affairs can be deduced.

There is obviously a problem for Popper in specifying degrees of falsifiability in theories, for this cannot be done by simply comparing quantities of empirical consequences, since any empirical statement will have an infinite number. This is because the conjunction of any state of affairs together with an event directly forbidden by a statement is a further event ruled out by the statement. So we must find ways of comparing the sizes of classes of basic empirical statements clashing with theories which do not involve numerical enumeration of consequences. One way is through the subclass relationships which may exist between the potential falsifiers of two theories, x and y. If the class of potential falsifiers of x includes the class of potential falsifiers of y and some more as well, x is more falsifiable than y. An example would be if x said that planetary orbits were circular while y said they were elliptical. In this case y would have greater logical probability than x (for it excludes less), while x has greater empirical content than y (for it says more). As the potential falsifiers of y are a proper subclass of those of x, x is more falsifiable than y, and as x and y speak of the same phenomena there is a sense in which x is more precise than y. Greater precision in this sense then involves greater falsifiability. Another type of example of the subclass relation involves a further aspect of universality from that considered earlier. Suppose that z says that all heavenly bodies have elliptical orbits, while y is as before. Then all the potential falsifiers of y are falsifiers of z, but not vice versa; hence z is more falsifiable than y and has greater empirical content, for z speaks in the same way of all of the entities covered by y, plus some more. It is to be noticed then in both these types of example greater falsifiability goes with greater empirical content, and hence with lower logical probability. (Remember that a tautology has logical probability $= 1$, while some vague triviality has a higher *a priori* likelihood of being true than some precise, wide-ranging prediction.)

Both precision and universality are usually seen as desirable in scientific theories. Universality in both its aspects connects closely with the methodological application of the principle of causality, the drive to leave nothing unexplained. In its new aspect, it encourages the attempt to connect apparently unconnected types of phenomena and the theories covering them through theories of higher universality. Thus Newtonian dynamics was able to connect Galileo's terrestrial and Kepler's celestial physics by showing both to be approximations to it. Higher universality would also be achieved in a successful reduction of, for example, biology to physics and chemistry, for it would show that one subject matter was in fact explicable in terms of the laws governing another.

There are cases where it is possible to compare the testability of two theories even though the subclass relationship does not apply, and so direct comparisons in terms of universality and precision cannot be made. This is if we can speak of one theory as having a lower dimension than another. What this means is that the falsification of the one requires more singular statements of the same sort than the other. Thus our theory y (planetary orbits being elliptical) has a higher dimension than our theory x (planetary orbits being circular), for at least six singular statements describing a curve are required to falsify y, while x requires only four. The theory of lower dimension is more testable. If a theory w says that planetary orbits are parabolic, then it cannot be compared with x in terms of subclass relationships, because circles are not special cases of parabolas, but the two are comparable by dimensionality, since w requires at least five singular statements of planetary positions for its falsification. It is to be noted that this account of degrees of testability may not be fully adequate for Popper's purposes. As we shall see in considering auxiliary hypotheses in chapter VI, hypotheses which Popper wants to compare in terms of falsifiability may not be comparable on his chosen criteria. We will also see that problems with comparing theories through subclass relationships also figure largely in the criticisms of Popper's account of verisimilitude.

Having established criteria for degrees of testability, Popper suggests that simplicity can advantageously be analysed as degree of falsifiability. He has already shown that theories of a lower dimension are more falsifiable than those of a higher dimension, which gives some support for his account of a notoriously imprecise notion. Universality and precision may also be part of what people are looking for in demanding simple theories, and these also increase with greater falsifiability. Popper's stipulations about simplicity may not produce theories which are simple in other respects (e.g., the formulas of theories simple on his criteria may be extremely complex). Because his analysis of simplicity is so stipulative, it must be admitted that the desirability of Popperian simplicity must depend on whether we think highly testable theories are desirable, rather than on any intuitions as to the desirability of simplicity in some other sense (for example, the number of primitive terms in a theory, or its economy and ready intelligibility of presentation).

We have seen that, while degrees of falsifiability and accounts of empirical content go hand in hand, falsifiability is inversely related to logical probability. Popper thus has two reasons for not basing our theory choice on notions of probability. If probability is assessed in terms of the support that evidence gives to a theory, then the choice will be inductive and so unacceptable. If, on the other hand, probability is assessed in terms of the initial logical probability of a theory, then we will be led to prefer theories with low empirical content, which will tell us little about the world. We must now see how Popper attempts to choose between scientific theories without appealing to inductivist, justificationary or probabilistic reasoning.

Popper's own original tool for theory choice is the degree of corroboration achieved by a theory. This is a non-inductive measure, for it is an analytic or tautological assessment of how a theory has stood up to tests in the past and in no sense adds to the probability of a universal theory, which remains at zero. Positive degrees of corroboration can be assigned only to theories that have not yet been falsified, while significant degrees will be given only to theories which have high content and which have survived severe tests. In contrast to inductivist attempts to analyse the confirmation of a theory in terms of its logical probability (in which high confirmation may be a symptom only of low content), high Popperian corroboration will be given only to theories with high content ($=$ low initial probability) and which have survived what, in the light of present knowledge, are severe tests. In other words, the theory, if true, will be adding significantly to our knowledge. As the logical probability of universal theories is always zero, in order to assess degrees of improbability (and hence of content) of such theories, we will need measures of the 'fine structure' of content, which are not the same as logical probability. Popper suggests that we use comparisons of simplicity and dimension here (cf. *LSD*, pp. 375–7). The point on severe testing is brought out in one of Popper's formal accounts of corroboration (*LSD*, pp. 399–402). Where $E(x, y)$ is the explanatory power of a theory x with respect to evidence y, and $C(x, y)$ is the degree of corroboration x is given by y, we have

$$(1) \quad E(x, y) = \frac{P(y, x) - P(y)}{P(y, x) + P(y)}$$

and

$$(2) \quad C(x, y) = E(x, y)(1 + P(x)P(x, y)).$$

Where x is a universal theory, Popper holds that $P(x) = 0$. If y follows from x, then $P(y, x) = 1$. So, in the case of a universal theory and a test implication deducible from it (with initial conditions), we will have

$$(3) \quad C(x, y) = E(x, y) = \frac{1 - P(y)}{1 + P(y)}.$$

So, degree of corroboration in such a case will depend on how $P(y)$ is assessed. If, in the light of background knowledge, $P(y)$ is high, then $C(x, y)$ cannot be high. Popper says this shows that often repeated tests cannot significantly increase the corroboration of a theory, because the fact that a test has often been made with the same result will increase our assessment of the probability of that result. Only a severe test, where $P(y)$ is low, can result in high corroboration of x. But the notion of a severe test cannot be fully captured by a purely quantitative assessment of $P(y)$, for a really severe test is always a sincere and genuine effort to refute rather than verify a theory (*LSD*, p. 414). So the definition of corroboration in (2) brings out necessary rather than sufficient conditions for corroboration.

None the less, we do see in (2) and (3) a crucial difference between

Popperian corroboration and accounts of inductive probability given by Carnap and others, in that quality rather than quantity of supporting evidence is what counts. Examples of improbable corroboration are the Einstein story considered by Popper or the antecedently highly improbable consequence of cloning as a corroboration of DNA theory. Not only is the degree of corroboration of a theory not a measure of probability (or a prediction of future success), but it cannot be given absolutely. It is always given in the light of the critical discussion of the time and also, implicitly, in comparison with the degrees of corroboration of competing theories. This is because severe tests of one theory will usually be severe because their improbability is given relative to background knowledge – that is, in relation to competing theories. Finally, unlike inductivist confirmation, theories which were once given high degrees of corroboration will, as they become part of background knowledge and so not severely testable, no longer be able to get high corroboration.

In *The Logic of Scientific Discovery*, from which I have mainly drawn the preceding sketch of his scientific methodology, Popper says that the ideas of empirical content and degree of corroboration are the most important logical tools developed there (p. 395). His subsequent work on the method of science rests on the same insights, but he has since introduced one more important notion, that of the verisimilitude of theories. The main point of this notion is to give some clarification of our intuitive desire to speak of some theories as being nearer the truth than others. If we take the logical consequences of an empirical statement which is false (e.g., 'It always rains on Sunday'), we can see that not *all* its non-trivial consequences need be false (e.g., if it rained last Sunday). We can then distinguish between the class of true statements which follow from it (truth content) and the class of false statements which follow from it (falsity content). The verisimilitude of our statement will then be defined as its truth content minus its falsity content. The intention of this definition is not that with it we can compare the respective verisimilitudes of unconnected theories, but that it enables us to compare comparative verisimilitudes, when we have two theories covering the same ground: where one is more universal or more precise than the other, a qualitative assessment can then be made between them in terms of their comparative contents and ability to survive tests. For example, if t_2 adequately explains all that t_1 does, and, in addition, explains more than t_1 and has stood up to some tests in the area on which t_1 is silent, then t_2 can be said to have greater verisimilitude than t_1. Equally, if t_2 and t_1 cover the same ground but differently, and t_2 survives a crucial experiment where t_1 was predicting a different outcome, then t_2 will again have greater verisimilitude than t_1.

Popper (CR, p. 235) does not see verisimilitude as supplanting his theory of severe testing and corroboration, but only as clarifying it. In the case just considered, where t_2 survived tests failed by t_1, the greater verisimilitude accorded to t_2 may allow us to continue to prefer t_2 to t_1 even after t_2 itself has been refuted. This would be the case if t_2 was more universal or precise than t_1 and its refutations were all in areas not touched on by t_1, providing its falsity content in these new areas was not greater than its truth content. Thus, Newton's dynamics, even though we know that it is refuted, is still preferable to the theories of Kepler and Galileo on grounds of comparative verisimilitude. Newton's theory continues to explain more facts more precisely than the other theories and to unify formerly unconnected problems: crucial experiments between theories always favoured Newton's theory, while the refutations of Newton's theory either did not bear on the other theories, or affected them adversely as well.

Verisimilitude is most important in cases where we know that the theories under examination are at best approximations, because it enables us to think of even false theories as being nearer to or further from the truth than other false theories. Naturally, it encourages us too to look for theories with greater empirical content, which go beyond their competitors in precision and universality and which challenge us to investigate new areas, because such theories have greater potential verisimilitude. The appraisals of comparative verisimilitude remain, of course, provisional, relative to our testing procedures and background knowledge, although verisimilitude itself remains an absolute notion, like truth. Once more, we have to conjecture that what appears to us verisimilar is so in reality. Verisimilitude, then, appears to be a useful addition to Popper's original methodological proposals, but it is fundamentally in harmony with them.

We must stress that for Popper neither the verisimilitude nor the degree of corroboration accorded to a theory are intended to have inductive overtones. Corroboration, he writes (OK, p. 18),

> being a report of past performance only . . . has to do with a situation which may lead to preferring some theories to others. *But it says nothing whatever about the future performance, or about the 'reliability' of a theory.*

Degree of corroboration (and the same goes for degree of verisimilitude), being both retrospective and based on the state of critical discussion at a particular time, must be sharply distinguished from probability in any inductive sense ('RC', pp. 1029–30):

> In this context it is crucial that it is not our corroboration statements but our *theories* which allow us to make predictions

. . . our theories do have predictive import. Our corroboration statements have no predictive import, although they motivate and justify our *preference* for some theory over another.

Judgments of degrees of corroboration are analytic or tautological and therefore not inductive. They only sum up the relationships existing between certain theories and their tests. Nevertheless the decision to use the most highly corroborated theories is far from tautological, but depends on the proposal to use the best-tested scientific theories in our possession. Is there a hint of inductivism here? Popper says not, on the grounds that his methods of theory choice are both rational and non-inductive, and that it is rational to use a theory chosen on rational grounds. Where Popper does (*CR*, p. 248 n) admit a whiff of verificationism in his methodology, however, is in his insistence on using well-corroborated theories – that is, theories which have survived severe testing. The reason for this is that we are looking for genuine guesses about the structure of the world, and the fact that a theory survives a severe test *ipso fatco* represents an increase in its truth content. Successful predictions are at least a necessary condition for the truth of an empirical theory, and clearly, in the growth of knowledge, we prefer theories which survive tests their rivals fail. Whether this can give very strong support to the surviving theories without some inductive reasoning and whether Popper's use of corroboration and even the explanation of corroboration itself are not fundamentally inductive will occupy us after we have considered some of his more detailed criticisms of inductive logic.

3 *Inductive logic*

Because of his acceptance of Humean scepticism about induction, Popper thinks that inductive logic, in the sense of an attempt to assign probabilities to theories on the basis of evidence, is basically a myth. Not only do we not want to work on initially probable theories (for they will promise little new knowledge about the world), but he rejects attempts such as that of a Carnapian (Bar-Hillel, 1955, p. 156) to propose favouring theories which are initially improbable but which are highly confirmed after testing. Such 'prudence' would be for Popper quite illusory, as any sort of confirmation is basically inductive. In any case, testing and any resulting 'confirmation' always leave us with an infinity of possible theories still compatible with the evidence. Far from seeking inductively highly confirmed theories, for Popper (*LSD*, p. 419),

what we do – or should do – is to hold on, for the time being, to *the most improbable of the surviving theories* or, more precisely, to the one that can be most severely tested. We tentatively '*accept*' this theory – but only in the sense that we select it as worthy to be subjected to further criticism, and to the severest tests we can design.

In other words, scientific work should not be guided by the illusory goal of prudence, but by the realizable procedure of continuous severe criticism, which implies high improbability at all stages in theories we concern ourselves with. These arguments, as I have said, are independent of particular attempts to develop systems of inductive logic; nevertheless, Popper has spent much time in criticizing such attempts in detail, so it seems worth while to spend a little time examining some of these criticisms, in order to underline some of the differences in attitude between Popper and the inductivists.

One of Popper's main lines of argument (*LSD*, pp. 387–95) is to suggest that attempts to define the confirmation accorded to a theory in terms of the probability calculus, as Carnap does, lead to the contradictory conclusion that there exist cases where a statement x is supported by z a statement y undermined by z, yet x is confirmed by z to a lesser degree than is y. To get this conclusion, all that is required is the assumption (basic to probabilistic accounts of confirmation) that x is confirmed by y if and only if the probability of x given y is greater than the probability of x on its own; in symbols,

(1) $Co(x, y)$ if, and only if, $p(x, y) > p(x)$.

Popper considers an example in which x is the statement 'six will turn up with the next throw of the dice', y the negation of x and z the information 'an even number will turn up'. Then we have the following absolute probabilities:

$$p(x) = 1/6; \quad p(y) = 5/6; \quad p(z) = 1/2$$

and the following relative probabilities:

$$p(x, z) = 1/3; \quad p(y, z) = 2/3.$$

Thus x is supported by z and y is undermined by z, but we also have $p(x, z) < p(y, z)$. So there are cases in which

(2) $p(x, z) > p(x).p(y, z) \leq p(y).p(x, z) < p(y, z).$

Replacing $p(x, z) > p(x)$ and $p(y, z) \leq p(y)$ with $Co(x, z)$ and $-Co(y, z)$ in accordance with (1), we get

(3) $Co(x, z). - Co(y, z).p(x, z) < p(y, z).$

But if probabilities are degrees of confirmation, we will get

(4) $Co(x, z). - Co(y, z).C(x, z) < C(y, z).$

If we read the instances of C in (4) as the degree to which one statement renders another more probable than the second one was on its own (i.e., as a measure of relative probability, as is Co in (1)), then (4), expressed in terms of probabilities, becomes

(4) $p(x, z) > p(x).p(y, z) \leq p(y).p(x, z) - p(x) < p(y, z) - p(y).$

This seems to be the contradiction Popper wants, because (4) is saying that we can have a case in which the probability of x given z is greater than that of x on its own, and the probability of y given z is less than or equal to that of y on its own, and yet the probability of x given z less x on its own is less than that of y given z less y on its own. Unfortunately for Popper's contradiction, however, in Carnap's system, despite some confusion in his exposition, C is not normally to be read in the way here suggested, but rather as equivalent to or a straight explicatum of absolute logical probability, i.e., as

(1′) $C(x, y) = p(x, y).$

So a correct Carnapian reading of (4) will have to take the instances of C along the lines of (1′). This will result not in the absurd (4′) but in the consistent (4″):

(4″) $p(x, z) > p(x).p(y, z) \leq p(y).p(x, z) < p(y, z).$

This way of analysing the situation is based on Michalos (1971, pp. 25–33). Michalos also provides a model to show the consistency of (4″), but this is hardly necessary here, because (4″) is of course the same as (2), for which Popper has already given us a model. Thus Carnap appears to be justified in claiming 1963, p. 998) that absurdity results from (3) only if the last conjunct is read as Popperian rather than Carnapian confirmation.

Of course, Popper's fundamental objections remain to the Carnapian (1′), in which confirmation is straightforwardly equivalent to logical probability. Popper's point about high probability being equivalent to low empirical content clearly carries some weight when we are considering initial probability, but it is less clear that his account of theory-choice provides a complete answer to Bar-Hillel's advocacy of a methodology combining high initial improbability of theories with high probability after testing. In other words, Popper does not show that a probabilistic theory of confirmation must always plump for low content at all stages. Obviously Popper would be wrong in thinking that we do in fact always accept the boldest surviving theory for all purposes, and there are grounds for thinking that Bar-Hillel's proposal bears an important relation to our actual practice, if a way could be found of assigning universal theories more than zero confirmation, however objectionable the inductivism involved is to

Popper. (It should also be noted that Carnap (1962, pp. 221, 243) does not think that inductive logic alone should determine methodological decisions; this is another contrast between Carnap's confirmation and Popper's corroboration.)

Some of the more general questions raised by Bar-Hillel about the desirability of improbability at all stages in our theories will crop up again in the following sections. Here we will now examine Popper's criticisms of Carnap's attempt to account for the confirmation of universal theories despite his agreement with Popper that all the probability of all universal theories is zero. Carnap introduces (1962, pp. 571–4) a notion called the qualified-instance confirmation of a law (cqi*), in which a degree of confirmation is assigned not to the universal law itself, but to the hypothesis (h) that the next observed instance relevant to the law will conform to it. The degree of confirmation accorded to this hypothesis depends on the number of past cases favourable to the law (s_2) and the number unfavourable to it (s_1) and on the logical widths of the predicates involved in speaking of past instances favourable (w_2) and unfavourable (w_1) to the law:

$$(5) \quad \text{cqi*} \, (h, e) = 1 - \frac{s_1 + w_1}{s_1 + w_1 + s_2 + w_2}.$$

(Logical width is a notion introduced by Carnap to determine the relative logical probabilities of individuals having a particular property, the probabilities being calculated on the way that property is expressed in a given language. Thus, where P_1 and P_2 are atomic predicates in a language, we are asked to grant that logically (though not necessarily in practice) the property defined by the molecular predicate P_1 & P_2 is stronger or narrower than that defined by the predicate P_1, while that defined by P_1 V P_2 is wider. For the calculation of logical widths, cf. Carnap (1962, pp. 126–7).) Popper's criticism of cqi* focuses on the point that a refuted theory may, in virtue of (5), obtain a higher qualified-instance confirmation than an unrefuted but little-tested theory. He continues his point (CR, p. 283), taking Carnap's own example of the law 'all swans are white':

> This law ought to be considered as *falsified* if our evidence consists
> of a flock of *one black*, and say, 1,000 white swans. But upon
> this evidence, the instance confirmation, instead of being zero,
> will be very near to one . . . More generally, if a theory is again
> and again falsified, on the average, in every nth instance, then
> its (qualified) 'instance confirmation' approaches $1 - \frac{1}{n}$, instead
> of 0, as it ought to do . . .

In reply to this, Carnap (1968, pp. 309–10) reiterated that on his system a universal theory, refuted or not, never has confirmation greater than zero. What qualified-instance confirmation does is to assign a probability to the next instance being as the theory predicts. In fact, earlier (1962, p. 208) Carnap had said that predictive inferences rather than universal induction are more important for science.

So, Popper's objection would hold only if Carnap's cqi* confirmed a theory rather than a singular predictive inference. None the less, even if Carnap is not open to the objection raised by Popper (quite apart from general objections to induction), Popper would surely be right in regarding the shift from the universal theory to particular propositions as unfortunate. Moreover, instance confirmation seems to put a higher premium on repetition of tests, in order to estimate probabilities, than on devising and improving genuinely explanatory theories covering all the phenomena of a given type. It is appropriate to note here that Howson (1973) has asked whether the logical probability of universal laws has in fact to be zero, as Carnap and Popper think. Howson suggests that some of Popper's arguments to this conclusion from Humean principles (those suggesting that the postulation of any 'after-effect' from evidence to conclusion involves a synthetic *a priori* principle to the effect that the future will resemble the past) would not apply to accounts of logical probability which saw the relationship in terms of partial entailment of the conclusion by the premises. In fact, Popper is favourable to such an account of probability logic ('PM', p. 369):

> Probability logic . . . generalizes derivational logic by considering not only conclusions which are entailed by the premises, but also partial conclusions which are only partially entailed by the premises . . . But it does not, *in doing so, allow us to conclude from the known premise to an unknown conclusion; in fact, what goes beyond the premise remains as probable or as improbable as it was before.*
>
> Induction, of course, is essentially an attempt to extend our knowledge; to conclude from the known to the unknown, by increasing at least the probability of something that is unknown . . . Whatever we may think of induction, it certainly is not analytic; it thus cannot be identified with probability logic.

Popper's position, then, is that probability logic is a legitimate generalization of deductive logic, but that it must be *distinguished from inductive logic*. No doubt, too, as Howson says, systems of logical probability can be devised in which universal statements do not have zero probability. But Popper's main reasons for insisting that universal statements do have zero probability are, as we have seen, given in the context of inductive attempts to probabilify universal laws. For this reason they are epistemological, rather than logical, and so would not appear to exclude purely logical calculi in which universal statements were given greater than zero probability. But they would exclude the attempt to use such calculi inductively, as the basis of an inductive logic, as Howson appears to concede when he agrees that one should be extremely sceptical of the truth of law sentences in infinite domains.

I shall consider later (in chapter VII) Popper's attacks on the logical and subjective interpretation of the probability calculus, which have connections with his attack on inductive logic. But what emerges so far is that the detailed attacks on Carnap's systems of inductive logic which we have examined are inconclusive (though these systems are surely highly vulnerable in view of the fact, noted by Salmon (1967, pp. 101–4), that in them the same theories attain different confirmation values depending on the language in which they are expressed, as can be seen even from my passing reference to logical width). The main force of Popper's attack on inductive logic must then be carried by his general scepticism about inductive inference. What we now have to consider is how far Popper's chosen methods of theory-choice would be able to survive similar scepticism.

4 Corroboration and reliance

Popper speaks of a well-corroborated theory as having demonstrated its fitness to survive by standing up to test (*LSD*, p. 251). This has been taken by some critics as an implicit admission of induction, in that he appeared to be saying that we would then be in a position to assess how far a theory might be able to survive future tests. This criticism was based on a misunderstanding of the biological metaphor, for clearly every species that existed until time t, but failed to survive after t, had proved its fitness to survive up to t. 'It would be absurd to suggest that Darwinian survival involves, somehow, an expectation that every species that has so far survived will continue to survive' (*OK*, p. 19). The point of the metaphor, then, is that a theory that is well corroborated at t might well let us down after t.

A biological species can become extinct in two distinct ways. Either it may be driven out of its original environment and be unable to cope with the new, or its old environment may change in a way it cannot adapt to. In both cases it is failing to deal with new problems, so its old answers to its old problems (and its fitness to survive relative to them) are not thereby invalidated. But what can't be guaranteed is the stability of its environment, even if it is not driven out. The situation is similar with a well-corroborated theory. Either some test implications in an as-yet-untried area may go against it, or the phenomena it has so far explained successfully may alter so that there is failure just where there had been success. It is this second possibility that Popper must be thinking of when he says that we cannot rationally rely on a theory, however well corroborated, because, if the only possibility of failure was in so-far-untried areas, it would be reasonable to rely on a theory where it had proved itself, even though we could not be sure of its total truth. Thus Popper should not see much value in Ackermann's attempt (1976, pp. 58–64) to reconcile inductivism with non-justificationism 'in a sufficiently complicated evolutionary metaphor' by seeing theories as species occupying ecological niches, the niches being the types of data the theory is primarily concerned with, and the theory surviving so long as there are no radical alterations in the data it is successful with, even though it cannot cope successfully with new types of data. (Ackermann's example is of Newtonian physics surviving in its ecological niche of naked-eye and classical instrument observation, although unsuccessful with micro-data.) Not only would Popper reject the implied instrumentalism of this view as incompatible with his drive for universality and truth, but it is just the inductivist assumption of a stable environment that he wishes to cast doubt on. So he would hardly build a substantial view on even a qualified acceptance of such a premise.

Popper provides a further contrast between his attitude to theory testing and that of the inductivists when (*LSD*, p. 419) he points out that, while they (e.g., Mill) eliminate theories in order to establish the survivor, he regards any such attempt as futile because the number of survivors consistent with any evidence remains (potentially at least) infinite. Popper says that we should tentatively accept the most improbable survivor as being the most worth working on for future criticism, and 'on the positive side, we may be entitled to add that the surviving theory is the best theory – and the best tested theory – of which we know'.

This last sentence is clearly important for Popper, for, in 'Replies to my Critics' (p. 1003), he castigates Lakatos for having overlooked it, when in the latter (1974, pp. 254–5) he speaks of the only function of high corroboration being to challenge scientists to work on overthrowing the corroborated theory. Yet there is something puzzling in this sentence, for, having spoken of an infinity of survivors, Popper speaks here of *the* survivor. Which is this? Presumably the most improbable survivor which is accepted as being the best unrefuted theory, but this need not be the best-tested theory, for two incompatible theories tested favourably by the same evidence will presumably be equally well tested and possibly tie in the best tested stakes. Also it is conceivable that of two as yet unrefuted but competing theories the less thoroughly tested one is preferred as the starting point for further research. Popper admits this distinction between the best theory and the best-tested theory, when he speaks ('RC', p. 1186) of further clarifying this distinction, referring to an addendum added to the 1972 edition of *The Logic of Scientific Discovery* (p. 419), in which he says:

> By the 'best' theory I mean the one of the competing and surviving theories which has the greatest explanatory power, content, and simplicity, and is least *ad hoc*. It will also be the best testable theory, but the best theory in this sense need not always be the best tested theory.

If in practice there were competing theories which were equally well tested, we should then choose the one with the highest corroborability and test that at the points of conflict with its competitors, and go on through its competitors until we found the one with the highest positive degree of corroboration (cf. *OK*, p. 15). Of course the problem of the potential infinity of its competitors would arise here too, but this would hold us up only if any of them were actually formulated. So the problem of the potential infinity of equally well tested theories can be dealt with in practice, but it points to an important difference between corroboration and the attempts by inductivists to establish a theory's truth by eliminating its competitors.

For an inductivist, successful tests are seen as confirming a theory; he will therefore have grounds for preferring the most probable surviving theory (that is, the one which least outstrips the new evidence), which will be his sense of the 'best-tested' theory. He will then appeal to his principle of induction to justify the reliance he places on the best-tested theory. Popper rejects any such principle, together with any idea that tests verify theories or any interpretation of corroborations as a degree of 'the rationality of our belief in the truth' of a theory (*LSD*, p. 415). The remark in *Conjections and Refutations* (p. 112) that we should choose for crucial tests those places at which we should expect a theory to break down if it were not true must, in the light of his general position on corroboration and his attack on eliminative induction, be taken psychologistically – as referring to the thoughts of experimenters. An objectivist reading of it – that a survival of a crucial test verifies a theory – is so un-Popperian that it is surprising to see Grünbaum (in 1976a, 1976c) using it to convict Popper of straightforward inconsistency between his attack on eliminative inductivists and his own theory of corroboration. In any case, for Popper, the preferred survivor is not necessarily the same as it would be for an inductivist.

Nevertheless, Grünbaum does have a point, that *if* high corroboration (or the combination of high actual corroboration with high potential corroboration) does not *support* the truth of a theory, what is its value? It is, of course, open to Popper to define the best theory as he wishes, and there is no reason why the best theory should be either the best-tested theory inductively (or in any other way) or the most probable theory on current evidence. Indeed, Popper can (and does) partially answer Grünbaum's question, by saying that the most improbable of the surviving theories is the one most likely to promote growth of knowledge, both in being the most open to quick refutation and, in view of its high universality, in encouraging us to test in new areas and hence to make new discoveries. These opportunities for growth in our knowledge would obviously be missed if we remained content with the most probable surviving theory, a fact which points to the stultifying effect of aiming at high probability at any stage (cf. *CR*, p. 219). It also explains how Popper can, without immediate inconsistency, claim (*OK*, p. 20) that degree of corroboration is a means of stating 'preference with respect to truth', for actual corroboration implies that the theory has not yet been shown to be false, while potential corroboration involves opportunities for growth of knowledge. But what now needs urgent consideration is whether choosing a theory through corroboration (or through corroboration and improbability or corroborability) – as defined by Popper – gives us any reason for acting on that theory.

When we act, we don't want to be told merely that certain theories have done well in the past and may be highly testable in the future, we want to know which theories to rely on. According to Popper (*OK*, p. 21) this is to ask for too much: 'From a rational point of view, we should not "rely" on any theory, for no theory has been shown to be true, or can be shown to be true.' But we have to act, and hence we have to choose, so we should prefer as a basis for action the best-tested theory or the most improbable of the equally well tested survivors. Why? (*OK*, p. 22):

> Since we *have* to choose, it will be 'rational' to choose the best-tested theory. This will be 'rational' in the most obvious sense of the word known to me: the best test theory is the one which, in the light of our *critical discussion*, appears to be the best so far, and I do not know of anything more 'rational' than a well-conducted critical discussion . . . [but] in spite of the 'rationality' of choosing the best-tested theory as a basis of action, this choice is *not* 'rational' in the sense that it is based upon *good reasons* for expecting that it will in practice be a successful choice: *there can be no good reasons* in this sense, and this is precisely Hume's result.

In this passage, it is clear that Popper is speaking of two types of rational preference. In the first type what we are interested in selecting is the theory which has been best corroborated, while in the second type what we are interested in selecting is the theory which is most likely to succeed. There is no reason, on Popper's anti-inductivist view, to suppose that these two selections will coincide, for we are never justified in supposing that an instance we have experienced (past success of a theory) can tell us about an instance we have not experienced (future success of the same theory, even in the area where it was previously successful). Nevertheless, Popper does say that it is rational to prefer as a basis for action the best-tested theory. He sums up his case (*OK*, p. 27) as follows:

> *A pragmatic belief in the results of science* is not irrational because there is nothing more 'rational' than the method of critical discussion, which is the method of science. And although it would be irrational to accept any of its results as certain, there is nothing 'better' when it comes to practical action; there is no alternative method which might be said to be more rational.

But, despite what Popper said earlier, if we did not think there were some grounds for expecting our choice to be successful, would we be justified in calling our choice of the best-tested theory rational as a basis for action? Maybe there is nothing rational when it comes to pragmatic preference. The mere fact that there is no 'better' or 'more rational' method than a given one (in this case choosing the best-tested theory) does not prove that that method is itself a rational way to achieve an end (in this case, successful action). In a randomized number-guessing game there is no better or more rational method than calling the number which is double that which last came up, but we would hardly call this a rational procedure. And, unless we deny Hume's conclusion, we have nothing more than chance to go on when it comes to predicting the future. Indeed, in warning us against trying to explain why many of our theories have worked up to now, Popper asserts (*OK*, p. 28) that our past epistemological successes are 'miraculously improbable, and therefore inexplicable', the results of an endless series of improbable accidents.

So Popper's view (*OK*, p. 26) is that any future event is quite compatible with the evidence we now have:

> If we assume that we are in a position to reflect on the evidence, and what it permits us to assert, then we shall have to admit that the sun may not rise to-morrow over London after all – for example because the sun may explode within the next half-hour, so that there will be no to-morrow.

This being so, it is unclear how Popper is in a position to tell us that it is more rational to act on a well-corroborated theory than to adopt any other policy when it comes to action. As we can never justify our belief in the truth of any theory (cf. 'IA', p. 82; *UQ*, p. 104), we might as well act on any theory – even on the most improbable surviving theory. But saying that does not show why the theory we chose, for whatever reason, is the best to act on.

Popper ('Supp. R', pp. 365–6) has commented on the objection in the last two paragraphs (which was first put forward in O'Hear (1975)). Popper says that the method of corroboration helps us to eliminate false theories. In doing this, it may help us to find the true theory, if there is one. In particular, it is better either than leaving things to chance (acting on bold guesses with no attempt at elimination) or than being dogmatic (simply sticking to one guess) or than having no method at all. But what has to be asked is why any of these procedures might not be just as good guides as to what might happen in the next moment, if Hume's point is correct. High corroboration shows only that a theory has done well up to now. Hume's point is that our world might suddenly change to being one where chance might be a good method or where previously falsified theories might be the best to act on or where we might be better off having no method at all. I cannot see how Popper is justified in claiming that these methods are, in the light of his acceptance of Hume's point, worse methods for basing practical decisions on.

Popper argued ('RC', pp. 1025–6) that any decision on which we are going to act must be open to the most telling criticism we can muster against it, and this means that we will use in our criticism the best tested scientific theories, because these are the ones which have best withstood criticism. Here we can only ask again why, from an anti-inductivist standpoint, such past success should be relevant to future action. In a way, Popper admits the force of this question, because he says that he sees his method as giving us no absolute justification for relying on our theories, adding that the world might suddenly become quite different from what it has been. However, as we can do nothing about this 'from a pragmatic point of view', it is 'obviously not worth bothering about'. This is surely disingenuous at this point. What we need here is a metaconjecture, that in at least some areas the world will be as our well tried and well criticized methods lead us to expect. This indeed is how Popper now speaks ('Supp. R', p. 366):

> we have metaconjectures that lead us to expect that the method
> of conjectures and refutations may be helpful in order to answer
> questions in certain fields, but not in certain other fields.

Of course such metaconjectures are fallible and may let us down, but if they are based on our past experience and used as a basis for future action, it is hard to see how there is not something implicitly inductive about them, or, indeed how they are very different from what Lakatos (1974, p. 260) calls a conjectural inductive principle, according to which we conjecture that some of our well corroborated theories might be true and, hence, presumably, reliable (cf. chapter IV below, pp. 63-4).

If the fact that a theory is well corroborated is not, non-inductively, a good reason to act on it, we are brought right back to asking why, for the non-inductivist, a well-corroborated theory is valuable at all. After all, as Grünbaum points out (1976a), part of what is included in a theory is its future consequences, and yet corroboration provides no support for them, and hence none for the truth of the theory as a whole. High corroborability (= high content) can be valuable non-inductively, as leading us to investigate new areas of research and so to avoid the conservativism of complacency with high initial confirmation, though to take this any further, and argue that good science is actually likely to result from this method, because it has in the past, is clearly itself inductivist. Moreover, as we have seen, inductivists need not advocate low initial content. More to the point, Popper himself wants more from corroboration than recommendations as to which theories are likely to be the best instruments for exploration, an attitude he condemns as instrumentalist (cf. CR, p. 248 n). In other words, he values corroboration as well as corroborability. If all that corroboration does is to tell us that one theory along with an infinite number of other possible theories has not been shown to be false, as Popper admits, it does nothing to justify any confidence in the truth of that theory; the sense in which we are entitled to believe that such a theory may be approaching the truth or be a genuine guess about the structure of the world is thus an entirely minimal one, because it is shown to be a genuine guess only to the extent that its hordes of possible competitors are as well. Despite occasional 'whiffs' of verificationism and possible lapses into verificationist rhetoric such as that picked out by Grünbaum, or the statement (CR, p. 231) that in weeding out false theories we get 'nearer to the truth', Popper does assert (OK, p. 21) that the most his method does positively is to 'make it reasonably certain that, if a true theory should be among the theories proposed, it will be among the surviving, the preferred, the corroborated ones'. But, as he also admits, this never at any point does anything to exclude the possibility that it will be not our theory but one of its competitors that will be true. Popper's scepticism is profound. Corroboration does not alleviate it. In the context of this scepticism the point of preferring corroborated theories remains obscure, while the virtue of highly corroborable theories seems to be purely instrumental.

5 Severe tests

Corroboration cannot add to the zero degree of justification a theory possesses at any time of its life. In other words, it does not give us any reason for believing in a theory's truth. Significantly, corroboration was originally introduced by Popper in 1934 before he considered the concept of truth to be sufficiently clear and free from paradox to be used in philosophical discussion. Later attempts to bring truth into the picture led eventually to the theory of verisimilitude, technical difficulties of which will be considered in the next section. But even if these could be overcome, the basic problem of the value of corroboration and of verisimilitude remains for the non-inductivist: why is the past performance of a theory any good reason for adopting it for the future? How can Popper justify his preference for well-corroborated (or verisimilitudinous) theories when he insists on the fact that neither measure does anything to justify any belief in the truth of the theory? (If they did, of course, they would justify a degree of reliance on the theories.) Why, in short, should a non-inductivist have any interest in the past performance of theories, or even in seeking universal theories at all? Popper appears to have no answer to these questions. That his methodology is attractive to so many is probably due to the fact that most people reading it are, for inductive reasons, interested in past performance, high corroboration and universal theories. And, as we shall see, an inductive Popperian might be rather similar to a Bayesian. Whether or not most people bring their inductive assumptions with them when reading Popper, what we will now consider is whether Popper himself can talk of corroboration without himself using inductive assumptions.

Popper (*CR*, p. 231) prefers severely testable theories to trivial theories which do not go far beyond the evidence '*even (and especially) if (they) soon turn out to be false*', because in discovering that a conjecture is false we learn much more than we would by sticking to the trivial theory. The notion of a severe test is used to rule out not only theories of low empirical content, but also theories that have already been much tested.

Clearly it is not in practice possible to carry out every single possible test of a universal theory because, owing to its unlimited scope, there is no limit to the number of possible tests of it. But then, by Popper's account, in order to assess the worth of a theory, there is no need to carry out all possible tests; what is of primary methodological significance is severe testing, a sincere attempt to refute a theory. We should concentrate, therefore, in testing a theory on just those places where it is most likely to fail. A theory is to be given a high degree of corroboration not by surviving a large number of tests, for the fact that a theory has survived a large number of tests by itself tells us nothing about how severely the theory has been tested, but only by surviving the most severe tests we have been able to put it to.

But how do we know when a theory is confronted by a severe test? A serious empirical test always consists in the attempt to find a refutation, a counter-example. In the search for a counter-example, we have to use our background knowledge; for we must always try to refute first the *most risky* predictions, the '*most unlikely* . . . consequences' (as Peirce already saw); which means that we always look in the *most probable kinds* of places for the *most probable* kinds of counter-examples – *most probable in the sense that we should expect to find them in the light of our background knowledge* [my italics]. Now if a theory stands up to many such tests, then, owing to the incorporation of the results of our tests into our background knowledge, there may be, after a time, no places left where (in the light of our new background knowledge) counter-examples *can with a high probability be expected to occur* [my italics]. But this means that the degree of severity of our test declines. (*CR*, p. 240).

So, we use our background knowledge to decide what is or is not a severe test of a theory, and the results of tests undertaken will themselves become part of background knowledge to later tests. The crux of the matter is the way in which the background knowledge is used. A natural way of reading what Popper says here is to see background knowledge being used inductively: enabling us to predict the likelihood of future events on the basis of past events.

However, there may be another way of understanding what Popper says. If we consider a theory as entailing a number of predictions as consequences, every time we test it and it passes its test, we reduce the number of places where it can fail us. This becomes part of our background knowledge. As there are now fewer places where the theory can fail, there is a sense in which, from our point of view, it has less possibility of failure than it had before we had this knowledge. Some places where it could have failed are now no longer possible places of failure. To that extent, the theory has less chance of failure than it had.

So long as we are thinking of the tests of a theory individually one by one, the fact that it has survived a finite number of tests is going to make very little difference to its overall possibility of success because of the indefinitely large number of all its possible tests. But if we are able to think of the tests of a theory as falling into various groups, it will be a quite substantial result to eliminate the need for carrying out tests of a certain type. But it is precisely this piece of knowledge, that a certain *type* of test can safely be eliminated, that involves inductive reasoning.

The elimination of a certain *type* of test is clearly what Popper was speaking of (*CR*, p. 240); to continue the passage quoted above, his view, in contrast to inductivist theories of confirmation for which every confirming instance has equal value, explains

> why an often repeated test will no longer be considered as significant or as severe: there is something like a law of diminishing returns from repeated tests (as opposed to tests which, in the light of our background knowledge, are of a *new kind*, and which, therefore, may still be felt to be significant).

Of course it is true that *if* our background knowledge includes a theory in the light of which some effect is deducible or probable, then background knowledge makes that effect more probable than it would be if no such theory was in our system. But what could lead us to think of a theory as part of our background knowledge in this way aside from the fact that it has survived tests in the past? This would clearly be an inductive step. From an anti-inductivist standpoint, however, the fact that a theory has survived a certain type of test on occasions can give us no reason to suppose that it is more likely to survive another test of the same type on the $n + 1$ occasion than it was on the first occasion of undergoing a test of that type. For what could be the basis of such a view other than a generalization from instances of which we have had experience to one – a different one, even if in some ways similar – of which we have as yet had no experience? In other words, treating well-corroborated theories as part of background knowledge is covertly inductive if it means that we now think of certain effects which follow from the theories as likely to occur, and so if they do, as unsevere tests of any theory.

Popper might reply here that we should repeat a test of a given type only to ensure that we have a reproducible effect, and that, if this hypothesis is corroborated, then we can treat what is being tested as unproblematic since further testing in the same area would only mean doing more tests of the same sort. But how, on non-inductive grounds, does reproduction of a given effect on some occasion(s) of testing give us reason to think that further testing would not be severe? In determining test severity, background knowledge does appear on any reading to be used inductively.

Even if this were not so, however, it is central to what Popper has been saying that tests may be spoken of as being of different types, but it is very doubtful that a non-inductivist is entitled to speak of a future test as being of the same (or different) type as past tests. A new test will have some properties in common with, and some distinct from, those of old tests. It counts as a test of the same sort if the properties distinguishing it from the old tests are those we believe on inductive grounds will not substantially affect the outcome. Suppose we are investigating whether metals dissolve in acids and that we have so far tested iron at sea-level. We now do two new tests, one of iron at 500 feet, and one of nickel at sea-level. We will be inclined to think of the iron test as simply a repetition, a test of the same sort as the previous one, but this is only because our background knowledge leads us to assume that such chemical experiments will have similar results whether they are done at sea-level or at 500 feet. Here again, background knowledge is being used in a predictive way, and our decision has an inductive basis.

What is ultimately at stake here is not simply a directive about which tests and experiments to carry out on a theory, but the basis on which we make judgments about the success or failure of theories under test. For, in a test situation, no theory is simply confronted with a brute experience and either corroborated or refuted. No test will bear decisively on any theory unless we assume among other things that all the other factors in the test situation are 'normal' (i.e., as our background knowledge expects them to be) and that any failure of a test-implication is actually due to the falsity of the theory being tested and not due to some unexpected deviation from our theoretical expectations of it caused by one of the countless other factors bearing on the test situation. Background knowledge no doubt assures us that many such deviations are unlikely and can be discounted – so long as we are inductivists and feel entitled to do what Popper (*CR*, p. 390) says we have to do anyway in testing a theory: accept background knowledge (i.e., the results of past testing) as unproblematic. But if we do not generalize from the past to the future, how can we ever discount the possibility that some failure does not occur in some theory we normally accept unquestioningly, which is involved in our thinking of our current test situation as normal? We could, of course, test that theory, but then in order to make the new test effective we would have to discount the possibility of other theories not failing us in the new case, and so our problem would recur. The conclusion is that Popper cannot achieve even theoretical theory preference through testing without making inductive assumptions; at various points in the testing process background knowledge (i.e., theories well corroborated in the past) has to be accepted, not as being 'worthy of further testing' but as a reliable guide to what is happening now and to what is likely to happen in the immediate future. So although Popper ('Supp. R', p. 363) is quite correct to say that there is nothing inductive in inferring an effect from a universal theory and the relevant initial conditions, inductive assumptions are being made in the way background knowledge had to be used in order both to treat a particular effect as a test of one particular theory and to assess its severity as a test of that theory.

Musgrave (1975) accepts that, if background knowledge is used so as progressively to increase assessments of the probability of repeated tests (as the passage from *CR*, p. 240, suggests), then there is a degree of inductivism about. In order to avoid this, he proposes that after 'sufficiently many' tests of a theory, the appropriate falsifying hypothesis (asserting reproducibility of the effect) is either simply accepted or rejected and consigned to background knowledge, after which further testing of that effect is deemed to have no severity at all. He says that we simply decide when sufficiently many tests have been made. This is not justified on grounds of probability (which would be inductive). Indeed, the decision cannot be justified at all, although we may be able to justify our choice of it on, presumably, non-inductive grounds. This is in line with Popper's view that preferring one theory to another (because it is more corroborated and corroborable) can be rational without having reasons for believing in the theory, and with Watkins's assertion (1968, p. 279) that 'there may be reasons having nothing to do with relative certainty for preferring one hypothesis to another'. Popper is also free to say (*LSD*, p. 280) that those among us who are unwilling to expose their ideas to the hazard of refutation do not take part in 'the scientific game', but as he cannot give us any reason for thinking that the decisions made on the basis of the game or those made within the game are likely to be true, he ultimately fails to show how playing the game is a reasonable thing to do for those interested in truth. Bartley's innocent comparison of Popperian methodology with a Wittgensteinian language game (cf. Bartley, 1968, p. 110) possibly so enraged Popper because of its closeness to the truth.

6 *Verisimilitude*

Verisimilitude was introduced by Popper in order to give some backing to the intuitive idea that one theory – even though false – might be preferable to a competitor as being nearer to the truth. The sort of example he had in mind was one in which theory t_1 is more precise or universal than theory t_2, has passed tests t_2 has failed and has failed only those t_2 has failed as well. In other words, t_1 is preferable to t_2 in terms of both content and true implications. This led him to combine the notions of truth and content so as to define the verisimilitude of a theory as its truth-content minus its falsity-content. (As will be seen, Popper's preferred definition is actually slightly more complicated than this.) Of course, our appraisals of verisimilitude will depend on our interpretations of the relevant tests, and hence on inductive background assumptions, as Popper indicates when he says (*CR*, p. 235) that the stability of such appraisals depends on the stability of our background knowledge. As we shall see further in chapter VI, revolutionary changes here may lead us to think that t_2 has succeeded where previously we thought t_1 had succeeded. Equally, the future use of such an appraisal will be as questionable as the use of corroboration. So talk of verisimilitude does not in itself help the non-inductivist to answer the difficulties raised in the previous section. Here, though, we will consider how criticisms by Tichý (1974), Harris (1974), Miller (1974, 1975) and Grünbaum (1976c) have shown the inadequacy of Popper's original attempts to formalize the concept of verisimilitude.

Popper says of verisimilitude (CR, p. 233):

Assuming that the truth-content and the falsity-content of two theories t_1 and t_2 are comparable, we can say that t_2 is more closely similar to the truth, or corresponds better to the facts, than t_1, if and only if either (a) the truth-content but not the falsity-content of t_2 exceeds that of t_1, (b) the falsity-content of t_1, but not its truth-content, exceeds that of t_2.

What the critics have shown is that for either of the ways proposed by Popper for comparing truth- and falsity-contents (CR, pp. 391–7; OK, pp. 47–52, 331–5), conditions (a) and (b) can be fulfilled together only when t_2 is true. In other words, on these accounts, false theories cannot attain what seems a reasonable minimum requirement for comparisons of verisimilitude, while, as Miller (1974, p. 174) remarks, we hardly need the sophistications of verisimilitude to tell us to prefer the logically richer of two true competitors.

Popper defines the content of a theory A ($Cn(A)$) as being the set of its logical consequences. Its truth-content (A_T) is the set of its consequences belonging to the true sentences (T) of the language, and it follows from his definition of A's falsity-content (A_F), as the relative content of A given A_T, that A_F is the set of A's consequences belonging to the false sentences (F) of the language.

The first way of comparing truth- and falsity-contents for verisimilitude is through subclass relationships (symbolized by $A_T \subset B_T$, where A_T is a proper subclass of B_T). Popper's conditions for verisimilitude now say that A has less verisimilitude than B if and only if their truth- and falsity-contents are comparable through subclass relationships and either (a) $A_T \subset B_T$ and $A_F \not\subset B_T$ or (b) $B_T \not\subset A_T$ and $B_F \subset A_F$. The comparability involved means that we can say $A_F \not\subset B_F$ only if $B_F \subseteq A_F$ and $B_T \not\subset A_T$ only if $A_T \subseteq B_T$. So on this account (the qualitative or logical account) A has less verisimilitude than B if and only if either (a) $A_T \subset B_T$ and $B_F \subseteq A_F$ or (b) $A_T \subseteq B_T$ and $B_F \subset A_F$; that is, either (a) A's truth-content is a subset of B's and B's falsity-content is a subset of or the same as A's or (b) A's truth-content is a subset of or the same as B's and B's falsity-content is a subset of A's

However, whenever B is false, neither condition can hold, so we can never compare two false theories for qualitative verisimilitude. A variation of Tichý's succinct proof of this is that, since B is false, there is a false sentence, say f, in Cn (B). Assume first that $A_T \subset B_T$. Then there is a sentence, say b, in $B_T - A_T$. But then $f.b$ is in B_F, but not in A_F (or b would be in A_T). Thus $B_F \not\subseteq A_F$, so condition (a) fails. On the other hand, assume that $B_F \subset A_F$. Then there is a sentence, say a, in $A_F - B_F$. Then $a \lor - f$ is in A_T, but not in B_T, for, if it were in B_T, then either $- f$ would be in $Cn(B)$ or a would be in B_F and, given that B is consistent, these possibilities are ruled out by the choices of f and a. So condition (b) fails as well.

Tichý points out, as an illustration of his proof, that one of Popper's own examples (in OK, p. 56) violates his conditions for verisimilitude. Let A consist of the sole sentence 'It is now between 9.40 and 9.48' and B of the sole sentence 'It is now between 9.45 and 9.48', the 'between' in each case excluding the upper bound. Assume it is 9.48; then, says Popper, B has more verisimilitude than A. It is true that $A_T \subset B_T$, but as B is false and the (only) member of B is in B_F, but not in A_F, $B_F \not\subseteq A_F$. Grünbaum points out that in this example B entails A, but not vice versa. However, in the more important cases in science we have incompatible competitors. Here, the situation is even worse for qualitative verisimilitude for, as Grünbaum says (and is in effect stated by Popper in his definition of truth-content (CR, p. 392)), since B will be false and incompatible with A, $- B$ will be in A_T, so we will not even be able to get $A_T \subset B_T$.

Popper's second method for comparing contents has even worse results for his conditions for verisimilitude. In this method, which involves assigning quantities to contents, the measure of the content of a theory A is defined in terms of its logical improbability, as $1 - p(A)$. In other words, the less A's logical probability, the greater its content. If we use the letters a, b, etc., to refer to the sets of statements implied by theories A, B, etc. and t to refer to the set of true statements of the language (all these sets being closed under the operation of logical consequence), A's content becomes $1 - p(a)$. If we follow Popper (CR, p. 392) in using $(a \lor b)$ to symbolize the product of sets a and b (which contains all their common consequences), A's measured truth-content $(ct_T(a))$, being, on Popper's view, the intersection of A and the system of all true statements, becomes $1 - p(a \lor t)$. This seems reasonable, as, if A is true, its truth-content increases directly with its logical improbability. A's measured falsity content $(ct_F(a))$ is given in terms of the probability of A, given its truth-content, i.e. $1 - p(a, a \lor t)$. Thus, if A is true, its falsity-content is zero. A's measured verisimilitude $(V_s(A))$ is its truth-content less its falsity-content, preferably, in Popper's view, to be multiplied by a normalizing factor and coming out as

$$(ct_T(A) - ct_F(A)) / (2 - ct_T(A) - ct_F(A)).$$

Given that we can overcome the drawback of these definitions being based on logical probability and so seemingly unable to make fine enough distinctions between universal theories, there are still two consequences following from them which render them practically useless for the comparison of false theories. This emerges from considering cases where the theories involved are not universal and can be assigned greater than zero probabilities.

If A is false, it is incompatible with t, so $p(a \lor t)$ becomes equal to $p(a) + p(t)$. So A's truth-content becomes $1 - [p(a) + p(t)]$. Because, by the probability calculus, the relative probability $p(a, b)$ is $p(a.b)/p(b)$, A's falsity-content can be rewritten as $1 - [p(a.(a \lor t))/p(a \lor t)]$, which in view of A's falsity becomes $1 - p(a)/[p(a) + p(t)]$. The first unwelcome consequence of this is that it is clear now that these computations of truth- and falsity-contents of any false theories will vary solely according to the absolute logical probabilities of the theories. As the definition of verisimilitude has as its sole variables the measures of truth- and falsity-contents, the same goes for computing comparative verisimilitudes of competing theories. In other words, once we know that a theory is false, no empirical facts will be relevant to determining its truth- and falsity-contents or its verisimilitude. Any two theories with the same logical probability and hence with the same content will, if false, have the same verisimilitude, which is surely undesirable in a measure supposedly discriminating between competing theories covering the same ground.

The second unwelcome consequence of this way of measuring truth- and falsity-contents has been pointed out by Miller (1974, p. 173). Popper's conditions for comparing verisimilitudes require either that the theory with greater verisimilitude has excess truth-content but not falsity-content over its rival or that the theory with less verisimilitude has excess falsity-content but not truth-content over its rival. In the case of two false competitors, these conditions can never be fulfilled. For as the content $1 - p(a)$ of a theory increases, so, if it is false, do *both* its truth-content, $1 - [p(a) + p(t)]$, *and* its falsity-content, $1 - p(a)/[p(a) + p(t)]$. So, with false theories, either of Popper's conditions for verisimilitude can be fulfilled if we calculate truth- and falsity-contents on either subclass or quantitative methods. The quantitative theory of verisimilitude does enable us to compare false theories for verisimilitude, but hardly in the way we want, as these comparisons are based entirely on the content of the theories and not on their actual accuracy.

Popper ('NV') admits the criticisms by Tichý and Miller of his earlier accounts of verisimilitude, and proposes yet another one. On this account, the nearness to truth of a theory A $(n_T(a))$ is equal to its content plus q, where $q = p(t)$, when A is true, and to its content minus q when A is false, i.e.

If A is true, $n_T(a) = ct(a) + q$.
If A is false, $n_T(a) = ct(a) - q$.

Content is, as always, inversely related to logical probability.

It is clear that, as q will be the same for all sentences of a given language, the nearness to truth of theories will depend solely on their truth-values and their content. While this is what would be expected of true theories, it is not satisfactory in the case of false theories. To adapt Popper's own example, if the time is now 9.48, the false statement 'It is now between 9.45 and 9.48' is, according to Popper, closer to the truth than the false statement 'It is now between 9.40 and 9.48', but this cannot be explained solely by appeal to the greater content of the first statement, for the false statement 'It is now between 9.34 and 9.35' surely has more content but less verisimilitude than either.

Faced with failure of the qualitative and quantitative theories of verisimilitude, Miller (1975) took up a hint from Popper (CR, p. 235) to the effect that theories can be ranked for verisimilitude if, on the occasion when numerical values for the same quantities can be derived from each, one is always nearer to the true value than the other. What Miller shows is that, when the theories involved are false, even if for one version of the theories it turns out that one of the theories makes uniformly more accurate predictions, logically equivalent versions of the theories will reverse the ordering. To illustrate this point, Miller's own example invites us to suppose that P and Q are two physical constants, with theory A asserting $P = 8$ and $Q = 0$ and theory B asserting $P = 7$ and $Q = 2$. In fact, $P = 0$ and $Q = 2$. Thus B is more accurate on P and Q. But now consider physical constants R and S, defined so that $R = P + Q$ and $S = P + 4Q$. The predicted and true (T) values will be as in Table 1. On R and S, A appears more

TABLE 1

	Constants			
	P	Q	R	S
Theories				
A	8	0	8	8
B	7	2	9	15
T	0	2	2	8

accurate. It can hardly be claimed either that P and Q are inherently simpler than R and S, for if P and Q are defined from them, we have $P = (4R - S)/3$ and $Q = (S - R)/3$. What Miller goes on to do is to show formally that the shared constants and parameters of any two theories can be replaced by new constants and parameters defined on the basis of the old ones in such a way as to yield theories that are logically equivalent (i.e., will make the same predictions on all measurements) but in which the original impressions of accuracy are reversed. The implications of this result for verisimilitude can be avoided only if we think of a theory stated in a certain way – using certain constants and parameters – as being more important, significant or fundamental than a logically equivalent one stated in another way.

Miller regards any attempt to think of some set of quantities as more fundamental than some other interdefinable set as a type of essentialism, in which the way a theory is expressed and the particular quantities it focuses on are specially significant. Against this, it can be urged that there are good reasons for making planetary motions or atomic masses more fundamental than other possible measurements in planetary astronomy and chemistry, because doing so 'permits an economical summary' (Rosenkrantz, 1975, p. 196) of the properties of planets or of matter. Popper himself suggested personally ('NV', pp. 156–7) that those parameters central to the problems the theories are designed to solve can be taken as fundamental, and then competing theories compared on their performances on those parameters. Against this, Miller contends that Popper himself wants theories to address themselves to new problems as well as to old ones, and, of course, with new problems judgments as to the relative importance of parameters based on what seemed central with the old problems may well be overturned. Popper answered this by emphasizing the relative and historical nature of appraisals of verisimilitude: that they are made relative to the past performance of theories on particular problems and tests, and that, therefore, *if* a new set of parameters ultimately appears as more central we will certainly overturn the old judgments, but until that happens there is no need to worry. From a non-inductive standpoint, however, what Miller's results show is that there is no reason to think that past performance is a good guide to future performance. In particular, quantities that were once highlighted as central (planetary distance with Kepler) may later appear to be no more central than other sets of quantities (all celestial distances are equally significant for Newton). If this is right, it is significant in showing that in this respect the problem of the non-inductive value of verisimilitude emerges from the heart of our assessments of verisimilitude. We can indeed make judgments on the accuracy of theories, but these will be relative to the particular parameters and constants we are focusing on, and there is no guarantee that they will appear so central in the future. Indeed, to think that they will be is not only inductive, but it may blind us to other and better possibilities.

Analogous criticisms can be made of attempts (such as that by Tichý (1974)) to analyse the relative verisimilitude of two theories in terms of the distance of the relevant constituents (i.e., complete consistent theories of the language) from the constituent which is the true theory in that language. In a simple propositional language, for example, these distances will be defined in terms of the numbers of primitive sentences negated in one constituent, but not in others. So for such a language with only three primitive sentences, h, r and w, where the true constituent is h & r & w, the false constituent $- h$ & r & w has more verisimilitude than $- h$ & $- r$ & $- w$, as we would expect. But, as Miller (1974, pp. 175–7) has shown, this appraisal may be reversed if we translate our theories into a language employing different primitive terms. In a language in which the primitive terms are h, m and a, and m is equivalent to $h \equiv r$ in our first language and a to $h \equiv w$, the truth will be h & m & a, our first false constituent becomes $- h$ & $- m$ & $- a$, while the second is $- h$ & m & a. Now the second theory is closer to the truth.

What Miller calls the language-dependence of this account of verisimilitude has been called by Mott (1978) its interest-dependence. How far relativity to our actual interests is an integral part of our pre-systematic idea in appraising verisimilitude is open to dispute. Popper ('NV', p. 147) explicitly rejects accounts such as that criticized by Miller which would make appraisals of verisimilitude vary with the language in which the theories are expressed. In view of his counter in the same paper to Miller's accuracy argument, however, perhaps he should not look so unkindly on such accounts so long as the languages in which the theories are expressed when the appraisals are being made reflect in their conceptual apparatus our actual interests. What does not appear to be in dispute, however, is that the most promising way to construct a formal theory of verisimilitude is through specifying means of measuring distances of constituents from each other. Such measures have been constructed for quantificational as well as sentential languages (cf. Tichý, 1978; Miller, 1978; Niiniluoto, 1978). However, such measures have not produced satisfactory results when they have not been tied down to specific languages or conceptual schemes, which still seems a problem from a strictly Popperian point of view, as Miller's arguments and Popper's remarks would indicate.

In *Conjectures and Refutations* (p. 235), Popper wrote:

Ultimately, the idea of verisimilitude is most important in cases where we know that we have to work with theories which are *at best* approximations – that is to say, theories of which we actually know that they cannot be true ... In these cases we can still speak of better or worse approximations to the truth (and we therefore do not need to interpret these cases in an instrumentalist sense).

The difficulties encountered with the verisimilitude of false theories are therefore particularly damaging to Popper's attempt to formalize verisimilitude. Miller's accuracy point might perhaps be simply side-stepped by stipulating that verisimilitude can still be compared between false theories having different degrees of content. Indeed, Popper clearly wants content to play a major role in determining verisimilitude – so much so that in the probabilistic definition and in 'A Note on Verisimilitude', the relative verisimilitude of false theories depends entirely on the content of the theories. (This also appears to be the case with Mott's 1978 attempt to construct an interest-free account of verisimilitude.) In the 'NV' account, as q will be small in any interesting language, a false rich theory may well have higher verisimilitude than a true trivial theory. One might object to this, saying that the perfect fit of a true theory is in one sense always preferable to the imperfect fit of a false theory (at least you will not *lose* any money by betting on the true theory), but this is not Popper's view, and, as far as increasing our knowledge goes, he is right. We will learn more from testing a rich (but false) theory than from testing a vague and trivially true one. Which, then, is closer to the truth, the false theory or the true one? Popper wants to say that, sometimes at least, the false theory can be. The pre-philosophic notion of closeness to the truth is surely vague enough to allow him to do so, and to include high content as a crucial factor in his account, although it should obviously not be the only factor. (Certainly it should not be if, as we have seen with the quantitative account of verisimilitude, increasing content in a false theory involves increasing truth- *and* falsity-contents. Harris (1974, p. 163) shows a similar result for the qualitative theory.)

If content is to be a factor in determining verisimilitude, it is in place to ask how the content of universal theories is to be compared, for which $p = 0$. Popper (*OK*, pp. 52–3) said that the intuitive comparability of Einstein's and Newton's theories could be established by showing

(a) to every question to which Newton's theory has an answer, Einstein's theory has an answer which is at least as precise . . .
[and] (b) there are questions to which Einstein's theory can give a (non-tautological) answer while Newton's theory does not.

In other words, Popper is proposing a class-inclusion account of content through the questions answerable by theories. Miller (1975) and then Grünbaum (1976b) have shown that, even in the case of Newton's and Einstein's theories, condition (a) is not fulfilled. Grünbaum takes the question 'Why is the orbit of a planet of negligible mass which is subject solely to the sun's field a perfectly closed ellipse around the sun?' and shows that, while this is answerable precisely by Newton (as what it asks is a consequence of his theory), all Einstein can say here is that the question is based on a false presupposition and, as such, does not arise. If Einstein's repudiation of the question is allowed to him as an answer, then, equally, Newton must be allowed a similar move when Einstein raises problems (about, say, the relativity of physical magnitudes) which cannot be stated in Newtonian terms. More generally, Popper himself ('Supp. R', p. 368) shows, following suggestions of Miller (1975, p. 165), that a predecessor theory can always answer questions which a successor which contradicts it cannot. Let c be a false statement which follows from the predecessor theory and which is corrected in the successor theory, and u an undecidable statement, then only the predecessor will be able to resolve the question 'is c-or-u true?' Of course this question is not of any great interest but its existence makes it seem doubtful that there can be a successful measure of content which is based purely on class inclusion of questions. As Popper himself goes on to admit, the likelihood is that the comparisons of content we are interested in will have to be made relevant to questions and problems that are of scientific interest at the time of the comparison, and that we will have to speak of a successor theory as having greater content than a predecessor as implying that it covers at least the range of *scientifically interesting* questions of the predecessor and either applies to some more situations than its predecessor or corrects some of the predecessor's mistakes (or both).

Measures of content and verisimilitude have not been constructed by Popper or anyone else which formalize the notion in such a way as to fulfil all Popper's original desiderata. His own measures are either inconsistent or make verisimilitude depend solely on logical content, while those advanced by others tend to make appraisals of verisimilitude vary with language. What is not any objection to any of these theories is that they all make use in one way or another of something which we do not actually know: the truth, considered as the set of true sentences. This would no doubt limit their practical applicability, but they are not presented as ways of solving practical questions, but as logical analyses of the notion, investigations of its consistency and implications. However, the question remains whether the fact that Popperian verisimilitude has not been shown to be satisfactory means that it should be abandoned. Popper thinks not, continuing to stress the importance of the idea. His recent account ('NV', p 158) of verisimilitude is at once looser and more guarded than earlier accounts. He says that we may conjecture that Einstein's theory is nearer to the truth than Newton's because

(i) Einstein's theory seems to have greater content, since it seems to solve all relevant problems which Newton's can solve (because Newton's theory can be obtained from it in approximation). On the other hand, there are several great problems on which Newton's theory has nothing to say while Einstein's has. (Example the redshift of light emitted in a strong gravitational field.)

(ii) The tests appear to show that the numerical results of Einstein's theory are in a few fields nearer to the target than those of Newton's theory. (Mercury perihelium movement; light rays grazing the surface of the sun.)

The idea of a theory implying another as an approximation on the 'relevant' problem and solving problems in other areas too gives some substance to the comparison of truth content, even if these cannot be made set-theoretically. The idea of a theory doing better than another on crucial experiments also has intuitive plausibility. These ideas are combined in the 1978 note on verisimilitude, where, after conceding the faultiness of the earlier definitions, Popper offers the following account:

> it appears intuitively that a statement b is nearer to the truth than a statement a if, and only if, (1) the (relativized) truth content of b exceeds the truth content of a and (2) some of the consequences of a that are false (preferably all those accepted as being refuted, and even more preferably, some others beyond them) are no longer derivable from b, but replaced by their negations ('Supp. R', p. 371).

Of course, Miller's accuracy point would still apply (as Popper recognizes), but if we are prepared to think of verisimilitude in terms of actual appraisals of theories we are interested in, in the formulations that seem significant to us, then, however implicitly inductive such thinking might be, we do have a basis for ranking theories. Popper admits ('Supp. R', p. 372) that a purely logical approach to the definition of verisimilitude might not be possible, and that the notion might be viable only when relativized to relevant problems or to the historical problem situation and, possibly, one might add, to appraisals in specific languages as well. Certainly, from an inductive and language-dependent point of view to think of verisimilitude in the way Popper speaks in the last two quotations given above is intelligible. It is also, as he points out ('NV', p. 157), consistent with his general emphasis on interpreting and appraising theories in the light of the problems they are designed to solve and which scientists were (or are) actually interested in.

IV

Reinstatement of Induction

1 Induction : a transcendental argument

In *Objective Knowledge* (pp. 23–4), Popper sees in men and animals

> [an] immensely powerful *need for regularity* . . . which makes them
> seek for regularities; which makes them sometimes experience
> regularities even where there are none; which makes them
> cling to their expectations dogmatically; and which makes them
> unhappy and may drive them to despair and to the verge of
> madness if certain assumed regularities break down.

Against the Humean account, according to which the regularities we
find around us impose themselves upon us through repeated experience, we saw that Popper argued that the experience of repetition
must be preceded by the adoption of a point of view, even a theory or
an expectation. The need to seek regularities and impose such theories
on our environment is 'clearly inborn and based on drives, or instincts.
There is the general need for a world that conforms to our expectations.'
Unfortunately, there is no reason why the real world should be such
a world. This is what we learn from Hume's attack on the principle
of induction. Our expectations can fail us; it is simply irrational to
rely on them.

Popper's philosophy of knowledge is, as he says (*OK*, p. 5), an
attempt to construct a rational system which does without irrational
beliefs in regularities. It exploits the human ability to formulate
theories and expectations exosomatically, as objectively stated theories.
Unlike other animals we can thus correct and criticize our theories .We
do not need to die just because one of our expectations comes unstuck.
But Popper's attempt to dispense with induction is unsuccessful. We
have found that inductive reasoning, removed from one part of the

picture, crops up in another. I shall now attempt to show that the underlying reason for this is that any coherent conceptualization of experience requires the assumption of a stable order in the world. To say this is to say something stronger than the analytic justification of induction, which says only that an inductive principle *happens* to be central to our science and common sense, but does not show why it is. It is also to give some reason for the apparent perversity of scepticism about induction.

The ability to distinguish in principle between what really exists apart from me and what is merely mind dependent is basic to any coherent conceptualization of experience, because such an ability is required for any being who is able to see himself as existing in an objective world at all. Without it, he could never decide that his perceptions reflected anything other than his own current states of consciousness. In fact, as I shall argue in chapter V, he could not even do this, because the categorization of one's perceptions itself depends on one's being in a world of objects, and that one recognizes that some of one's perceptions are perceptions of such objects. What I want to show here is that in this recognition one has to transcend in an inductive way the sensory data one is given in immediate experience (Kant's intuitions) – that one does move from what one has experience of to what one has no experience of on the basis of the experiences one has. The argument of chapter V shows that, without seeing oneself in a world of objects, one will be unable even to talk about or categorize one's sensory input, while what is at issue here is that *within* one's sensory input which reflects the world of objects.

A world which has existence apart from me is one which I take to have existence apart from my perceiving it. However, my whole experience of it is through my perceptions; I have no other contact with it. From this it follows that there must be something within my perceptions which allows me to think of some of them reflecting a reality apart from them, which would have been there even if I had not been perceiving it. In our actual experience we distinguish between those things whose existence is not constituted by their being perceived (tables, chairs, other people) and those inner states such as pains, headaches, after-images and the buzzings and flashings whose existence *is* their being experienced. What *esse est percipi* amounts to here is that on the basis of his inner experiences alone the experiencer can find no application for the distinction between a 'real' pain and a 'merely imaginary' one. In practice, the distinction may have an application because of the correlations that have been made between the pains we feel and externally observable facts such as injuries to parts of the body, dental decay and so on. So what is it within our experience that reflects a world of *externally* observable facts, of a reality whose existence is independent of its being perceived? Like Kant, I am assuming that we do have a use for the concept of such a reality; what I want to bring out here is its basis in experience.

If we consider typical cases of objective realities we will find ourselves thinking of such things as chairs, tables, trees, houses and other enduring three-dimensional objects. From the perceptual point of view, such objects are characteristically re-encounterable according to orderly expectations. If we are able to recognize such objects, then significant tracts of our experience will be organized in such a way that, on the basis of past patterns within our experience, we are able successfully to predict future experiences. My recognizing that a certain object is a desk leads me to expect that I will have certain experiences in the future, for example, that I will see the desk again when I look in a certain direction, that it will continue to feel hard to my touch and so on. One thing that makes it possible to think of things as existing even while unperceived is that, after having moved from them, I am able to perceive them again in a regular pattern, which is based on the regularities noted within the past perceptions which I took to be perceptions of those objects. So, the existence of un-perceived things is reflected by the presence within my perceptions of inductively projectible regularities. If such regularities did not obtain, it would not be possible for me to think of my perceptions as being perceptions of objects which endure even while unperceived. If I cannot see myself as existing in a world in which objects exist while unperceived, it is hard to see how I could think of my perceptions as being perceptions of things that would have been there even if I had not: that is, I could not see myself as being in a world independent of me, and, in such a case, I would have no grounds for distinguishing appearance from reality. Hume is thus right, and Popper wrong, to place the recognition and projection of regularity at the heart of our conceptual scheme; it is our biological good fortune that on the whole the regularities we are disposed to notice lead to successful projections.

Our notion of an objective world, then, is reflected by the degree of continuing order and regularity that is to be found within our perceptions. What this implies, of course, is not that if our perceptions were not ordered or ceased to be ordered in various ways there would be no objective world, but that we would not be able to say that there was. Consider the chaos of experience which the surviving astronaut entered in the last part of the film *2001*. His experience up till that point had been like ours, but the vast majority of the expectations built up on his past experience were suddenly shattered. He would, therefore, have been unable to tell whether his inductively based expectations had been substantially refuted or his perceptual faculties had undergone some transformation so that they were no longer capable of delivering veridical information. The point is that at the onset of experiential chaos he lost the ability to apply the distinction between objective and subjective experience, and questions about the reality or otherwise of what he was experiencing – including the question as to whether induction had failed – became for him necessarily undecidable.

What the argument of the previous paragraph, which derives in part from Blackburn (1973, pp. 159–63), suggests is that, in order to recognize that our perceptual faculties are sound and telling how things actually are, we need to have a large proportion of our inductive expectations fulfilled. Only then will we be in a position to think that significant changes in the course of nature are due to nature rather than to some disorder in ourselves, because only then will we have any grounds in general for trusting our senses. Empirical evidence can then point definitely only to piecemeal changes in nature. Later on, of course, we might begin to recognize a new order in the originally apparently chaotic perceptions, which would be some reason for thinking that it was the world rather than us that had changed. But, even if this did happen, it would not follow that induction had not been a reasonable course to follow in the past. Not only had success up to the cataclysm been remarkable, but, further, the connection between order in our experience and objectivity suggests that our new world picture will equally be based on and reflected by inductively pro-jectable regularities within our new experience. Without such regulari-ties, there would be no basis for a distinction betweenappearance and reality. In addition, as I shall show in chapter V, without being able to think of some of our perceptions as perceptions of enduring objects, we would not even be able to categorize our perceptions as being perceptions of a certain sort. This suggests that the same order within our perceptions which enables us to think of ourselves sometimes perceiving real states of affairs also enables us to categorize our per-ceptions. To sort out our perceptions at all, then, implies that we can sometimes successfully speak of objects and that, therefore, our perceptions are given to us in an ordered way. That this need not be so and that the order may break down (either in the perceptions or in what they are perceptions of) is clearly what gives Popper's scepticism about induction its force, but the view that induction is dispensable, while still being able to talk significantly and make discoveries about the real world, cannot be so easily maintained.

That a belief in induction is not something which can be dropped without substantial alterations elsewhere in our conceptual scheme is why the failure of Popper to develop a truly non-inductive science is not a chance result, but one with deep roots. The rationality of induc-tion (and hence of action on inductive policies) is of a piece with the rationality of belief in an external, objective world. Indeed, induction can be taken to be required for our knowledge of objects spatially as well as temporally removed from our current experience, on the grounds that knowledge of their continuing and orderly existence involves, from the perceptual point of view, an equal jump to things beyond what we have actually experienced. It is central to our ability to make judgments to the effect that what is being experienced is objectively there that we can also make judgments to the effect that some things exist which are not objects of current experience and that some of our perceptions are of enduring, re-encounterable objects of this sort. The fact that this latter type of judgment is necessarily one which goes beyond that of which we have direct experience makes it in a broad sense inductive, and because of the connection between objectivity and order, it will in practice be inductive in a more precise sense: what we will expect to be there and to happen when we are not perceiving them will be just those things predicted by projecting the regularities we have encountered in the experiences we have had.

The conclusion to be drawn from this examination of the connection between induction and belief in an external world is that the use of inductive policies is to be seen, not as Popper does as an irrational biological flaw, but as a necessity for any conceptual scheme which provides any basis for a distinction among our experiences between the real and the imaginary. This does nothing in any absolute way to guarantee that the world might not suddenly become chaotic, but it does show that a basic feature of a rational approach to experience – the ability to mark out what is objective in it – depends for its continuing application on the assumption that the world is not going to behave like this. It is worth emphasizing that an important part of my argument is that, if our inductive expectations were suddenly to let us down, we would be unable to know whether our perceptions were still veridical. Thus, I am not simply saying that our ability to distinguish between true experience and illusions depends on our once having experienced an orderly world, but that it depends on the continuance of whatever order we had previously recognized. But to assume this is just what, according to Popper, is deeply irrational, and which should be eliminated from our conceptual scheme. That, as I seek to show, it cannot be so eliminated is the underlying reason for one's natural feeling that scepticism about induction is forced and unreal; this reasoning also provides some substance to the analytic justification, which fundamentally seeks to stress the connection between reason and induction, but which fails to show the necessity for this connection. In the final analysis, what is surprising is not that inductive generalization on past experience should be part of our conceptual scheme (rearing its head even in Popper's attempt to construct a methodology free from inductive reasoning), but that the regularities within human experience on which human beings have generalized should have proved to be as useful in predicting the course of nature as they have. But this is a question for biology – to explain how we are so adapted to our environment – rather than for philosophy.

2 *A 'whiff' of inductivism*

The transcendental argument of the previous section cannot guarantee the success of inductive inference, either in general or in particular cases. On this, Popper and I would agree. The difference between us is whether we can do without induction. My argument suggested that the distinction between the objective and the subjective presupposed an inductive principle. A general failure of induction (in the sense of the assumption of continuing regularities within our experience and the general success of our inductive inferences) would lead to a break-down at this fundamental point. The strange thing is that Popper appears to agree with just this point.

Not only does he say (*LSD*, p. 252) that science is an attempt to uncover a pattern of regularity among natural phenomena and, as such, 'presupposes *the immutability of natural processes* or the "principle of the uniformity of nature"', but he also speaks ('RC', p. 1027) of the cosmos as being almost entirely such as to make the acquisition of knowledge impossible because of the absence of observable regularity:

> Our theories tell us that the world is almost completely empty,
> and that empty space is filled with chaotic radiation. And almost
> all the places which are not empty are occupied either by chaotic
> dust, or by gases, or by very hot stars – all in conditions which
> seem to make the application of any physical method of acquiring
> knowledge impossible. There are many worlds, possible and
> actual worlds, in which a search for knowledge and for
> regularities would fail. And even in the world as we actually
> know it from the sciences, the occurrence of conditions under
> which life, and a search for knowledge, could arise – and
> succeed – seems to be almost infinitely improbable.

So Popper seems to agree that regularity in the world around us is essential for human knowledge, at least inasmuch as this is acquired by 'physical methods'. This is just what I have been trying to establish in arguing that our conceptual scheme relies on inductive assumptions. We can agree with Popper that these assumptions are not 'logically valid' – i.e., they could fail us. But he is saying here that a world of continuing regularity is required for knowledge of it to be possible. This is not far from admitting that there is a sense in which inductive assumptions have to be made by us in our attempt to live in and understand the world.

We have seen, too, how a high degree of corroboration says nothing about the future performance of a theory, or, to put it bluntly, about its truth. We may 'feel in our bones' that the past successes of our theories give us reasons for thinking that our theories, especially if they are well tested, are near the truth, but not only would such reasons be inductive, but to think this would be to forget that the scientific approach to knowledge is one of testing, not one of justifying. Popper's attitude has always been consistent here, as can be seen from the following passage from the 1934 *Logic of Scientific Discovery* (p. 278), which he quotes in 1974 ('RC', pp. 1002–3):

> Science is not a system of certain, or well established, statements; nor is it a system which steadily advances towards a state of finality. Our science is not knowledge: it can never claim to have attained truth, or even a substitute for it, such as probability. Yet, science has more than mere biological survival. It is not only a useful instrument. Although it can attain neither truth nor probability, the striving for knowledge and the search for truth are still the strongest motives of scientific discovery.

What is worrying in Popper's position here is that, although in science severe testing can give us reasons for preferring some theories to others, we are never given an extra-scientific reason for preferring the severely tested statements (such as that they are true or probable). In fact, without inductive inference, even being told some theories are false is not much help, for there is no reason to think that theories that have failed us in the past might not succeed in the future.

Lakatos (1968, also 1974) suggested a way out for Popper. He says that Popper's arguments against induction can be regarded as refuting a justificationist attitude to induction, such as using it to 'prove' that inductively established theories are bound to succeed, or assigning them *a priori* degrees of probability. Such moves may fail, showing their logical invalidity as proofs. On the other hand, there would be nothing wrong in speculating that our world was such and we were such that theories we put forward in it which gain high degrees of corroboration through the tests we are able to devise for them progressively capture more of the truth about that world. The fact that this is advanced as a piece of speculation shows that we are aware of the lack of proof that this is so, although we may think of the speculation as being supported by and in turn explaining the success of our technology. Lakatos asks (1974, p. 260) whether there is any reason to exclude from rationality a conjecture that highly corroborated theories are true and whether we should thus

> relegate the *application* of science to its 'animal' 'biological' function. Popper's master argument against a justificationist principle of induction (namely that it leads either to infinite regress or apriorism) is, *in this case*, invalid; Popper's powerful argument only applies to a principle which would serve as a premise to a *proven* measure function of (spatio-temporally local) verisimilitude (one like Popper's degrees of corroboration). A conjectural inductive principle would be abhorrent only to the sceptico-dogmatist, for whom the combination of total lack of proof and strong assent indicated mere animal belief.

We could add to Lakatos's last sentence that the centrality of some form of inductive principle to any conceptual scheme shows that 'total lack of proof' of the principle does not militate against its indispensability. Given, then, that the assumption of regularity in the world is essential both for rationality and (as Popper admits) for science, what would be the best way of uncovering it? Popper is surely correct in emphasizing from among the methods at our disposal the advantages of severe testing of our theories over dully 'confirming' theories through the repetitive amassing of favourable evidence and over blindly sticking to old theories. Blindly sticking to old beliefs will lull us into a false sense of security while merely repetitive testing as opposed to testing for regularities in unlikely places will add little to our present view as to where regularities might or might not be found. But this is implicitly admitted by an inductivist such as Mill, and comes out explicitly in the application of (the inductivist) Bayes's theorem to scientific testing made by Grünbaum (1976c, pp. 108–10) and Salmon (1967, pp. 115–20). One version of Bayes's theorem has the following form:

$$P(H, B.C) = \frac{P(H, B) \times P(C, B.H)}{P(H, B) \times P(C, B.H)} + P(-H, B) \times P(C, B. - H)$$

If B is background knowledge and C a test statement implied by a theory H, this formula represents the support given by C to H in the light of our background knowledge. Where C is predicted by H, $P(C, B.H) = 1$, so the support given by C to H increases the more improbable C is given $-H$. Of course, as not only H but many theories incompatible with H will imply C, it might be said that $P(C, B. - H)$ will always be high, but we have seen already that Popper's degree of corroboration is plagued by a similar problem at this point. If, in both cases, we restrict our universe of theories to those *actually* formulated and competing, we may be able to say that, given our background knowledge, on the theories to hand, C is unlikely if H is false, and so we may assign a low value to $P(C, B. - H)$. We will also be able to see how, on Bayes's theorem, an effect that is well known will give little posterior probability to an H undergoing a test, because the likelihood of C will already be part of our background knowledge. In one respect Bayes's theorem in this interpretation differs from Popper's methodology, but is perhaps closer to what we may want to say, namely, in saying that high initial implausibility of H is a disadvantage. The problem in deciding this dispute is that, while Popper reads high $P(H, B)$ as a symptom of low content, Salmon reads it as indicating plausibility in a more general sense, referring to the theory's presentability in its current scientific context. We seem to want both, and, given that for all universal theories $P(H, B)$ is straightforwardly zero, what is involved here is a choice of means of measuring the 'fine structure' of probability. If Popper agreed that boldness was not the same as sheer implausibility, he might be persuaded to agree that, on one way of measuring it, high $P(H, B)$ is not an advantage in a scientific theory and that at least part of what he wants by boldness (high informative content) is captured reasonably well by low $P (C, B. - H)$ – meaning that C is unlikely on current background knowledge.

However far Popper would sanction this reading of Bayes's theorem as defining the degree of corroboration given by evidence to a theory (and he does speak of 'limited formal analogies' between the two (*LSD*, p. 263, n 1)), he would obviously reject any attempt to probabilify through it. So would Lakatos. What Lakatos is suggesting, however, is that theories arrived at through the best means at our disposal (which will certainly include severe testing) are, by virtue of that fact, conjectured to be true. Popper explicitly rejects any such 'whiff' of inductivism, admitting only that we may guess that 'the better corroborated theory is also the one that is nearer to the truth' ('RC', p. 1011), but denying that corroboration itself is a measure of support for the theory's truth. But what right do we have to make such a guess if the measure of corroboration is not (conjectured by us to be) a measure of a theory's truth? As Popper also tells us that it is rational to act on the best-tested theories, one is tempted like Lakatos to conclude that the difference between him and Lakatos's proposal to regard corroboration conjecturally as a synthetic function indicating nearness to truth (and not just an analytic report on the present state of critical discussion) is a merely verbal dispute, were it not that accepting Lakatos's proposal would forge the missing – and strenuously denied – link between the scientifically acceptable and the true. If in turn we based the assumption of a synthetic corroboration principle on the hope that we are biologically well adapted to our environment, we would have some answer to the problems arising from the countless incompatible theories which are yet compatible with all the tests we can make and from the apparent importance of particular formulations of logically equivalent theories. This would be by suggesting that our adaptation to our environment does mean that the ways we arrive at, formulate and test our theories will be likely to have some correspondence with the way things are in the world.

Despite his many disclaimers, there are two places where Popper does consider an argument to the effect that we have a positive reason to believe that the world may be similar to what science teaches us. The argument is based on the extreme improbability of a merely accidental correspondence between a logically very improbable and wide-ranging scientific hypothesis and reality. If such correspondence is found through a theory surviving severe tests, it could hardly be an accident, but there must be some truth-likeness or verisimilitude in the theory. Popper (*OK*, pp. 101–3) does not want to say straightforwardly that such theories would therefore be true, because incompatible theories 'can agree in many fine points in which it would be intuitively highly improbable that they agree by sheer accident'. Although this rules out Grünbaum's view that Popper holds that survival of severe tests helps to verify theories, Popper is prepared to say that an 'accidentally very improbable agreement between a theory and a fact can be interpreted as an indicator that the theory has a (comparatively) high verisimilitude'. This, of course, connects with the 'whiff of verificationism' noted earlier when we saw Popper requiring actual corroboration from acceptable theories. In this context, the distinction between indicators of truth and of verisimilitude is comparatively unimportant. Even to admit that we have a positive reason for thinking a theory has some verisimilitude is to come close enough to inductivism.

It is difficult to see how Popper does not admit just this when he considers the argument again ('RC', pp. 1192–3). Although the passage is long, I will quote it in full as little further comment will be required:

> There is a probabilistic though typically non-inductivist argument
> which is invalid if it is used to establish the probability of a
> theory's being true, but which becomes valid (though essentially
> non-numerical) if we replace truth by verisimilitude. The
> argument can be used only by realists who not only assume that
> there is a real world but also that this world is by and large
> more similar to the way modern theories describe it than to the
> way superseded theories describe it. On this basis, we can argue
> that it would be a highly improbable coincidence if a theory like
> Einstein's could correctly predict very precise measurements not

predicted by its predecessors unless there is 'some truth' in it. This must not be interpreted to mean that it is improbable that the theory is not true (and hence probable that it is true). But it can be interpreted to mean that it is probable that the theory has both a high truth content and a high degree of verisimilitude; which means here only 'a higher degree of verisimilitude *than those of its competitors* which led to predictions that were less successful, and which are thus less well corroborated.' The argument is typically non-inductive because in contradistinction to inductive arguments such as Carnap's the probability that the theory in question has a high degree of verisimilitude is (like degree of corroboration) inverse to the initial probability of the theory, prior to testing. Moreover, it only establishes a probability of verisimilitude relative to its competitors (and especially to its predecessors). In spite of this, there may be a 'whiff' of inductivism here. It enters with the vague realist assumption that reality, though unknown, is in some respects similar to what science tells us or, in other words, with the assumption that science can progress towards greater verisimilitude.

If, despite the qualifications over the sense of verisimilitude, we are entitled to conclude from this passage that reality is at least to some extent as science teaches us and that the methods of science do get us nearer the truth, then are we not equally entitled rationally to rely on the findings of science? Naturally, our reliance will be cautious, as we will be aware of the fallibility of our findings, but few inductivists would claim that inductive methods give us infallible knowledge. It is not surprising that some commentators have seen this passage as an enormous concession by Popper to his critics. Certainly, with its 'whiff' of inductivism, it brings Popper's philosophy more in line with common sense and with what one would want to say about our knowledge of the world, but it also means that he can no longer complain about corroboration and theory testing being taken by his less cautious readers to have inductive implications.

V

Observation and Theory

1 *Fries's trilemma: the unjustifiability of observation statements*

Popper's account of scientific theories is based on the idea that our general theories are tested by making particular observations. It might then be expected that he would contrast a level of descriptive discourse which is theoretical with a level which is observational in such a way that the observational level is not itself theoretical; even though to achieve an actual falsification we have to hypothesize that the observed effect is reproducible, statements recording the observations would be free from the sort of doubt that the theoretical statements are open to. Of course, in practice some actual test statements (such as those yielded by electron microscopes) will involve theoretical assumptions, but we feel that even in such cases there may be a way of speaking about the results which is theory-free. In any case, at the basic every-day level of observation – in our talk about tables, chairs and colours – we do not seem to be involved in theorizing, and even the most abstruse scientific theories (such as nuclear physics) ultimately have some bearing on things at the everyday level.

It is a central plank of Popper's epistemology, however, to deny that there is any untheoretical level of description. So even if the results of scientific testing were reducible to talk of colours and everyday objects, it would still be theoretical. What does Popper mean by speaking of the theoretical nature of all observation statements in this way, and why is it important to him?

We have already seen in his attacks on the Baconian methodology and the Humean account of the acquisition of empirical beliefs Popper's insistence on the selectivity of observations and on the logical priority of systems of classification over perceptions. This point can be put in traditional empiricist terms by saying that, in order to make any sense

68

of the chaotic, indefinite barrage of sensory stimulations which we are undergoing at any moment, we have to have some idea of what things to pick out, what things to count as members of the same stimulus class. Popper's argument from the approximateness of any similarity between two different things or events to the necessity in observation of a criterion of similarity can be supplemented by the fact that experience can, in theory at least, be organized in more than one way. In our actual observations, we look at things in one way, rather than another. An example of this might be that we naturally tend to notice the material objects around us (people, chairs and tables) and to divide the world up primarily into such objects. Theoretically, it might be equally possible to see the world primarily in terms of similarly coloured surfaces, although this would obviously not be so useful to us. Finally, it is well known that, within limits, different peoples have different ways of dividing up qualities such as colours, and that there is nothing in nature that compels us to adopt one way rather than another; two examples of blue for us might well be examples of different colours for South Sea Islanders. It has also been experimentally shown that the ability to recognize and distinguish between various shapes is not independent of knowledge of geometry and perspective, and the same goes *mutatis mutandis* for sounds. In general, then, Popper is correct in claiming that observations are made on the basis of certain inborn or learned predispositions to classify things in one's environment in particular ways and that these predispositions can often be related to particular biological or social needs and interests. However, it is not so clear that the schemes of classification used in observation are to be thought of as theories in the sense that they involve hypotheses or expectations of future events such that the observations made on the basis of those classificatory schemes would be held open to later falsification, in the same way that a general scientific theory is open to later falsification. Popper, however, holds just this, and in this respect he holds that they are theoretical just as much as explicitly universal theoretical statements, such as scientific laws.

In *The Logic of Scientific Discovery*, Popper raises the question of the justification of the statements we make about the world around us in terms of what he calls Fries's trilemma. On the one hand we have language and on the other the world. In language, we make statements *about the world*, and what has to be established is the grounds on which we should accept or reject these statements. J. F. Fries, an early-nineteenth-century German philosopher, thought that there were three options open to us here. Either we simply accept some statements *dogmatically*, or we attempt to justify them. But if we want justification through reasoned argument, we become committed to the view that statements can be justified only by yet other statements, and hence to an *infinite regress* of justifications. (We remain enmeshed in language.) Fries's third option is what Popper calls *psychologism*, which is the view, favoured by philosophers of a traditional empiricist cast, that we can break out of the net of language without being reduced to dogmatism, because there are some statements which can be directly confronted with perceptual experience. Statements of this type are often called basic statements, and non-basic statements are to be accepted or rejected according to whether or not they are supported by true basic statements. There has been much controversy over what precisely basic statements are like. Some people have thought of them in terms of simply observations, like 'Here is a glass of water', while others, impressed by the possibility of errors in such observations, examples of illusions and so on, have taken basic statements to be those recording our current sensations ('I seem to see a glass of water here'). According to Popper, psychologism draws the strength of its appeal from the fact that statements describing what is given to us directly in experience cannot, as a matter of psychological fact, be doubted, but in his view feelings of conviction even here do not constitute proof.

Popper denies that any statement can be justified by experience, because he thinks that the universal terms used in describing what I see ('Here is a *glass of water*'), or, more guardedly, how something appears to me ('This looks *red* to me'), essentially transcend the experiences they are applied to. In saying this, he is not merely pointing out that in calling something 'red' I am placing that object at a certain point on a certain scheme of colour classification; what he is suggesting is that descriptive terms ('water', 'glass', 'red') are covertly theoretical in the sense that their application in a given case gives rise to implications beyond one's immediate observational experience. This is the doctrine of the dispositional nature of all descriptive terms, and in holding to it Popper is, as he is aware, blurring the sharp distinction between universal statements ('All men are mortal') and singular statements ('N.N. died on 7 June 1970, in London'). Asserting a singular statement about the world commits one just as much as asserting a universal statement to an open-ended set of predictive implications because of the dispositional character of the descriptive terms. Popper holds that all descriptions as well as general theories and descriptions employing terms such as 'breakable' or 'soluble', which refer to the dispositions that objects of certain types have to behave in certain ways in given conditions, are theoretical or hypothetical (or dispositional, as he would call it) because the universal terms which appear in them 'cannot be correlated with any specific sense-experience ... By the word "glass", for example, we denote physical bodies which exhibit a certain *law-like behaviour*, and the same

70

holds for the word "water"'' (*LSD*, p. 95). While one might agree that an analysis of this sort would, if true, show that 'Here is a glass of water' is theoretical or dispositional, it might be objected that it does not show that appearance statements like 'This looks red' or even 'This looks like a glass of water' are dispositional, because my more guarded claims do not imply that there *is* a glass of water present and are not committed to any object exhibiting law-like behaviour. Popper (*CR*, p. 118) extends the argument about the dispositional nature of descriptive terms to cover appearance statements as well:

> In my opinion *all universals are dispositional*. If 'breakable' is dispositional, so is 'broken', considering for example how a doctor decides whether a bone is broken or not. Nor should we call a glass 'broken' if the pieces would fuse the moment they were put together; the criterion of being broken is behaviour *under certain conditions*. Similarly, 'red' is dispositional: a thing is red if it is able to reflect a certain kind of light – if it 'looks red' in certain situations. But even 'looking red' is dispositional. It describes the disposition of a thing to make onlookers agree that it looks red.

So when I say that something in front of me looks red, I am saying something about what other observers would be inclined to say about it. He concludes that 'the customary distinction between "*observational terms*" (or "*non-theoretical terms*") and *theoretical terms* is mistaken, since all terms are theoretical "to some degree".' Even so, it may not follow from this that the *use* of all terms is theoretical. Can't I use a descriptive term in such a way that I am committed to no implications about what a thing is or what it would look like to others? In saying 'X looks red *to me now*' am I not doing just this? Are not assertions of this sort completely restricted to my own current experience, in no way dispositional?

As Popper points out, Carnap at one time argued that in recording our own current perceptions in this way, we had a type of statement (known as a protocol sentence) which was not theoretical, and so not in need of any further check or confirmation, and that it should be possible to base a rational science on such sound foundations. Carnap's programme suffered from problems involved in assessing the relevance of given protocol sentences to the theories they were to test. If, for example, an astronomical theory predicted that a certain planet would be in a certain place at a certain time, this prediction would have to be translated into a protocol sentence about the perceptions an observer would have in looking through a telescope directed at a given angle at the appropriate time. Apart from the involvement of yet more protocol sentences in establishing that what we had was a telescope properly directed, etc., would it count against the theory if an observer who was inexperienced, drunk or short-sighted failed to have the predicted perceptions? Clearly some criteria for normal observers and normal conditions of observation are needed in order to eliminate irrelevant protocol sentences, but such criteria would be from the observational point of view heavily theoretical, and so the programme does not free science from theory in the way it was intended. Nevertheless it might still be right that protocol sentences are purely observational and completely non-theoretical, as far as future implications go, even though they are not in principle uncriticizable.

Popper is in some places inclined simply to rule out protocol sentences from science on the grounds that statements about someone's current perceptions are not more easily inter-subjectively testable than statements about things in the world (cf. *LSD*, p. 99). The defender of the untheoretical nature of protocol sentences would hardly be impressed by this, but if we add to it Popper's view that all universal terms are dispositional, we do get an argument for their theoreticality. For the predicate 'looks red to me now' is a universal term; it can be predicated of many things, so I think we have to conclude on Popper's view that in predicating 'looking red to me now' of some object we are making some sort of theoretical assertion, though maybe a more guarded one than if we were to predicate 'looks red' or 'is red' of that object. In defence of this position, it could be urged that mistakes about how things look to me are possible; I might miscategorize the look of the thing in such a way that on being presented later on with a clear red colour sample, I might wish to retract my earlier assertion about how the object had looked to me. So, in saying that some X looks red to me now, I am committed to the theory that I will in the future be inclined to assent to the proposition that X looked to me then like the red colour sample I am now looking at. The inter-subjective testing of my original protocol sentence will presumably involve other people checking on whether or not I do assent to judgments of this sort, so a connection can be made out between what Popper says about their testing and their theoretical nature. For Popper, then, *every* description (even descriptions of the content of my present perceptual experience) is dispositional or theoretical. Description necessarily transcends experience; it involves going far beyond what can be known with certainty on the basis of a momentary perceptual experience. It should be clear that this is quite a different thesis from the first one we examined, which denied the possibility of pure, undirected observation. It is possible to agree that observation requires a scheme of classification or set of concepts without holding that observation statements are dispositional in the sense that they have future implications which some future experience would necessarily make us, if we were rational, retract our earlier classification. This conclusion would follow only if the classifying or direction of interest involved in observation required that the judgments we make were dispositional in this sort of way.

Before examining this point more fully in the next section, we must see on what Popper bases testing of theories (and so, ultimately, scientific knowledge itself) if there is no untheoretical mode of description. His fallibilism means that just as there is no certainty about general theories in science or in everyday life, so there is no certainty about the particular observations by which theories are judged. They too are 'soaked in theory' and so equally 'affected by the hypothetical or conjectural character of all theories' (CR, p. 387). However, although the singular existential statements which record the occurrence of observable events in space and time and which serve as tests of general theories (what Popper calls basic statements) are hypotheses, they are testable hypotheses. As such, agreement can be reached about their success or failure, potential or actual, in surviving further tests. I say potential, because it may be generally agreed that a particular basic statement has been established well enough and needs no testing. But suppose it is a fact that it needs testing, won't the new tests themselves be theory-soaked? Popper answers that they will be and points to the infinitely regressive nature of the situation: 'this procedure has no natural end', he says (LSD, p. 104), but adds that in practice we stop somewhere – 'every test of a theory must stop at some basic statement or other which we *decide to accept*'. So basic statements are not any special type of supposedly ultimate statement, such as a protocol statement. Indeed, protocol statements, not referring to inter-subjectively observable states of affairs, would not have the required testability to function as basic statements in Popper's scheme. Basic statements are simply those observation statements which are accepted for some purpose as not being in need of further testing. As such – and this reflects actual scientific practice – they can be highly theoretical compared with statements about everyday objects. A formerly basic statement could, of course, be further tested, in which case it would no longer be basic for the purpose in hand, but when within a given investigation we come to observations on which researchers are likely to reach agreement, we tend to treat the corresponding statements as basic. If such habitual agreement on some class of relevant observation statements could not be reached,

> this would amount to a failure of language as a means of universal communication. It would amount to a new 'Babel of Tongues': scientific discovery would be reduced to absurdity. In this new Babel, the soaring edifice of science would soon lie in ruins. (LSD, p. 104)

73

Popper speaks a lot about testing basic statements, without saying much about how they are to be tested. A problem is involved here owing to the fact that they are statements about particular events. By the time we want to test a basic statement, the actual event will in all probability be past. What then of our original statement's testability? Popper does speak (*LSD*, p. 105) of re-examining the test certificates issued by research departments and even of testing the perceptual faculties of the researchers. But in the scientific context the possibilities of checking testimony in this sort of way seems rather limited and not particularly fruitful. Popper also wants to say that any observation statement has an indefinite number of implications about the future behaviour of the objects observed. As I shall argue in the next section, this is not true, but even if it were, it is not easy to see how basic statements about states of affairs remote from us in time or even in space could be re-tested now. What I suspect Popper has in mind when he talks of testing basic statements is testing whether the same effect can be observed in relevantly similar conditions. This would certainly be in line with his assertion (*LSD*, pp. 45–6) that non-reproducible observations (or 'occult effects') are not part of scientific knowledge. Indeed he says there that science could never decide whether unrepeatable and unique events do occur. But, suppose a large amount of plausible testimony was presented in favour of an apparently unrepeatable event (including perhaps my own witnessing of the event along with a number of normally reliable observers), would it not be unreasonable simply to reject the testimony as mistaken? Science, on Popper's account, must reject the event as chimerical, however unreasonable this might be to a historian's eye. If, in the light of this, it is true that Popper is really thinking of the testing of the reproducibility of the observed effect when he speaks of testing basic statements, we would, even while rejecting his argument as to the theoretical nature of all individual observation statements, accept that all *scientific* statements have a theoretical element because in science even basic statements are acceptable in so far as they are taken to report on reproducible effects.

Popper, however, insists that all observation statements are theoretical even though they are only about particular events. What makes basic statements basic is not that they are justified by experience or anything else. From Fries's trilemma of dogmatism or infinite regress or psychologism, Popper takes elements of all three options: dogmatism because we *decide* to accept certain statements as basic; the infinite regress because we *could test them further* if we wanted to and because being unproven, they can be seen as having need for further testing; psychologism because, in Popper's terms, experience may *motivate*, but can never justify, our decisions regarding basic statements. He insists that there is nothing absolute about the empirical basis of science. We take what we take as the basis because we are temporarily satisfied that it is firm enough. Presumably we think our testing procedures are well corroborated and so we can accept the judgments they deliver us, but Popper seems far more concerned to emphasize the uncertainty of our basic statements and the gap between them and the motivating experiences than to provide an account of what their acceptability consists in or to explain in what sense (if any) they are better based than the propositions of the theories they are used to test. It is true that he criticizes Neurath for throwing empiricism overboard by failing to give any rules for the acceptance or rejection of the protocol statements on which he (Neurath) wanted to base knowledge (*LSD*, p. 97), but Popper's own rules for the acquisition of his basic statements do (as he would be the first to insist) nothing to justify them. In fact he stresses (*LSD*, pp. 106–11) the conventional nature of these rules (of which an example is that only basic statements relevant to theories under test are to be accepted). He goes on to say that the difference between him and the conventionalists is not that they, rather than he, have an element of decision and agreement in their epistemology, but that he exercises decisions over singular (basic) statements, while they assert that universal statements are decided by agreement. Popper goes on to compare the scientific community deciding whether to accept a basic statement with a jury deciding a matter of fact. He says that, although the jurors may have individual reasons and motivations for their decision, what counts and what can be challenged is only the formal correctness of the procedures by which they reach their decision. Whether this is true of juries or not, it seems a peculiarly obscure way to deal with basic statements. Something surely needs to be said about the support (even if it is less than absolute) given to them by experience and about the epistemological status of the procedures scientists use to reach their verdicts on them; otherwise it is hard to see why we should ever be satisfied even momentarily to rest science upon them.

2 *The verification argument*

Although Popper is in no sense a verificationist, the argument he uses to establish that all observation statements are theoretical is what has been called the verification argument (by Norman Malcolm (1963, p. 3), who actually refers to Popper's use of the argument). Popper's main reason for thinking that 'This is broken', 'Here is a glass of water' or 'This is red' are theoretical statements is that, in making such assertions, we are committing ourselves to the truth of an indefinite number of statements about the future behaviour of the objects in question, which are implied by the original statements, but which we are not yet in a position to verify. A glass will shatter if broken; something broken will not fuse the moment its parts are placed together; something that is red will look red in certain situations.

This last case is worth dwelling on, for it brings out clearly the full extent of Popper's position. Something's being red commits us to holding that it will look red in certain situations, while the fact that it looks red in a particular situation describes the disposition the object has to make onlookers agree that it looks red in the same or similar situations. But, then, this theory can be tested by seeing if various people do agree, and there seems nothing theoretical about that: I agree, A agrees, B agrees, and so on. Is it a matter of theory that each of these onlookers assents to the proposition that the object is red? Here at last, it seems, is the bedrock of non-theoretical fact. But someone who is arguing along Popperian lines here has no need to be put off by this. Person A assenting to 'X is red' may be dispositional in that other people are disposed to assent to his assenting, or perhaps in that A will act in various specified ways on the proposition 'X is red'. (Suppose A is myself. Does this mean that I can never be sure whether I think X is red?)

The move that is being made all the time is to show that judgments which are apparently categorical and non-dispositional are in fact hypothetical and dispositional. A judgment of the form 'X is F' is always to be understood either as 'If X is put in conditions $c_1, c \ldots c$- to observers $O_1, O \ldots O$-, then the observers will agree that . . .' It is clear that such an analysis *can* in a formal sense be given of any categorical descriptive judgment whatever. What has to be examined is whether categorical judgments do in fact always have the meaning attributed to them by the dispositional analysis.

To say, as Popper does of 'looking red', that 'X is F' implies that in certain conditions certain observers will agree that it is F is to blur the distinction between what *is* said and what *ought* to be said. This distinction is brought out by Wittgenstein (1967, p. 90) as follows:

> If someone asks me: 'What colour is this book?' and I reply
> 'It's green' – might I as well have given the answer 'The
> generality of English-speaking people call that "green"'?

What is wrong with this answer is that it suggests that there is no difference in this case between an appeal to the rule which establishes the meaning of a term and a simple appeal to head-counting. Of course, in a border-line case of greenness, the head-counting reply might be appropriate, but the successful working of language requires that, in central cases at least, native speakers have a shared knowledge of what *ought* to be said, logically distinct from beliefs about what would be said. It is true that the rule determining the use of a term like 'green' might be arrived at by a child or a translator partly through seeing how adult or native speakers actually use the term (though Popper would be the first to insist that more than this would have to be involved, and that observations of the use of the term would be part of the learning process only given some prior hypothesis as to its use), but what is learned is not just that most people tend to use 'green' only in certain circumstances, but rather an idea of what those circumstances are, which will enable the learner to distinguish between correct and incorrect uses of the term. In other words, in contrast to a descriptive scientific hypothesis, he will not be obliged to treat deviations from what he takes to be the rule determining the use of 'green' as counting against his hypothesis as to what the rule is: mistakes of perception and usage in other speakers are allowed for. Indeed, the antecedent existence and acceptance of prescriptive rules determining what ought to be said are what give language users something genuinely to agree or disagree about when deciding whether something was, say, green or not. The undoubted fact that most people would say that the same things were green shows only that they accept the same rules and speak the same language, not that talk about what should be said can be reduced to an anthropological survey of what most people would say, or that saying what something *is* is equivalent to saying what most people would say about it.

Popper might claim at this point that I have misrepresented his view that 'looking red' is dispositional because it describes the disposition of a thing to make onlookers agree that it looks red, on the grounds that he was not referring to their agreement on the meaning of the word 'red', but to their tendency to agree on particular empirical judgments. In so doing, I have substituted a point about words for one about the world. Against this, however, it should be stressed that in central cases of redness there is no clear distinction to be drawn between my knowing what 'red' means and my being right about what things are red. Indeed, in a case where I guardedly claimed that an object looked red *to me* at a certain time, and I did not mean that it was a border-line case of redness, then, provided that there was no reason to doubt that I understood the meaning of 'red', it is hard to see how I could miscategorize what I saw, or how the disposition of onlookers could even be relevant to my claim. Strictly speaking, this would be enough to cast doubt on Popper's claim that *all* observational judgments are implicitly dispositional, but a stronger objection can be made to his position by considering the way in which colour talk is learned. It is learned through being given paradigmatic cases of blue objects, red objects, etc., and being categorically told that they are blue, red, etc. For a normally sighted man in normal conditions to doubt that such an object is, for example, 'blue' is to show that he does not yet fully grasp the meaning of 'blue'. Once a man has grasped colour vocabulary, on the other hand, he does not *predict* that all normally sighted people will in normal conditions be disposed to agree with him that a blue colour sample is blue; this is because such colour samples will be used to determine *whether* people are normally sighted, English-speaking individuals in normal conditions. In other words, the categorical judgment that a certain object is blue is used to establish other dispositional judgments; it is not itself dispositional because it is precisely through the categorical assertion of such judgments that the meaning of 'blue' is taught and the normality of observers and conditions assessed.

Categorical judgments seem to be possible with qualities such as colours and the successful making of such judgments in central cases is a criterion of a man's having learned colour talk. This is because the meaning of colour terms is established through the use of paradigm cases and, in a sense, exhausted by it. I am not, in making such a judgment, clearly committed to any implications about the future behaviour of an object which now appears red. In contrast to this, many other descriptive terms do appear to have implications regarding the future powers or behaviour of the objects they are applied to. As examples, terms such as 'witch', 'pump', 'dog' and 'table', all in different ways, seem to refer to more than the immediately apparent qualities of the objects in question. In the case of terms like these, the verification argument would seem to have a point in its claim that the powers and future behaviour of the objects concerned are relevant to the truth of my present judgment that someone is a witch or that something is a pump, a dog or a table. Indeed, in the case of 'witch' the implications of the term as regards powers seem to rule out the possibility of ever correctly calling someone a witch, whatever her apparent qualities might be.

Popper's crucial statement of his position here reads (*LSD*, pp. 94–5):

> Every statement has the character of a theory, of a hypothesis. The statement 'Here is a glass of water' cannot be verified by any observational experience . . . By the word 'glass' we denote physical bodies which exhibit a certain *law-like behaviour*, and the same holds for the word 'water'.

The reason Popper gives for treating 'Here is a glass of water' as a hypothesis is quite sound. It is also perfectly true that people might sometimes be mistaken in thinking that what they had was a glass of water. The 'glass' might be plastic, the 'water' hydrochloric acid. Nevertheless, it is not clear that verification of 'Here is a glass of water' can *never* take place. Popper presumably would accept that it is possible to falsify the hypothesis that the glass was made of plastic, or of ice, or of paper, or that what we had was an illusion, produced by mirrors or back-projection. He makes considerable play (e.g., in *SB*, p. 513) with the fact that, in dealing with optical illusions (such as the Müller–Lyer illusion), even after we know what is really the case we continue to 'see' incorrectly, but this in itself hardly supports a general scepticism about verification, because to say that conclusive verification is sometimes possible does not entail that we should always naively accept the first (or even the last) impressions of our senses. It is quite compatible with a highly critical attitude to naive realism, but insists that there are occasions when further suspension of judgment is otiose. Popper's scepticism about verification, on the other hand, seems to be based on a quite general feeling that we can never rule out every possible mistake, and that, even after every considerable test has been performed, something could in the future happen to make us want to revise our original hypothesis.

Like most philosophical scepticism about knowledge, this position has no practical import. We do not act as if we might at any time have to revise well-tested empirical judgments about everyday realities such as glasses of water. Perhaps the shortest and most effective way with the verification argument is to meet it head on and simply to assert that there are cases where it would be most unreasonable to revise an empirical judgment because of some future happening. Suppose all conceivable tests relevant to the glass were successfully undertaken and cross-checked and yet when we next examined the glass it had melted and coagulated (i.e., it did not exhibit the law-like behaviour of glasses). Would it be more reasonable to abandon the claim that we originally had a glass, or to look for a cause of the new behaviour of the glass? Even if no cause could be found, there is no reason to suppose that we would be obliged to withdraw our original judgment that what we had was a glass. So long as only our glass was affected, it might well be more reasonable to suppose that there was an un-explained event here rather than that our original testing procedures were inadequate either in theory or in practice, because, if, as we are supposing, the testing procedures were detailed and well executed, to cast doubt on them would reflect seriously on our testing procedures in general. It could be less harmful to our whole system of knowledge to live with a single as-yet-unexplained event than to admit a general doubt about our procedures for verification. Of course, as I suggested in the previous section, Popper would tend to dismiss a single un-repeatable event as 'occult' and chimerical, but it seems dogmatic, to say the least, to assert that in every case of an unrepeatable event we have to opt for a mistake in the original testing procedures or testimony rather than for the possibility of some freak occurrence. If it later became clear that our melted glass was not actually an isolated occurrence and that this was often happening to glasses, our original testing procedures would surely be vindicated, and we would have to look for some reason for change in the behaviour of glass in certain conditions. If, finally, many of our expectations about the behaviour of materials began to let us down – about steel, paper, plastic and so on – this would be evidence for a general change in the world, rather than evidence against our original verifying procedures. Even though too widespread a deviation from what we expect would result in a general breakdown of our ability to make objective judgments at all, the fact that we could sometimes get evidence for a change in the behaviour of glass or other materials depends on assuming the adequacy of the procedures we originally used to verify the presence of the material in question. In other words, the future behaviour of the glass, even if bizarre, need not make us revise our original judgment that we had glass before us.

3 *Hypotheses and evidence*

Even if Popper is wrong about the dispositional nature of appearance statements and about the impossibility of verifying any material-object statement, his discussion of observation does have something important to teach us. It is that the general success of our observation talk depends both on the existence of order in the world and on the correspondence between our perceptual faculties and that order. That these conditions should apply is indeed something transcending sense experience. The problem with Popper's account is that, in talking of all empirical judgments as hypothetical, he implies that what holds for those things which, within our conceptual scheme, we *call* hypotheses actually applies to all empirical judgments. Now, in calling something a hypothesis or theory we imply that there is some evidence which we could give for it which is more certain or obvious. However, it is doubtful whether for some of our empirical judgments (e.g., that I am now sitting at my desk, or that the paper before me is white) there is anything which could play the role of evidence.

In the situation in which I am currently engaged in writing at my desk, it is hard to think of anything more certain than that I am at my desk. There is no reason for me to think that either my mental state or the situation here are in any way abnormal. I have come in through the door, found everything in order, opened the window, consulted some of my books, and started writing. If I were seriously to doubt any of this, I would have to be given some reason to do so which was more convincing than any of the beliefs I have mentioned. But what sort of reason could this be? I do not mean that I have evidence for my beliefs here. Quite the contrary, it is because I can think of nothing counting as evidence for them that in this type of case it is impossible seriously to imagine that any of the circumstances which would lead me to give them up (e.g., my being drugged) are actually obtaining. To question a bedrock belief like this would appear not to be possible within our system of theory and evidence; it would be rather to cast doubt on the system as a whole.

It might be suggested that corroboration from other people could be relevant as evidence here. But if I don't believe that my judgment that I am at my desk is reliable, why should I any more believe that the judgment that other people are saying certain things to me is reliable?

The proposal that goes to the heart of the matter here is the one which says that my judgments about the objects around me are hypothesized on the basis of my current sensations. This is because reports of my sensations appear to be more guarded than my judgments about enduring objects, such as desks or doors, whose truth seems to transcend my momentary experiences. Popper explicitly denies that sensation reports are untheoretical; thus, he writes ('EP', pp. 163–4) characteristically that 'sense data, untheoretical items of information, simply do not exist. For we *always* operate with theories, some of which are even incorporated in our physiology. And a sense organ is akin to a theory.' Nevertheless, part of the plausibility of his claim that judgments about glasses of water are theoretical surely derives from his insistence that the terms in those judgments 'cannot be correlated with any specific sense-experience' (*LSD*, p. 95). What I now want to show is that, although our observations are undoubtedly dependent physiologically on sense experience and although reports of sense experience might occasionally function as evidence for our statements about things (e.g., when the light is bad and we use a report of how something appears to us as evidence of how it is), statements reporting observations of enduring objects cannot in general require evidential support from sensation reports, because sensation reports are logically dependent on talk of enduring objects. The distinction between sensations and sensation reports is important because sensations as such can hardly be evidence for anything. Unless a sensation were recognized as being a sensation of a certain sort, it is difficult to see how it could be relevant to assessing the truth or falsity of any observation. So, although observing things entails having appropriate sensations, it is only when the sensations are categorized as falling under concepts and can accordingly feature in sensation reports (e.g., 'There is a desk-like shape in my visual field') that they can function as evidence for my observations. So if categorization of sensations in general presupposes recognition of objects, sensation reports cannot be evidence for all talk of objects. In other words, it is only when sensations are in an organized enough state to yield us perceptions of objects that they themselves can be categorized to yield evidence for anything.

A preliminary point to notice is that the ability to speak of something looking red to me, or appearing to be the shape of a desk, presupposes mastery of talk about red objects and desks. The only way we have of referring to those sensations relevant to talk about things in the world is through our talk of objective realities. I can significantly say that something looks red to me only if, on being asked what red looks like, I can correctly point to something that is red. If my speaking of my sensation as red is not grounded in a mastery of what objectively is red, then there is no way in which my talk of my red sensations could be shown to be about the same type of sensations as other people talk about when they speak of their red sensations. In other words, the expression 'looks red' will have no public sense unless it is logically secondary to the expression 'is red'.

What has just been said shows that appearance talk is parasitic on objective talk. It does not yet show that we need object talk. Perhaps publicity of sense requires only that there is agreement among speakers on recognition of possibly momentary qualities, not that the qualities themselves must persist through time as the enduring qualities of enduring objects. After all, we do succeed in objectively referring to such momentary occurrences as explosions and flashes of lightning, where there are no persisting examples to ensure that what we are now calling an explosion or a flash of lightning is similar to what we called an explosion or a flash of lightning in the past. The problem here is one of fixing the meaning of the terms involved. In practice, of course, this problem is not difficult, because definitions of these momentary occurrences can be given in terms of other terms whose meanings have been fixed and through the connection with the regular behaviour of enduring objects (such as clouds and bombs). What we have to assume here is that everything we have to categorize is of only momentary duration and that no appeal is made to enduring physical objects.

All that there is to go on here are memories of what had previously been referred to as lightning. Is this enough to fix a sense for the term? The difficulty is that, if I appeal to *my* memory of what I previously called 'lightning' in order to check my present use of the term, on analysis it emerges that I am using the same memory to check itself. This is because what leads me to my present use of the term must itself be my memory of what I had called 'lightning' in the past – i.e., what I am really trying to check *is* my memory of what I called 'lightning' in the past. Alternatively, if I say that what I am trying to check is my knowledge of what 'lightning' means, this knowledge comes into play both in my present use of lightning' and in my summoning up of a particular memory experience from the past. In saying that *that* was what I called 'lightning' in the past, I am relying on my current idea of the meaning of the term – but this is what is at issue. It seems that, whether I decide my present use of the term is right or wrong, my present use of it is really uncheckable, if all I have to go on is my own memory, because I will be using the *same* memory that has resulted in my present use of the term to identify the past sensation with which I am comparing my present sensation. Because in these circumstances 'whatever is going to seem right to me is right', as Wittgenstein puts it (1958, p. 92), all I have here is a simulacrum of checking. With such I cannot succeed in objectively fixing a sense for my terms, even for myself.

It might be thought that the memories of individuals for the meanings of terms could be provided with independent checks through the memories of others, but an appeal to the memories of others would be quite illegitimate in this context, because it assumes the continued existence of the other people from one time to the next, as well as their continuing recognizability. If this was the only way that the sense of descriptive terms could be fixed, then the logical dependence of sensation talk on talk of enduring objects would be admitted.

My argument about the impossibility of fixing senses for our terms without some assumption of enduring objects has, of course, been based on Wittgenstein's private-language argument. As I have presented it the argument shows that there can be no successful fixing of sense which appeals to nothing beyond an individual's sensations, because there is then no way even in principle of showing whether any particular term is being used consistently or not. Ayer (1954) has objected to Wittgenstein's argument on the grounds that an isolated individual on a desert island could successfully invent words to describe features of his environment even before the arrival of any Man Friday. All he would have to rely on in his use of his descriptive terms would be his memory of the objects they were meant to stand for. In this way, the castaway would, in Ayer's view, be in exactly the same position as the man who has only his memory to go on in what he says about his sensations.

I can accept Ayer's claim that the castaway could invent some sort of language appropriate to his environment, and I think that he would do this in the first instance by associating a particular sign (either mentally or physically) with some standard example of the type of object the sign is to stand for. He might, for example, select a particular pebble as his blue colour sample, to use to check his future use of 'blue'. Now the fact that he has an enduring sample for blue makes a crucial difference between the case of the castaway and that of the man privately naming his sensations. It is true that the castaway, in checking on his current use of 'blue', has to remember that the pebble is his blue sample and that it is a colour sample, as opposed to a shape sample. Why his checking, as opposed to that of the sensation namer's, is not a meaningless ritual, is because the castaway is using a *different* memory to check his memory that blue is *that* colour quality. What he is checking is the quality that he remembers has been called 'blue' and he checks it through the separate memory that, say, the first pebble on the right in his tray of colour samples is the sample of 'blue'. The sensation namer, as we saw, is held up not because he has to rely on his memory, but because he has only *one* memory, which he has to pretend to check by appeal to itself. Consideration of the castaway reinforces the suggestion that a descriptive vocabulary has to be firmly rooted in assumptions about enduring objects, for his use of his blue colour sample depends on the belief that it will persist through time, remaining the same colour. Whichever way one looks at it, then, concepts of enduring objects will be presupposed in any talk of qualities or sensations.

The conclusion that sensation talk is logically dependent on talk about enduring objects connects closely with the argument in chapter IV that the application of the distinction between appearance and reality requires that at least some of our experience is seen as experience of objects existing apart from us. That there is a world some of whose objects exist independently of our perceptions of them is not something that can be conclusively or directly verified in our experience. On the other hand, any successful categorization of experience requires the assumption that there are such objects. Although this assumption is logically prior to the successful categorization of experience, circumstances could be imagined in which one lost one's bearings, in which the regularities within one's experience began to fail so that objects never did what was expected of them. It is possible to imagine a breakdown of regularity so total that one was unable to think of any objects as continuing to exist independently of one's perceptions of them. What our analysis of induction showed was that in such circumstances one would lose the ability to speak of anything as objective, while the conclusion of this section is that in a totally chaotic world, without the ability to perceive enduring objects, even the continuing classification of one's experiences would become impossible. There would be no markers to secure sense for one's descriptive classifications, other than the dubious guarantee afforded by one single and uncheckable memory. In addition to the relevance of the private-language argument here, in a chaotic world there would be no general reason to trust one's memory on anything, because one's memories of what had happened could no longer be cross-checked through the expectations engendered by those memories.

The fact that, if we ceased to find regularities in our experience, there would be a breakdown of our conceptual scheme, so that talk of objects and classification of experiences became impossible, does not show that the regularities we do perceive are *evidence* for our talk of objects. It is rather that both talk of objects and the systematic recognition and description of one's experiences require that there is a certain continuing regularity within one's experience. This regularity is, as I argued in chapter IV, reflected in one's perceptual experiences of objects, but, as I argued here, the actual recognition of one's experiences itself requires a prior recognition of objects. There must, then, be some talk or recognition of enduring objects which is not related to appearance talk as hypothesis to evidence, but which is established without recourse to talk of, or recognition of, appearances. This is reflected in the fact that sense-impression talk is characteristically in terms of physical-object talk. To say that there is a desk-like shape in my visual field implies that I already know what would justify me in calling something a desk. Even if the justification were given initially in terms of appearance statements which did not mention actual desks, in spelling out the meaning of these statements we would finally have to reach statements which did not mention appearances: statements directly about colours and shapes, for example, which in their turn rest on the possibility of enduring objects acting as appropriate samples. Thus, sooner or later, we should arrive at an account of the criteria for the application of a material-object concept, in which no appearance statements figured fundamentally. The evidence for physical-object statements must in the end be explained in terms of talk about other physical objects.

Because I have been talking here about hypotheses and the evidence for them, and about the classifications of objects and appearances, I have naturally tended to speak of the relationships between statements and terms of one sort and another. But it is important to underline that, in saying that because appearance talk presupposes physical-object talk it cannot serve as evidence for it, I am not relying on a general principle to the effect that whenever talk of one sort (*A*-talk) presupposes talk of another sort (*B*-talk), *A*-talk cannot always provide evidence for *B*-talk. This principle is not universally valid, as may be seen from considering a case of some illness where describing some features as symptoms of that illness presupposes talk of that illness, while we are never, in fact, in a position to speak of the presence of the illness without evidence from symptoms. The point about physical objects and sensory data is not intended to rest on a possibly accidental linguistic dependence of the one on the other, but on the point that the stability needed to classify anything at all (including sensory data) would be provided only in a world and for beings who were already able to successfully operate a classificatory scheme for enduring objects.

Of course, Popper would not want to think of sensation talk as evidence for my hypotheses about my desk, my pen, my paper, etc., and he would agree that talk of objects is something brought to the world rather than inferred as a result of a passive perception of regularity within our experience. The problem has been to see in what way he can maintain that such statements necessarily remain hypothetical once his claim that they are unverifiable is abandoned, and it is seen that within our system there is nothing with respect to which some of them are hypothetical. The conclusion of this section may throw some light on this, because it is to suggest that the assumption of an order of enduring objects in the world, reflected in our perceptions of regularity in it, is necessary for any successful observation talk, even about our own sensations. In addition, language requires a measure of perceptual agreement among different observers, such that they can agree on basic statements. Failure of the world order, or failure within our perceptual organization, individually or collectively, would indeed bring about the 'Babel of Tongues' Popper alludes to. There is no guarantee that this might not happen, in which case our procedures of verification and our material-object talk would fail. There is no guarantee that any or all of our procedures are incorrigible. Circumstances could be imagined in which we would be unable to decide whether something was a desk (because we could have no knowledge of what it would be like next), or even what colour it was. Thus Wittgenstein (1968, p. 306):

> We learn the word 'red' under particular circumstances. Certain
> objects are usually red, and keep their colours. Most people
> agree with us in our colour judgments. Suppose all this changes:
> I see blood, unaccountably sometimes one, sometimes another
> colour, and the people around me make different statements.
> But couldn't I in all this chaos retain my meaning of 'red',
> 'blue' etc., although I couldn't now make myself understood to
> anyone? Samples, e.g., would all constantly change their
> colour – 'or does it only seem so to me?' 'Now am I mad or did
> I really call this "red" yesterday?'

But, given that the conditions are such as to enable us successfully to speak of the world and its contents, it can only be misleading to think that the fact that I am now at my desk is an unverifiable hypothesis. It is true that from the point of view of immediate perceptions inductive jumps are involved in speaking of objects, but it does not follow from this that any talk of objects has to be inferred from reports of perceptions. Although a general failure of inductive inference would go hand in hand with an inability to speak of objects at all, the crucial point of this section has been to show that the categorization of perceptions itself presupposes the recognition of some things as enduring objects. Thus any inferences from perceptions to objects would in the end rest on earlier recognition of objects.

In our system of discourse there are indeed occasions when statements about the direct observation of everyday material objects, such as chairs, tables, people and animals, are not hypotheses, both because it is impossible to think of anything functioning as evidence for them, and because it is hard to see how anything in practice could effectively count against them. For a statement to refute some other statement, it has to be more certain than it, but doubting clear-cut everyday judgments about enduring objects would be reasonable only given a general breakdown of world order or perceptual order in which we would also lose the ability to categorize even our perceptions.

It is in clear-cut cases of everyday judgments about enduring objects that we should look for cases of non-theoretical (or basic) observation statements. They are basic because of their unquestionability for us and because of the way they refer to inter-subjectively observable present situations; as such they provide the point at which our language connects closest with the world, and the natural point of departure for entry into foreign languages. Popper, as we have seen, needs some such starting point for his empiricism, or his system is hardly less conventionalistic than that of Neurath. He is unable to say anything about the 'motivation' of his basic statements. His problem here is undoubtedly exacerbated by the way in which he relativizes basic statements to communities of researchers. Obviously, statements about cloud-chamber observations are theoretical from the point of view of everyday observation, but the conclusion that everyday observation statements must be equally theoretical, by overlooking their role in the fixing of the senses of descriptive terms in our learning of language, wrongly implies that there must be some theory with respect to which they have the sense they have and some evidence with respect to which they are supported or undermined.

This conclusion has been vigorously attacked by Feyerabend, on two important grounds. The first is to suggest, largely by examination of examples (Feyerabend, 1965, pp. 180–1), that

> statements that are empirically adequate and are the result of observation (such as 'here is a table') may have to be reinterpreted, not because it has been found that they do not adequately express what is seen, heard, felt, but because of changes in sometimes very remote parts of the conceptual schemes to which they belong . . .

87

The examples Feyerabend concentrates on are cases like the observation of demonic possession, phlogiston and Galileo's example of the walker's impression that the moon is following him over the rooftops. Obviously he is quite right to suggest that in these cases what is reported as being observed is affected by (now rejected) theories. But he does not show that in a dispute on any of these matters all parties could not agree on some more basic level of description as to what it was they were observing. Such disagreements may be fruitful in bringing out the fact that certain levels of description may not be as basic to particular conceptual schemes as their protagonists originally thought. But although (as we shall see later) Feyerabend is inclined to deny this, it is hard to see how, without agreement at some level of description, there could be any communication between the parties, or even any higher-level disagreement about what it was they were observing, because it is unclear how they could be sure that they were each referring to the same phenomena. This is precisely because of the central role played by what I am calling basic statements in connecting language to the world.

Feyerabend's second line of argument is to point out that, although sometimes theories are tested by observations, observations are also judged by theories, both because we will often ignore observations when they clash with theories and because we decide what observations to accept on theoretical grounds. He goes on to suggest (1970b, pp. 70–1) that reliance on experience at all in science is only a psychological quirk, but, if this were so and if there were no general principles for deciding when observations clashing with theories were to be ignored, it is hard to see how empiricism could survive at all. (Feyerabend actually sees himself as attacking empiricism as such, so this conclusion would not really worry him.) Nevertheless, he is right to say that we do have general ideas as to the conditions for reliable observation and that the senses are generally reliable; there can be no particular objection to speaking of these ideas as theoretical. Does this then make all observations theoretical? It does not follow from my denial of this thesis that any actual observations are absolutely incorrigible. In other words, I accept that the general conditions which make successful observation possible could alter at any minute. In this sense, all observation could be said to be based on the theory that these conditions obtain. But, within this assumption, there remains a distinction between a theoretical and a non-theoretical level of observation statements. What I have argued in this section is that without the ability to treat some observations of enduring objects as certain and non-hypothetical we would lose the ability to fix the sense of any descriptive terms at all.

The position I have argued for in this section has been that enduring objects are the necessary foundation for a classificatory scheme of any sort, even for one that classified only sensory data. To say this does not rule out all point in speaking of objects as posits, relative to sensory data. In saying that, one may be intending correctly to rule out any logical or epistemological analysis of objects in terms of sensory data. Further, one may be objecting to a naive realism according to which the perceiver makes no contribution to what he perceives. I have stressed all along the need for the perceiver to have both an initial scheme of classification and one which is roughly in tune with his world. On all these points, Popper and I would be in agreement. Where, in this section, I have parted from him is in what I understand of his claim that all observations are theoretical. This is misleading in two main respects: first, in that it suggests that there is always some evidence for any observation, and second in that it overlooks the way in which some of our talk about enduring objects provides a necessary basis for the rest of our conceptual scheme.

VI

Falsification and Scientific Explanations

---

1 *Realism and instrumentalism*

What I want to show in this section is that the emphasis on falsifiable predictions in Popper's account of scientific explanation brings his philosophy close to instrumentalism, despite his explicit commitment to realism.

According to Popper (*OK*, p. 191), the aim of science is 'to find *satisfactory explanations* of whatever strikes us as being in need of explanation'. This is done when we are able to formulate an *explicans* which will have as a consequence not only the *explicandum* but other, independently testable, consequences. In order to prevent an explanation being offered which simply conjoined the *explicandum* with some otherwise unconnected testable statement, Popper requires further that the *explicans* takes the form of a statement of universal law from which, given suitable initial conditions, both the *explicandum* and the other consequences can be deduced. It is to be emphasized that this account of explanation (which Popper takes to apply to the social sciences as much as to the physical sciences) is completely free of any psychological overtones. There is no suggestion that the *explicans* is itself intuitively obvious, or even less unfamiliar than the *explicandum*. In fact, Popper sees the general direction of scientific explanation as being from the known to the unknown, because the universal law statements will typically involve reference to the underlying structural properties of matter, including unobservable entities and forces, which are supposed to be the causes of the phenomena we do observe.

Because of this last feature of scientific explanation Popper claims (*LSD*, p. 431) that science can teach us 'that the world is utterly different from what we ever imagined'. He insists that scientific theories, and in particular the parts of them which refer to the unobservable structural properties of matter, are to be interpreted realistically. They are not merely instruments for predicting observable effects or models to aid our thinking about the world: they actually tell us what the world is like. Unfortunately instrumentalism, in one form or another, is not so easily disposed of either in general or in particular for Popper, whose fallibilism entails that we can never have any good reason for believing a theory to be true and that science progresses through the continuing replacement of false theories by other (probably) false theories. From a fallibilist and non-justificationist point of view, it would seem a natural step to take those parts of theories which give pictures of how matter is organized in a non-literal way as, say, heuristic devices simply to be disposed of when their predictive usefulness comes under attack. Before seeing how close Popper comes at times to taking this step, we will look at the general case for instrumentalism.

If we think of a scientific law involving talk of causal powers, then, as Hume has argued (1888, p. 162), we are immediately beyond the realm of the observable:

Suppose two objects to be presented to us, of which one is the cause and the other the effect; 'tis plain, that from the simple consideration of one, or both these objects we never shall perceive the tie, by which they are united, or be able certainly to pronounce, that there is a connexion betwixt them.

In other words, instances of causal relationships do not present us with the observation of powers or forces linking one of the objects to the other. We may be able to observe intermediate happenings between the cause and effect we are examining, but the observation of these happenings will not satisfy the quest for powers, because we will still have to see the forces linking the intermediate happenings to themselves and to the original cause and effect.

Apart from talking of forces, scientific theories nowadays frequently refer to entities whose existence is highly problematic. While such things as bacteria may be thought of as too small for the naked eye, but are still accessible to sight through the use of microscopes, which are not themselves too discontinuous with spectacles and magnifying glasses, the closest we can come to observing an electron is through what, on the basis of more high-level theory, are taken to be its effects in a cloud chamber. Of course, the theories which speak of electrons have effects which are less remote from observation, on the basis of which the theories can be tested, but it is not clear that because of that we are entitled to speak of the real existence of the unobservable particles, particularly when they are attributed combinations of properties which would be extremely bizarre in objects which were observable.

An apparently simple way of dealing with problems connected with the unobservable entities and forces referred to in scientific theories is instrumentalism. On this account, scientific theories are seen simply as instruments for deriving predictions of observable events. Popper points out (CR, pp. 166–74) that for Berkeley, a thoroughgoing instrumentalist here, Newtonian talk of forces of attraction was strictly meaningless because such forces could never be observed. Causal explanations in physics could not be true: at best they were useful tools for calculating the movements of bodies. The theoretical question of their truth dissolves into the purely pragmatic one of the limits of their applicability. Everything in a theory that lies between the statements of initial conditions and statements of the effects – all references to forces, intermediate entities, analogical and pictorial elements relating the structure of one class of phenomena to that of another, in short everything that contributes to the theory's conception of what the world is like – is regarded as no more than part of a bridge helping us to derive correlations between one set of observable states of affairs and another. As such, it has no need to mirror the real world at all, any more than a screwdriver should mirror the screw or the hand except at the points of contact.

Popper's opposition to instrumentalism begins with a concession to it, in the form of a denial that science will bring us to the ultimate essence of things. He sees the search for greater universality and depth in explanations as having no natural end, whereas talk of ultimate essences clearly implies that there is some natural end to scientific questioning. In Popper's view the drive for universality and depth is itself anti-instrumentalist, because it leads us to probe into more fundamental properties of matter and thereby to link apparently un-connected phenomena. As universality and depth are analysed by Popper in terms of testability, however, an instrumentalist could agree that they are desirable properties of a tool, because the more applications a tool has, the more useful it is. Popper argues further against instrumentalism on the grounds that realism is more critical because, while instrumentalism can admit a proliferation of conflicting views, realism will seek to knock out all but the best. Against, this, Feyerabend has urged that a proliferation of theories may actually enhance criticism by encouraging a diversity of viewpoints, against which a realist emphasis on the *one* victorious theory may actually promote less imaginative criticism. (Popper ('RSR') actually seems very close to this point of view himself. The significance of this shift from his earlier emphasis on strict refutation will be examined in the next section.)

Whatever conclusions are reached about the significance of degrees of depth and criticizability for the dispute between instrumentalism and realism, what the realist has to show is that theories are not merely instruments, but actually give us knowledge of the real world. Here, of course, Popper is in a fix, because he thinks that we cannot know this, beyond saying that some theories have survived some tests. His main argument against instrumentalism (CR, pp. 111-14) is to point to the fact that scientists reject falsified theories, even though a falsified theory may still be a useful instrument in certain areas (such as navigators using pre-Copernican astronomy). Instrumentalism, according to Popper, cannot account for the fact that scientists treat the predictions of their theories as potential falsifiers, and not simply as defining the limits of possible areas of application.

As it stands, this argument is surprisingly weak. After all, *some* scientists (such as Heisenberg) are instrumentalists, as Popper himself recognizes. An instrumentalist could reply to Popper that he is interested in testing his theories precisely to determine how far they can be applied, and that he seeks theories of ever wider and deeper applicability for all sorts of pragmatic and technological reasons. He could also point out that Popper's argument has so far given us no strong reason for a realistic interpretation of the parts of theories which do not deal directly with observables. In any case, do scientists simply discard refuted theories? Do they not, more characteristically, seek to incorporate earlier theories into their new theories, as approximations? Popper is, of course, aware of this. We have alluded to the incorporation of the results of Galilean terrestrial and Keplerian celestial mechanics into Newtonian dynamics in connection with verisimilitude, and Popper (OK, pp. 197-202) examines this very case again in order to illustrate increasing depth and universality in scientific explanation. He shows there how Newton's theory, while contradicting both Galileo's and Kepler's, could accommodate both these theories as excellent approximations. Newton, then, corrected the earlier theories while explaining why they were within limits successful (OK, p. 202):

> The original explanatory task was the deduction of the earlier results. Yet this task is discharged [by Newton] not by deducing these earlier results but by deducing something better in their place: new results which, under the special conditions of the older results, come numerically very close to these older results, and at the same time correct them.

Is there anything here an instrumentalist need disagree with? Is more being said here than that the observable effects, successfully accounted for by the old theory, must also be accounted for by its successor? What does Popper's realism amount to here?

The real weakness of instrumentalism is that it makes the success of successful theories an extraordinary coincidence. If what lies between the initial conditions and the predicted effects does not mirror the real world, how does the theory work at all? Realism answers this question by saying that theories are successful to the extent that they are because their explanatory elements – the powers and unobservable entities, and the analogies they use – do reflect in some way what the world is like, and that their observable success is evidence for this. Taking this seriously must surely mean, as Putnam has argued (1976), that a scientist is committed to incorporating not only the true *observational* consequences of an old, refuted, but partially successful theory into a new theory, but also to showing that the explanatory mechanisms of the old theory are in some way partial (or perhaps misdirected) reflections of the truth, according to the new theory. Is science in fact realistic in this way? At first sight, it seems not: indivisibility of atoms has not survived Dalton, nor constancy of mass Einstein. These ideas were surely central to the theories of which they were a part. On the other hand, Watkins (1974) has argued, from a Popperian point of view, that in a successful scientific reduction, although the new theory will repudiate the ontology of the old, it will not only predict the effects correctly predicted by the old theory but it will also show how the phenomena in question appeared to behave as the old theory said they did. Thus the kinetic theory of heat replaces the idea of the calorific theory that there is a fluid heat-substance obeying deterministic laws with the idea of molecular bombardments obeying statistical laws, but the effects of this activity are shown to be very much what they would be like if they were caused by an underlying fluid-like substance.

Whether or not science is in fact realistic in Putnam's sense, what we have to decide is whether Popper thinks that it should be, and whether his realism amounts to more than the belief that there is a world apart from us, unknowable, except perhaps at the points where we can observe it, and where we can kick it and it can 'kick' back at us and our theories (as Popper himself says in explaining what his realism involves ('QM', p. 15)). His denial of the distinction between theory and observation might seem to commit him to a fuller realism than that; indeed, he uses this very denial (*LSD*, p. 423) to criticize Berkeley's instrumentalist attack on occult forces. However, when he considers (*LSD*, p. 253) what we would have to do with our theories if there was some change in the course of nature (such as the sun failing to rise tomorrow), he says that the principle of the invariance of natural laws demands that the new theory would have to explain the old *results* as well as the new, but not, apparently the old explanations: 'The revised theories would not merely have to account for the new state of affairs: *our older experiences would also have to be derivable from them.*' What is striking about this is that it is definitely the old phenomena rather than the old explanatory structures that would be 'saved', but one wonders why this should be so, given that the explanatory structures (which, after all, were based on the old phenomena) had really been realistically intended. Had they told us nothing about the structure of the world, and, if so, should the principle of invariance not equally apply to them?

Popper may be unwilling to require that there is some continuity of explanatory structure from one theory to another because of the justificationist tone of such a requirement. His own account of scientific explanation in terms of testable and falsifiable universal laws and initial conditions remains close to instrumentalist accounts in its stress on the contact points between theories and experience. He is himself uncomfortably conscious of this (*LSD*, p. 61, n.*):

> My explanation of explanation has been adopted by certain
> positivists or 'instrumentalists' who saw in it . . . the assertion
> that explanatory theories are *nothing but* premises for deducing
> predictions. I therefore wish to make it quite clear that I consider
> the theorist's interest in *explanation* . . . [is] irreducible to the
> practical technological interest in the deduction of predictions. . . .

But what Popper appears to remain ambivalent about is the status of those parts of theories which lie between the initial conditions and the predictions.

The real weakness of instrumentalism is its lack of depth; its inability to give an account of the role played in science by ideas of what the underlying structures of things are like. It affords such ideas at most a role in motivating scientists, and it disappoints hopes that science can teach us what the world is really like. Popper, of course, wants science to do just that, but he declines to provide any means for even partially justifying the theoretical discoveries of science. This tension is surely reflected in his attitude to what he calls the meta-physical in science – the ideas implicit in major scientific theories of the fundamental nature of reality. In the early days, he identified the metaphysical with the non-falsifiable and the non-scientifically signi-ficant (cf. *LSD*, p. 198), although he insisted on metaphysical specula-tion as an important source of theories which were falsifiable and scientific and as a stimulus to scientists to devise such theories (cf. *LSD*, pp. 277–8 and 314). Later, he realized that metaphysical ideas, although unfalsifiable directly, could still be rationally criticized (*LSD*, p. 206n), and subsequently, wanting to bring them more into the centre of science, he introduced the idea of metaphysical research programmes, which he saw as determining beyond the purely formal criterion of falsifiability what type of explanation was, at a given time, to count as acceptable and worth testing (cf. 'IA', p. 120; *UQ*, p. 151

and 'RC', p. 1047). Presumably this means that metaphysical research programmes will substantially determine the types of entity and relationship acceptable in scientific explanations and, more generally, the world picture within which theories are to be considered for plausibility. However, it remains unclear in the light of this stress on falsification whether the metaphysical core can have for Popper, any more than for his instrumentalist opponents, more than a heuristic status in science, valuable as an external stimulus, but not part of what science actually tells us. We will be in a better position to answer this question after considering, in the next section, Popper's attempt to define the scientific in terms of the falsifiable and the restricting effect such a definition has on science.

2 *The demarcation criterion*

We saw at the outset that Popper locates the interest in a philosophical study of science in what we will thereby learn about the growth of knowledge generally. Science provides us with the clearest case we have of knowledge growing systematically. Hence the claim (*LSD*, pp. 38–9) that the 'first task' of the logic of knowledge is to put forward a concept of empirical science, which draws a clear line between science and metaphysical ideas, for it is Popper's view that it is only when science treats ideas as falsifiable (i.e., non-metaphysically, in his terms) that systematic growth occurs. A criterion demarcating science from metaphysics (and, incidentally, from other fields as well) will enable us to see clearly what it is in science that accounts for its growth, after which we will be able to apply what we have learned to other fields. What I want to show in this section is that Popper's demarcation criterion and the view of scientific growth through falsification on which it rests are both mistaken. Popper's mistake here incidentally accounts for his discomfort in attempting to explain the place of metaphysics in science. More importantly, though, from examination of the failure of the demarcation criterion we can learn something about science which is both of general application and Popperian in spirit.

The demarcation criterion advanced by Popper (*CR*, p. 39), says that 'statements or systems of statements, in order to be ranked as scientific, must be capable of conflicting with possible, or conceivable, observations'. In demarcating between science and other fields in terms of falsifiability, Popper was not intending to distinguish between meaningful and meaningless statements. He is not, therefore, substituting an analysis of meaning in terms of falsifiability for the logical positivist one in terms of verifiability. As we have already seen, Popper sees non-falsifiable metaphysical statements as having an important role even in science, and would therefore hardly propose to regard them as meaningless. In fact he attacks the verification theory of meaning both because it would render meaningless not only meta-physical statements but also the unverifiable universal law statements of science and, more radically, because he has a deep aversion to discussions of meaning in philosophy. As he says (CR, p. 40): 'I personally was never interested in the so-called problem of meaning; on the contrary, it appeared to me as a verbal problem, a typical pseudo-problem.' Most of the arguments Popper advances in favour of this view, however, boil down to pointing out the limitations inherent in explicitly defining concepts. Verbal definitions of terms must always leave us with some terms undefined, while in science and everyday life we are able to operate perfectly well with terms which are vague and not precisely defined (see chapter I, pp. 7–8; cf. OS, vol. 2, pp. 18–20). However, if conceptual analysis at its best – for example, in Ryle's hands – has little to do with formulating definitions, even less have philosophical investigations into the relationships between language and the world (such as those of Wittgenstein, Austin or Davidson).

Popper certainly does not show that meaning is not a proper field for philosophical analysis. Nevertheless, it is important to keep clear that, in demarcating science from non-science, he is not trying to distinguish between genuine and pseudo-propositions, as many people have misunderstood him here. Neither is he interested in providing a simple definition of science. Indeed, he says (OK, p. 29) that it was only after he had solved the problem of induction that he realized the importance of the criterion of demarcation; presumably because his analyses both of inductive reasoning and of the virtues of Einstein compared with Freud, Adler and the Marxists emphasized the import-ance of the refuting rather than of the confirming instance.

Not only is Popper's demarcation criterion not involved with meaningfulness or definitions; there is a sense in which it does not demarcate statements or theories at all. Rather, as he says himself (CR, p. 33), it distinguishes between 'a genuinely empirical method and a non-empirical or even a pseudo-empirical method'. Yet surely, it will be objected, what the criterion demands is that a scientific theory makes falsifiable predictions, and whether a theory or a statement does this is something inherent in the theory itself. Up to a point, this is true. Theories that are not falsifiable and which cannot sensibly be treated as falsifiable cannot be scientific, but the converse is not true. For it is always possible for defenders of formally falsifiable theories to treat them as unfalsifiable by explaining counter-examples away. In Popper's view, this is what happened with Marx's originally falsifiable theories, and why Marxism has degenerated into pseudo-science. Even in physics it is perfectly possible to 'save' theories in the face of falsified predictions in any number of ways. Dirac on occasion simply denied the reports of falsifications. Oersted and Faraday (falsely) blamed the insensitivity of instruments for failure to detect predicted effects. Prout preserved his theory that atomic weights were whole numbers by modifying a subsidiary hypothesis, in this case by changing the formula for water. (All these examples come from Agassi, 1975, pp. 167, 175–6.) Or anomalous observations can be explained as being due not to the falsity of the theory under test, but to the presence of as-yet-undiscovered factors interfering with the anomalous effect. Popper's initial response (*LSD*, p. 83) is to say that such moves as these destroy the scientific status of the theory under test unless they themselves make new predictions and so increase the falsifiability of the system as a whole. Scientific character, properly speaking, attaches not to a theory alone, but also to the way it is treated: the theory must be testable and adverse tests must actually be held to count against it. A genuinely scientific method of investigation, then, is one which proposes testable theories and which takes the tests seriously.

Both the logical nature of the criterion and its implications emerge clearly from a discussion of conventionalism in *The Logic of Scientific Discovery* (pp. 78–84). Popper takes conventionalism to say that in physics we impose our theories on nature. They are a merely logical construction which defines an artificial, scientific world by reference to the system of theories we choose, and it is this world of which science speaks. According to conventionalism we judge, for example, whether our instruments and perceptions are scientifically accurate by seeing if the measurements and observations which they give us from the real world conform to the scientific world picture of our theories. Thus, for a conventionalist, acceptable observations will be only those which conform to his theories (which he chooses on grounds of simplicity and coherence rather than on narrowly empirical grounds). In Popper's view, conventionalist moves to deflect criticism will usually be '*ad hoc*': by blaming the instruments or observers for actual observations which contradict the chosen system of theory, or by introducing auxiliary hypotheses which merely 'account' for the discrepancies without making any new predictions, or by imposing arbitrary restrictions on the applications of the theory, they may be said to decrease rather than increase the degree of falsifiability of the theory. It is to be stressed that Popper's use of the term '*ad hoc*' is not the same as that of all writers on the subject; some people (e.g., Grünbaum, 1976d) will also refer to what Popper thinks of as content-increasing auxiliary hypotheses as '*ad hoc*', and, as we shall see, the whole issue of the scientific viability of *ad hoc* hypotheses, even in Popper's adverse sense, is open. However, what is clear is that the conventionalist is treating his system as empirically unfalsifiable. In view of the fact that the physical system chosen by the conventionalist may in practice be the same as that of a Popperian realist, the conventionalist may argue that Popper's demarcation criterion fails because it is not possible to divide systems of theories into falsifiable and non-falsifiable ones. To this, Popper replies (*LSD*, pp. 81–2):

> These objections of an imaginary conventionalist seem to me incontestable, just like the conventionalist philosophy itself. I admit that my criterion of falsifiability does not lead to an unambiguous classification. Indeed it is impossible to decide, by analysing its logical form, whether a system of statements is a conventional system of irrefutable implicit definitions, or whether it is a system which is empirical in my sense: that is a refutable system. Yet this only shows that my criterion of demarcation cannot be applied immediately to a *system of statements*. . . . The question whether a given *system* should as such be regarded as a conventionalist or an empirical one is therefore misconceived. *Only with reference to the methods applied* to a theoretical system is it at all possible to ask whether we are dealing with a conventionalist or an empirical theory. The only way to avoid conventionalism is by taking a *decision*: the decision not to apply its methods. We decide that if our system is threatened we will never save it by any kind of *conventionalist stratagem*.

In fact, as we shall see in chapter VII, when discussing probability statements, it is possible to *decide* to treat logically non-falsifiable statements as falsifiable by adopting methodological rules specifying conditions under which they will be held refuted. Since much of science is concerned with probability statements, the fact that scientists do treat probability statements as falsifiable is important for Popper, who wants to maintain that falsifiability is the criterion of the scientific. So the criterion is ultimately methodological. It is not linguistic. It does not enable us to tell whether a system of statements is scientific simply by looking at it. We also have to look at what people are doing with it.

Popper says that a scientific system will never be saved by conventionalist stratagems, but that any saving hypothesis – to explain the failure of a prediction – must itself make new predictions and so increase the testability of the system as a whole. A good example of a content-increasing saving hypothesis (and one accepted as such by Popper), which was actually successful as well, is the discovery by Adams and Leverrier of the planet Neptune. The orbit of Uranus appeared eccentric on Newtonian astronomical principles, when they were applied to an initial set-up consisting of the positions and masses of the sun, Jupiter and Saturn and the mass of Uranus. Neptune was actually discovered because the eccentricity of Uranus's orbit was explained not in terms of the failure of Newtonian principles, but on the grounds that there was an extra-Uranian planet interfering with Uranus's orbit. In other words, what was rejected was the assumption that the sun, Jupiter and Saturn were the only factors apart from Uranus which needed to be taken into account. Modifying the results of Grünbaum (1976d), the first thing we note is that it is not clear on Popper's formal criteria for degrees of testability that the Adams–Leverrier hypothesis is more testable than an alternative which denied that there was any significant extra-Uranian planet and simply recorded Uranus's actual orbit as an exception to Newtonian principles. Being logically incompatible, the two theories cannot stand in a subclass relationship to each other, so the first mode of comparison of degrees of testability cannot be used. Nor is it clear how the second, that comparing the minimum degree of composition of respective falsifiers, is to be applied. Certainly what we have here is not like the parabola–ellipse–circle relationship used by Popper to explain comparison of degrees of testability through dimensions. In fact, the Adams–Leverrier hypothesis, although clearly more precise in giving an idea of where to look for possible falsifications, may in some circumstances actually need more basic statements to falsify it; while its competitor would always be falsified by any single observation of a sufficiently large extra-Uranian planet, if such a planet were observed, the Adams–Leverrier hypothesis might need quite a number of observations before it could be falsified, for certain predictions about the mass and orbit of the new planet are involved in its explanation of the orbit of Uranus and these predictions may well require several basic statements for their falsification. Whatever may be the truth of this criticism of Popper's criteria for degrees of testability, there is a clear intuitive sense in which the Adams–Leverrier hypothesis is preferable in terms of precision and content to the imaginary alternative which, in effect, simply limits the application of Newton's laws.

Unfortunately, and more seriously for Popper's position as a whole, as Lakatos (1970) has shown, the admission that saving hypotheses of this sort are allowed in certain circumstances means that scientific theories fail in practice to forbid any observable states of affairs. They thus become, practically speaking, unfalsifiable and, on the demarcation criterion, unscientific. The alternative would be to admit that formally strict falsification is impossible, but, as in the case of probability statements, to make a methodological decision to reject any theory which is confronted by counter-evidence and to disallow saving hypotheses of any sort. But this would naturally be disastrous for Popper's account of science, as many discoveries, like that of Neptune, have resulted from showing that an apparent counter-example to a theory is to be accounted for by predicting the existence of some hitherto unknown factor in the environment of the test, and responsible for the failure of the test to confirm the theory as it was originally being applied.

Lakatos brings his point home by emphasizing that, once the assumption is made that unknown factors rather than the theory under test may be held responsible for the failure of a test, it never need be admitted that the theory under test is to blame for the failure to observe what was predicted. Further, no theoretical limit can be drawn in advance to the number of saving explanations before a theory or its defenders lose their scientific status. After all, telescopic observation might have failed to discover Neptune, but, as Lakatos points out, a saving explanation could be devised to explain why the new planet was not observable telescopically, perhaps because it was obscured by a cloud of cosmic dust. Failure to observe this by satellite could also be explained by another saving hypothesis. . . . There is no natural end to a chain of hypotheses, each explaining the failure of its predecessor in terms of yet another interfering factor. Moreover, if a member of a chain of saving hypotheses turns out to be correct, the original theory together with the saving hypotheses will be triumphantly vindicated, and any earlier objections to continuing the chain will appear highly reactionary.

Predictions in science are not made by a theory (such as Newton's) alone; for the theory to be applied in such a way as to yield a falsifiable prediction we need to know the relevant initial conditions. In order to be certain that the theory is to blame for a falsified prediction, we must further be certain both of the initial conditions and that we have taken all relevant factors into account. It is this last assumption (the *ceteris paribus* clause) that will often be attacked by saving or auxiliary hypotheses. Popper, it is true, speaks of a saving hypothesis (such as the postulation of a new planet) together with the core theory and the initial conditions as together forming a new system, and he will allow new systems of this sort where they are more falsifiable than a system consisting of an old system plus an empty explanation of some anomaly (one in effect simply recording the anomaly, while making no new predictions). But this way of looking at saving hypotheses obscures the fact that their role is precisely to deflect criticism from the original 'core' theory, so as to treat it as virtually unfalsifiable. Lakatos is thus justified in asserting (1970, pp. 100–1) that

> *exactly the most admired scientific theories simply fail to forbid any observable state of affairs . . . such theories never alone contradict a 'basic' statement*: they contradict at most a conjunction of a basic statement describing a spatio-temporally singular event and of a universal non-existence statement saying that no other relevant cause is at work anywhere in the universe.

Popper himself realizes that this is Lakatos's key passage and that the example of the discovery of Neptune contains the key argument for his thesis that scientific theories fail to forbid any observable states of affairs, for he comments on both ('RC', pp. 1005–9), concluding that if Lakatos's thesis were true his philosophy of science would be 'completely mistaken' and 'completely uninteresting'. I shall argue later that this is not necessarily so: that, even granted Lakatos's claim, Popper's demarcation criterion can still tell us much about an important element in the conduct of scientific research, but what Popper seems to appreciate more clearly than Lakatos is that once Lakatos's basic thesis is admitted it is not (as we shall see) going to be possible to shore up falsificationism at all, even by making it much more sophisticated. This is because every attempt to specify in advance conditions in which observable states of affairs will necessitate the abandoning of some scientific theory dogmatically denies the possibility of a content-increasing saving explanation which might actually be true.

Popper's reply to Lakatos ('RC', p. 1007) is designed to show that the story about Neptune is not typical, because there are many other cases in which falsifying instances to Newton's theory could not be treated in that sort of way:

> While it is of course true that cases of the sort Professor Lakatos discusses could exist, it is also true that vast numbers of observable orbits could not possibly be dealt with by such auxiliary hypotheses. Assume we were to accept that a planet moves on the same geometrical orbit as at present, but with constant velocity. Or assume that the velocities of some planets were to decrease rather than increase when approaching their perihelion. Or assume the orbit of Mars were, in every fourth Mars year, *not* to show any perturbations (and thus none of those we attribute to Jupiter). Or assume the orbit of some planet were to be approximately rectangular. None of these cases could be dealt with and explained away by a method similar to the one suggested by Professor Lakatos within Newtonian theory. Thus we have many, many, potential falsifiers: and Professor Lakatos's story is not in his sense 'characteristic'.

I have given Popper's reply in full because he considers that it clinches his criticism of Lakatos. I find this doubtful, because what he seems to have done is simply to produce further-reaching and more complicated counter-examples. This in itself says nothing about the logical possibility of deflecting criticism. One could postulate, for example, that these strange orbits were due to powerful rockets on the planets involved. But there is no point in actually thinking up explanations within a Newtonian framework, or in denying that the difficulties of doing so may be considerable, once Lakatos's central point is grasped: that such explanations are always possible and, if there is some good reason for doing so (if the theory under attack is well established or looks like being widely useful), there is nothing *per se* unscientific in seeking one or even in living for a time with an anomaly, in the hope that a successful saving explanation will be devised eventually.

Popper goes on to suggest that if Newton's theory of gravitation were taken to say that all attractive forces are gravitational, then it is long and soundly refuted because of the existence of electrical and magnetic forces. This is particularly strange in this context if 'refuted' is to be taken as 'falsified' (as Popper does) because the thesis as stated looks like a metaphysical one to the effect that all attractive forces are explicable in terms of gravitation plus postulated masses. Now, why is this 'obviously' not the case? After all, the chances before Newton of explaining motion in terms of a theory which states that bodies move basically in straight lines did not look too good from the observational point of view. Isn't the difference between the two only that it is going to be much more complicated within the theory to explain the deviations we think of as due to electrical and magnetic forces than it is to explain the deviations of moving bodies from straight paths? But who can say that it would be impossible to do, by postulating hidden and as-yet-unknown masses and so on? Clearly, put like that, because of the complicatons involved, there appears little point in doing it, but the desire to save a well-established theory could justify the attempt. Grünbaum (1976d) points out that Pauli postulated the existence of the neutrino simply to preserve energy conservation in the theory of radioactive nuclear disintegration long before any test was envisaged or there was any other theoretical basis for it. Popper goes on to give examples of scientists who point out in advance what kinds of results would lead them to reject their theories. Even here we have (from Agassi, 1975, p. 195) the malignant example of Dirac who did do this, but refused to accept the results as such when they came, and was eventually proved to be right to do so. In any case, the fact that scientists specify refutations in advance could be more because they value simplicity in theories than because it would be logically impossible to get round the 'refutation'. What Popper does not show is that refutations need logically be decisive, nor, crucially, does his demarcation criterion give guidance on when the attempt to defend a theory becomes 'unscientific'.

It is important to realize the effect which the admissibility of saving hypotheses has on the use of falsification as a criterion of demarcation between science and other activities. If the falsification principle is applied rigidly, then much good science is going to become unscientific, which is clearly absurd. If, on the other hand, evasion of falsification is permitted, especially through the strategy of directing attention away from the theory under test onto criticism of the assumption that other things are not equal in the test situation, the demarcation criterion loses any practical value it might have in enabling us to know when we are being truly scientific in rejecting a theory that could be saved from falsification, as opposed to being unscientific in attempting to save it from falsification. The point is that, if falsification can never be conclusive, it is hard to see how apparent falsification can be absolute grounds for rejection. As I have said, it is always possible to 'explain' why things went wrong and, if necessary, to explain the apparent failures of the explanations, if they too are apparently falsified. Popper and Lakatos, it is true, put restrictions on the type of hypothesis permitted as saving explanations, hoping in this way to rescue falsificationism. But the condition of new and independent testability is elastic in application, because Lakatos at least is rightly careful not to insist on the immediate corroboration of the new predictions, for it is quite possible that corroboration might come only after several more saving hypotheses have been introduced to explain the initial failure of the new predictions. We are clearly now some distance from being able to write Marxism off as unscientific simply because its proponents have introduced new hypotheses to explain the refutations of some of Marx's original predictions: and who is to say that some of these saving hypotheses may not themselves have made reasonably successful, if not very precise, new predictions about movements in Third World countries and disaffection among alienated groups in urban societies? Analogous remarks can equally be made about Freud's successive revisions of his theories.

We have considered the case of the discovery of Neptune, in which a saving hypothesis and the core theory it was saving were both vindicated. This case is particularly interesting because an analogous solution was invoked to solve analogous problems with Mercury. The difference between the cases is that the intra-Mercurial planet Vulcan, unlike Neptune, did not exist to be observed. But this in itself did not lead to a rejection of the core theory. Mercury's anomalous perihelion was regarded as a problem for Newtonian astronomy, but one that would, likely as not, eventually be solved. The anomaly of Mercury became a refutation of Newton's theories only when it became clear that a rival theory (Einstein's) actually was closer to the truth about Mercury. For the impression given by Popper's falsificationism – that theories failing tests are to be rejected – is not a good reflection of scientific practice, in which theories are actually rejected only when some other theory is seen to do better.

Is scientific practice to be criticized here? In so far as in the imperfect state of our knowledge any theory will have dozens of empirical problems confronting it, it would surely be absurd to reject a theory simply because problems appear. What scientists do most of the time is to attempt to iron out difficulties; in so doing, they may both improve the theory and make discoveries (as the case of Neptune shows), or they may not. But the fact that they do not does not show that they might not. So it would be irrational just to abandon a theory with nothing better to put in its place. When we have a competitor, however, the situation is transformed; for, as Feyerabend has argued (1965, p. 250), when crucial experiments between the rivals are performed, the victorious theory will not only get the right result, it will also implicitly explain why its rival did not. (This accounts for the feeling we noted in Bacon and Mill that a confirming instance has more probative value for a theory when it is at the same time a counter-example to some other theory.)

However, we should be careful of taking too sanguine a view of crucial experiments as decisive moments in scientific history. Lakatos, who also insists that theories are actually rejected in conflicts with other theories rather than in conflicts with experience alone, has this to say (1970, p. 173) on the role of crucial experiments in leading to decisions on core theories (what he calls research programmes):

> *There are no such things as crucial experiments*, at least not if these are meant to be experiments which can *instantly* overthrow a research programme. In fact, when one research programme suffers defeat and is superseded by another one, we may – *with long hindsight* – call an experiment crucial if it turns out to have provided a spectacular corroborating instance for the victorious programme and a failure for the defeated one.

Long hindsight is required here because we may misjudge the situation. Even though the majority of scientists claim that a defeat has been inflicted,

> if a scientist in the 'defeated' camp puts forward a few years later a scientific explanation of the allegedly 'crucial experiment' within (or consistent with) the allegedly defeated programme, *the honorific title may be withdrawn and the 'crucial experiment' may turn from a defeat into a new victory for the programme.*

In other words, even crucial experiments can legitimately be explained away and the tables turned in favour of apparently defeated theories. Luck and ingenuity can make false research programmes appear successful and progressive on Popperian and Lakatosian criteria for a considerable time, as Lakatos himself admits (1971, p. 100). So falsificationism of a sufficiently sophisticated type to admit saving hypotheses at all will fail to give us definite heuristic advice even when confronted with crucial experiments between theories. In such circumstances it may be as scientific to attempt a defence of the defeated theory as to proclaim its demise. A major objective of the demarcation criterion was to get scientists to realize that it is unscientific to defend what has been refuted, but the criterion is of no practical value because we can never tell absolutely that this is so. This is because of the natural and justifiable tendency for core theories (or research programmes) to become unfalsifiable metaphysical systems.

Even appeal to verisimilitude, assuming that concept can be saved from the objections of Tichý and Miller, will not help us much in controversial decisions between theories. Popper (*CR*, p. 235) allows that

> it always remains possible, of course, that we shall make mistakes in our relative appraisal of two theories, and the appraisal will often be a controversial matter

but he goes on to say that

> as long as there are no revolutionary changes in our background knowledge, the relative appraisal of our two theories, t_1 and t_2, will remain stable.

Talk of revolutionary changes should not blind us to the significance of the admission here. Whether background knowledge is taken to consist merely in the idea that we know all the relevant factors in a given test situation, or whether it refers more generally to the beliefs and procedures admitted as plausible at a given time, argument over the force of crucial experiments is always liable to develop into discussions of the correctness of the relevant background knowledge. Despite general stability on background assumptions, there can be no ultimate logical or methodological objection to men who prefer to see crucial experiments casting doubt on some of these assumptions rather than on their theories. In many important cases of inter-theoretical dispute, consensus on background assumptions will be significantly absent. In the light of all this, the significance of Popper's reply to Duhem (*CR*, p. 112) may be underlined. Here he admits that theories can really only be tested against experience in conjunction with background knowledge, and that we may later change our assessments as to where the force of a test is to bear. But to say this is tantamount to saying that there can be no clear or easy demarcation between a scientist attempting to deflect a criticism of his theory and a dogmatist doing the same.

The demarcation criterion undoubtedly points to an important feature of scientific theories: that, in conjunction with other theories and assumptions, they are to make falsifiable predictions, and, other things being equal, content-decreasing stratagems are to be avoided by explaining anomalies through making new predictions at the same time. But these conditions may well be satisfied by students of form, astrologers and cranks predicting the end of the world or the arrival of beings in flying saucers. Nor can we dismiss any of these as being unscientific simply because they explain away the failure of their often very precise predictions. As Kuhn has pointed out (1970a, p. 8), medieval astrologers appealed to the problems involved in getting precise enough data about an individual's birth in order to explain why they did less well in predicting a man's future than on his general propensities or natural calamities. However,

> only after astrology itself became implausible did these arguments
> come to seem question-begging. Similar arguments are regularly
> used to-day when explaining, for example, failures in medicine
> or meteorology. In times of trouble they are also deployed in
> the exact sciences, fields like physics, chemistry and astronomy.

In other words, the acceptability of saving hypotheses in a given area depends on the scientific acceptability of the central core of theories and assumptions which are being saved. Just this point has been made by Grünbaum (1976d), who has argued that even *ad hoc*ness without new testability may be scientifically acceptable when the core theory is worth preserving, while, if the core theory is not worth preserving, *ad hoc*ness even with independent testability may be unacceptable. The problem is that it is often difficult to assess (except retrospectively) the acceptability of the core. Judgments here will naturally be influenced by the number and extent of saving hypotheses the core theory engenders, but this judgment is not amenable to an open-and-shut decision procedure, nor are judgments of the acceptability of one research programme as against another.

What is wrong with the demarcation criterion is that it overlooks the importance of the metaphysical or unfalsifiable status of research programmes to the growth of science, for growth would actually be hindered were theories not allowed to stand despite 'falsifications'. The strange thing is that Popper himself knows and admits this. He actually advocates (*CR*, p. 312n) the dogmatic defence of theories, especially in the early stages:

> The dogmatic attitude of sticking to a theory as long as possible
> is of considerable significance. Without it we could never find out
> what is in a theory – we should give the theory up before we
> had a real opportunity of finding out its strength; and in con-
> sequence no theory would ever be able to play its role of

bringing order into the world, of preparing us for future events, of drawing our attention to events we should never otherwise observe.

Moreover, not only is a degree of dogmatism in science not anti-thetical to the critical attitude; it is actually required by it ('RSR', pp. 86–7):

> a limited amount of dogmatism is necessary for progress: without a serious struggle for survival in which the old theories are tenaciously defended, none of the competing theories can show their mettle.

Dogmatism here can mean nothing other than the treating of core theories as unfalsifiable. But when is much dogmatism too much? We are now far from being able to decide what is scientific by any simple appeal to the demarcation criterion, even if we have a general pre-disposition in favour of empirically less-troubled theories.

Popper's advocacy of dogmatism as instrumental to scientific pro-gress is given a nice sociological twist by Kuhn (1970b, p. 262), who suggests that variability of judgment among scientists on theory choice is essential for scientific progress, because otherwise theoretical systems differing appreciably from the norm will never be developed sufficiently to become serious contenders. But, commenting on a passage from Lakatos we have already quoted, he underlines the fact that the correctness or otherwise of these maverick decisions is some-thing that can be assessed by the scientific community as a whole only 'with hindsight'. But to say this effectively deprives these decisions of their function, for

> the scientific community cannot wait for history, though some individual members do. The needed results are instead achieved by distributing the risk that must be taken among the group's members.

Naturally, Popper would advocate the flourishing of many competing theories in many stages of development (far more in fact than Kuhn, for whom 'normal' science exists when one main theory holds the field unchallenged). But it is hard to see how many theories can flourish without some degree of protective dogmatism on the part of their adherents, and how this is consistent with the demarcation criterion. Thus Lakatos comments (1971, p. 121) that

> until now all the 'laws' proposed by apriorist philosophers of science have turned out wrong in the light of the verdicts of the best scientists. Up to the present day, it has been the scientific standards, as applied 'instinctively' by the scientific élite in

particular cases which have constituted the main – although not
the exclusive – yardstick of the philosophers' universal laws. . . .
Is it not hubris to demand that if, say, Newtonian or Einsteinian
science turns out to have violated Bacon's, Carnap's or Popper's
a priori rules of the game, the business of science should be
started anew?

As we have seen, Lakatos's own proposals have no practical value,
since they involve decisions which, on his own admission, can be
assessed only retrospectively.

What has emerged so far is that, contrary to the intentions of Popper
in formulating his demarcation criterion, there is no precise point at
which holding one theory as opposed to another becomes unscientific,
or pejoratively dogmatic. Dogmatism and metaphysics are essential
elements of the scientific attitude. Moreover, there is inevitably a
degree of uncertainty in deciding precisely when to accept one theory
and to abandon another. The 'instinctive' attitudes of the scientific
élite no doubt have a role to play, just as in art criticism. The existence
of doubt and controversy on border-line cases in art, as in science,
does not, of course, preclude rationally based consensus on other
cases and, as we shall see in more detail in the next section, need not
lead to relativism. The *Mona Lisa* is a great work of art, and Newton's
theory a great scientific achievement, whereas daubs sold in chemists'
shops and the astrological columns of newspapers are rightly rejected
by experts. In science, as in art, reasons can be advanced one way or
another on these matters, and, *among people experienced* in them, agreement exists on the types of reasons relevant to making decisions, even
where there is sometimes intractable disagreement on precise assessments of particular cases. The existence of such disagreements is not
in itself a reason for concluding that what is said in art or science is a
totally irrational matter of fashion. In science, indeed, the critical
attitude is actually promoted by the controversies which result from
such disagreements.

The main result of our examination of the demarcation criterion is
that on it much science becomes irreducibly metaphysical, because of
the protection necessarily accorded in research to core theories. This
is not, of course, to deny that counter-evidence is and should be taken
seriously. We would certainly want to say, along with Popper, that
theorists who blithely ignore counter-instances to their theories or
refuse to specify what would count as counter-evidence are being
unscientific. But dogmatism comes in when theorists refuse (sometimes
even without being able to advance auxiliary hypotheses which
increase the testability of the system as a whole) to allow counter-
evidence to bear on what can be called the metaphysical core of their

theories. For the promise given by this metaphysical core of further discoveries, its past success, its generality and fruitfulness in connecting with other theories and problems can all be as important reasons in its favour as the existence of an amount of counter-evidence is a reason against it. Indeed, without the interest resulting from these other factors, testability on its own will hardly bring a theory to the centre of the scientific stage. As Agassi has pointed out (1975, p. 149), if it were true that testability alone were what determined the quality of a theory, aerodynamics would be of more scientific interest than much contemporary physics, to say nothing of a metaphysical system, such as atomism, which has inspired and guided so much fruitful research; it would also be a better theory than Newton's three laws of motion and the law of gravitational attraction when they were being treated by Newtonians as, for all practical purposes, unfalsifiable.

Once it is seen that unfalsifiable theories can still sometimes be criticized, there is no overwhelming need for resting the whole weight of scientific rationality on empirical falsifiability, nor for a rigid distinction in the history of scientific theories between their metaphysical and their scientific incarnations. Popper now argues a metaphysical theory can be criticized by asking questions such as (*CR*, p. 199):

> Does it solve the problem (it is addressed to)? Does it solve it better than other theories? Has it perhaps merely shifted the problem? Is the solution simple? Is it fruitful? Does it perhaps contradict other . . . theories needed for solving other problems?

In the light of this, less stress could perhaps be placed on the comparison of competing scientific theories on the basis of their empirical predictions and more stress on overall comparison of them, ontology and metaphysics included. This would certainly be in line with the claims we noticed at the end of the last section that metaphysical research programmes determine our attitudes in many ways to particular scientific theories.

One of the difficulties with assessing Popper's demarcation criterion is that it was obviously originally devised to give substance to intuitions about the merits of Einstein's theory compared with Freud's, Adler's and Marx's. In other words, it had an evaluative function. But this was conflated with an attempt to describe what distinguished empirical science from other disciplines, including metaphysics, mathematics and logic. The criterion fails on both counts. Science includes as an integral part what, on the criterion, is metaphysics. Intellectual respectability, in the sense of criticizability and advance through criticism, is not confined to theories such as Einstein's, as Popper himself clearly admits. Indeed, in reply to some remarks of Bartley (1968) to the effect that, in his concentration on the problem of demarcation between science and metaphysics, he had failed to attack the more general problem of the critical or rational approach to problems of all sorts, Popper ('PDR', pp. 95, 98) wrote that

> the demarcation between science and metaphysics is a special case of the wider problem of demarcating criticizable from non-criticizable theories

and that

> empirical refutation is just part of the general critical work of improving theories (including metaphysical theories) by searching for errors.

Rationality, then, consists primarily in eliminating errors and learning from them. This process is not peculiar to empirical science, nor is empirical science furthered by empirical testing alone, although it is undoubtedly true that change because of empirical testing is one important mark of the scientific and serves to distinguish it from conservative and empiricially closed systems such as African magic (cf. Horton, 1967). But in science, at the same time, other considerations, such as a theory's overall problem-solving potential, are also important in determining the direction of growth. If Popper himself ultimately sees the demarcation criterion as part of the general work of demarcating between criticizable and non-criticizable theories, the importance of distinguishing between science and non-science seems to diminish in comparison with the importance of distinguishing what counts as a critical as opposed to a dogmatic approach in each particular field of activity. Popper himself has, of course, made a start here with his analyses of theories in metaphysics, ethics and the philosophy of history, but before turning to these, we must look in more detail at the status of the critical attitude in science, given the failure of the demarcation criterion.

3 Relativism in science

Our examination of the demarcation criterion led us to the conclusion that dogmatism has an essential role to play in the development of scientific theories, and that apparently refuted theories can at times be rescued by saving hypotheses. This thesis of fallibility and possible impermanence of judgments on the standing of scientific theories must, however, be carefully distinguished from another, more radical, thesis to the effect that rational judgments between theories are altogether impossible, and that theory change is largely a matter of fashion. The thesis of the last section emphasized the fact that judgments between theories could be rationally made, but that defeats in crucial experiments could be turned into victories by further elaboration of a defeated theory. A defeat, then, required some action on the part of the defenders of the theory. What was uncertain after a particular injury was the extent of the damage, not that repairs were necessary. The radical thesis rules out any talk of theories competing, let alone enjoying ascendancy (if only for a time), on the grounds that different theories are literally non-comparable, and that when comparisons are made they are bound to be biased, as they are always made by assuming the correctness of the point of view of one of the competitors. It is this relativism that we need to examine in this section, as at least part of its plausibility derives from positions of Popper himself, notwithstanding Popper's hostility to it.

I argued in the last section that the failure of the demarcation criterion to provide a scientific decision procedure was not in itself enough to show that scientific rationality is a myth. But for Popper a more fundamental problem remains: given his own basic epistemological position that we can never *justify* any empirical statement, is scientific rationality a myth? What reasons can *he* have to justify his claim that he can sometimes justify preferences between theories if this does not amount to at least partially justifying the preferred theories themselves?

Popper does believe that proofs exist in logic and mathematics, and that because of this we can prove that some rules of inference are valid within particular languages. We are able to criticize empirical theories when they are formulated in an appropriate language because a rule of inference is, in Popper's view, a rule for transmitting truth from premises to conclusions. So a false conclusion from a valid inference will demonstrate the falsity of a premise. This, of course, leads to the method of falsification, and to Popper's view (*CR*, p. 64) that logic is the 'organon of criticism'. We increase the criticizability of our systems by using the strongest available logic; by appreciating the logical relations between various empirical statements, we will be given non-arbitrary reasons for accepting or rejecting some of them.

The importance of logic in argument cannot be overestimated. Nevertheless, to realize the logical relationships between statements does not on its own tell us which way to turn in a factual matter. To take an oversimplified example: even suppose an observation statement q is taken as actually following from a theory p, and we find $- q$, we will be justified in rejecting p only if we can be sure that $- q$ is true. We may know that we cannot have p and $- q$, but knowing that does not tell us which to reject. Until it is added to some *epistemological* foundations, giving us positive reasons for preferring one statement to another in such cases, logic is going to help us little in deciding which empirical statements we should accept. Effectively and rationally to prefer one empirical statement to another, we must know more than that they are mutually inconsistent. Does this mean that some substantive assumptions are required before we can progress here?

Popper mentions (OS, vol. 2, 1961 addendum) four ways in which he believes criticism can proceed without assumptions which are treated as being established. First, the assumptions being used to criticize the theory could actually be part of the theory. The effect of this would be to demonstrate an inconsistency in the theory, but we would still not know which of the inconsistent premises to reject. Second, the theory could be shown to be in conflict with some generally accepted assumptions. But we would not know from that alone which way to turn here. Einstein's theory rejected common-sense assumptions about time, but it is not clear from that alone that the assumptions are to be rejected. Third, the assumption may be part of competing theories, and crucial tests might be arranged. But, in such a case, the test statements would have to be accepted as true. Fourth, we can show that a theory does not succeed in solving its problems. But presumably an important part of the evidence showing this will be the theory's conflicts with various observation statements. We are left with the impression that even in these cases, the validity of criticism, beyond showing logical inconsistency, does depend on treating some empirical statements as true.

It is all very well for Popper to say (OS, vol. 2, p. 379) that 'even if we were to admit that all criticism starts from certain assumptions, this would not necessarily mean that, for it to be valid criticism, these assumptions must be established and justified'. For, in using the criticism to guide the choice between one theory or statement and another, one is treating some statements even temporarily as established and justified. What one now needs to show is the justification for doing this. To say that no justification can be given is tantamount to sceptical dogmatism (because, although some statements are accepted, it is made clear that they are dogmatically rather than rationally accepted), while to say that they are accepted because they have withstood other criticism is simply going to invite the same questions about these tests.

A relativistic opponent of Popper would no doubt accept Popper's view that the justification of empirical statements is impossible, with particular emphasis on the theoreticality of observation statements, but he would conclude from this that comparison between systems with differing empirical presuppositions is unavailing because there is no rational way of deciding between them. Even if Popper's method of falsification through crucial experiments were more conclusive than it appears, it would not help in cases of competition between radically alternative systems because each protagonist would tend – dogmatically and unjustifiably – to interpret the observational data in the light of his assumptions and to reject the interpretation of his opponent.

Popper (*OS*, vol. 2, ch. 23) argues against the idea that one is imprisoned by one's unjustifiable presuppositions on the grounds that in discussion one can recognize such presuppositions for what they are when challenged by a competing viewpoint or when, in working on a concrete problem, one realizes that what is causing problems is an assumption previously regarded by everyone as self-evident (as when Einstein was led to reject as a prejudice the common-sense notion of time). Moreover, it is not having presuppositions that is harmful, but only sticking to them when doing so obstructs progress in knowledge and they emerge as *prejudices*. So relativism can be avoided, even granted the existence of unjustified presuppositions, if one is sometimes able to recognize when one's presuppositions are really prejudices. But the point made by Kuhn is that this is just what – imprisoned within one's framework – one is unable to recognize.

It must be admitted that the examples Kuhn gives (1962) tend to tell against rather than in favour of his imprisonment thesis. Even though earlier I accepted some of Kuhn's criticisms of Popper's demarcation criterion and argued that theory comparison cannot be rigorously formulated in terms of verisimilitude, it does not follow that there are never extra-theoretical reasons for preferring one way of looking at things to another. More particularly, it is one thing to say that a theory in an undefended state is less adequate or more cumbersome as an explanation of some data than a competitor, or less universal than its rival, or more in conflict with other acceptable theories, and quite another thing to say (as a rigid interpretation of the demarcation criterion might lead us to do) that it would be *unscientific* to attempt to defend the original theory by refining it and working on *ad hoc* hypotheses to explain its apparent inadequacies.

Kuhn is right to stress as he does the irreversibility of scientific progress because much day-to-day work in science is devoted to making theories more adequate to the data they are supposed to explain. Competing theories will have to show themselves at least as capable of dealing with what is already dealt with. In an ideal case, it might be possible to show that not only does a new theory cover all or almost all of the successfully explained data of a competitor, but that it also explains some of the data which the competitor in its present state cannot explain *and* that it seems potentially more fruitful in that it explains or promises to explain data not even potentially within the scope of the competitor. In such a case, not only is rational comparison between theories possible, but, without an extension of the original theory, it would surely be rational to choose the new theory as the one to work on. In practice such a judgment would probably come down to one against even attempting to extend the original theory, especially if a lot of the new competitor turned out to be confirmed. This is not to say that anyone who attempted to extend the original theory would necessarily be irrational or even unscientific, but only that choices between theories have to be made and that they are not necessarily *arbitrary*.

The comparison between Einstein's theory of gravity and Newton's provides a case in point, according to Popper ('NSD', p. 57):

> [It is] simply false to say that the transition from Newton's theory of gravity to Einstein's is an irrational leap, and that the two are not rationally comparable. On the contrary, there are many points of contact (such as the role of Poisson's equation) and points of comparison: it follows from Einstein's theory that Newton's theory is an excellent approximation (except for planets or comets moving on elliptic orbits with considerable eccentricities).

In addition, Einstein's theory of gravity is embedded in a general theory of even greater scope than Newton's. In practice, such comparisons will be infrequent. Theories do not usually map onto each other so closely and so satisfactorily, with all (or even most) of the indications pointing in the same direction. Hence the fruitfulness of scientists coming to *disagree* on the potential of competing theories, and working on both. But what the relativist has to show here is that theory-preference (in judging either the present explanatory power of competing theories or their future potential, or both) is *necessarily* arbitrary.

At this point, the relativist will go to the heart of his (and Popper's) position on the theory-ladenness of all world-pictures, including their observational components, and say that the sort of comparison claimed by Popper to obtain between Newton and Einstein is simply not possible, because there is no theory-neutral ground available on which to base judgments of explanatory success and potential. Even the observation of the allegedly crucial experiments will take place in accord with one theory or the other, and hence simply reinforce the position from which each protagonist started.

An example of Kuhn's is to the point here. Consider the change of aspect which took place when men stopped seeing a swinging stone as an example of constrained fall and saw it instead as a pendulum. For the Aristotelians, what we think of naturally as a pendulum was a case of a heavy body attempting to reach its natural resting place (the centre of the earth), yet being prevented from doing so because of the spoke or chain it is hanging from, and able to reach to its lowest point only after tortuous movement and some time. By contrast, we see a pendulum: a swinging body repeating the same motion over and over again, the extent of swing depending on the length of the chain rather than on the heaviness of the body. Galileo, to whom we attribute this insight (though in fact he had been partially anticipated by Oresme), saw other properties of the pendulum and constructed much of his dynamics around them.

> Why did that shift of vision occur? Through Galileo's individual genius, of course. But note that genius does not here manifest itself in more accurate or objective observation of the swinging body. Descriptively, the Aristotelian perception is just as accurate. When Galileo reported that the pendulum's period was independent of amplitude for amplitudes as great as 90°, his view of the pendulum led him to see far more regularity than we can now discover there. Rather what seems to have been involved was the exploitation by genius of perceptual possibilities made available by a medieval paradigm shift. (Kuhn, 1962, p. 118)

The data – how phenomena are perceived – are transformed in a paradigm shift. Kuhn compares such transformations to those shifts of vision undergone by subjects of *Gestalt* experiments and suggests that this may be why scientists who solve problems by articulating new models often speak of 'lightning flashes' or of 'scales falling from the eyes' when describing their first moments of vision shift. What Kuhn is claiming (1962, p. 127) is that scientists (and the rest of us) are not in a position to judge between competing paradigms, because what they see is determined by the paradigm within which they work (usually within which they have been brought up):

> As a result of the paradigm-embodied experience of the race, the culture, and finally, the profession, the world of the scientist has come to be populated with planets and pendulums, condensers and compound ores. . . . Compared with these objects of perception, both meter stick readings and retinal imprints are elaborate constructs. . . . This is not to suggest that pendulums, for example, are the only things a scientist could possibly see when looking at a swinging stone. (We have already noticed that members of another scientific community could see constrained fall.) But it is to suggest that the scientist who looks at a swinging stone can have no experience that is in principle more elementary than seeing a pendulum.

Commenting on the pendulum example and on others like it, such as Lavoisier's seeing oxygen and all that it implied, where Priestley had seen only dephlogisticated air, Kuhn says (1962, p. 120) that 'though the world does not change with a change of paradigm, the scientist afterward works in a different world'.

This is the thesis of the incommensurability of paradigms and ultimately of breakdown of communication across cultures or paradigms. What we see is different depending on our point of view: there is no common ground to enable discussion and comparison of theories to begin, because all our possible experience is a product of our theories. In view of Kuhn's curious success in doing what is on his views supposed to be impossible (helping us to see the pendulum both as an example of constrained fall and as something more 'elementary' – a swinging stone), Popper can be forgiven for his making rather short work of Kuhn's claims and talk of living in a different world ('NSD', pp. 56–7):

> A critical discussion and a comparison of the various frameworks
> is always possible. It is just a dogma . . . that the different
> frameworks are like mutually untranslatable languages. The fact
> is that even totally different languages (like English and Hopi,
> or Chinese) are not untranslatable, and that there are many Hopis
> or Chinese who have learnt to master English very well. . . .
> An intellectual revolution often looks like a religious conversion.
> A new insight may strike us like a flash of lightning. But this
> does not mean that we cannot evaluate, critically and rationally,
> our former views in the light of new ones.

It would only be perverse to pretend that nothing could be said about the advantages of seeing a swinging stone as a pendulum rather than as a contrained falling body. Even the fact that Galileo could and can be seen as *opposing* the Aristotelian view shows that there is some experiential common ground between the two positions, from which comparison could start. They were explaining the same thing, and even if they were seeing the thing differently, we can see the two and evaluate the merits of the two ways of seeing it. The case of comparing competing theories is, in fact, quite different from a Gestalt switch, for there you cannot at the same time see a figure as both a duck and a rabbit, whereas we can surely think about both the Galilean and the Aristotelian account of the pendulum at the same time.

It might be felt, however, that, even if Kuhn's own examples, which are all from Western science, do not give great support to the thesis that different conceptual schemes are incommensurable, this still does not rule out the possibility that there could be incommensurable ones, employing quite different classificatory schemes and even alternative logics. Where Kuhn's examples let him down is that they do not seem to rule out all talk of experiential common ground acceptable to both parties of a scientific dispute, on the basis of which comparative judgments between theories might be made. So long as translatability obtains even at a very basic observational level (at the level of swinging stone, rather than at the level of pendulum or constrainedly falling body), it is hard to see how complete incommensurability between theories can obtain. Feyerabend, indeed, sees this point very clearly and bases his thesis of the incommensurability of theories on mutual untranslatability. He speaks (1970a, pp. 223–4) of children (in different stages of intellectual development) and of some adults (scientists acquiring new theoretical perspectives, anthropologists living with new tribes) replacing one conceptual scheme with another in such a way that the 'phenomena' of a succeeding stage are not correlatable with the phenomena of earlier stages. He says (1970b, p. 89) that scientists moving from one incommensurable scheme (special relativity) to another (classical mechanics) do so 'with such speed that they seem to remain within a single sphere of discourse', whereas in reality they are moving from one world view in which they have learned to live to another in which they also know how to operate, but between which there is no genuine translation or comparison. The data and the perspectives of the one simply disappear when they move into the other; any 'seeing' of the data of the one from the perspective of the other is a matter of conceptual illusion.

Feyerabend is driven into talking of untranslatable alternative conceptual schemes because he realizes some of the implications of translatability for the relativism of incommensurable alternatives. But this immediately places him in a dilemma, because, without understanding (and hence translating) another conceptual scheme, how can we know that it presents a genuine alternative to our own? But, if we do understand it, then it must be translatable, and so not an entirely incommensurable alternative. This problem applies even to the example of the scientist who moves from one scheme to another. Without a translation from one to the other, when he is looking at the world from the point of view of Scheme A, he will be aware only of the existence of Scheme B, but not of its content, and so at most that he has failed to translate it into the terms of Scheme A, not that it really differs from Scheme A to the extent that it is really untranslatable. I do not want to comment further on the psychological implausibility of this example, because an argument has been put forward by Davidson (in many places, including 1973, 1974, 1975 and 1977) which would rule out on logical grounds talk of wholesale conceptual alternatives among different tribes successfully speaking apparently different languages among themselves about the same world.

What Davidson seeks to show is that having a language at all depends on having a largely correct view of the world. He starts by considering what is involved in making sense of the utterances of others. Even if we think that something other people say is false, we have to assume a great deal of reason in and behind what they are saying or we will have no clear idea of what it is they are being unreasonable about. For example, if someone says that a blue table is red, we will have to assume that he can correctly identify tables in general, that he knows that they are objects fairly stable and enduring in nature, that he is correctly referring to the same table as us, that his colour classifications are similar to ours, that he uses 'is' to make a present-tense assertion, and so on. Without assuming agreement on all these matters (some factual, some linguistic) we will be unable to know what his disagreement with us consists in. Davidson actually takes this principle of massive agreement in belief being the basis of disagreement rather far. He says (1975, p. 21) that we should not be too confident that the ancients believed the earth was flat, given that they did not think of the earth as one of a gaggle of large, cool, solid bodies circling round a very large hot star. The point is that we and the ancients, in making statements about the earth, may have been thinking of rather different objects, and without further discussion it is not too clear just what their error consisted in. Even if we do not agree that in talking about the earth we do not identify what we are speaking of in the way Davidson implies (and that we identify the earth in a way that does allow us to be sure that we and the ancients are speaking of the same thing in speaking of the earth), Davidson's general point that common identification of a given subject matter requires many shared beliefs about what it is that is being referred to does seem to be correct.

Shared beliefs will not only be required in order to pick out individuals. They will also be required in understanding other people's property talk. We will have to assume that they do not believe that colours are constantly changing or that chairs naturally turn into tables if we are to understand what it is they are saying when they tell us that they have put a blue chair in the kitchen. We will also have to assume that they draw inferences in much the same way as us or we will be unsure of what follows from statements they make.

It will be said that the most that has so far been shown is that shared belief is required for mutual understanding, not that most or even any of the beliefs need be true. Davidson's answer to this is to emphasize the place accorded to error in his argument. An erroneous belief is the belief it is, only because it says what it says about the things it is referring to. Unless the subject matter of the belief is secured through correct identification, there is nothing that the belief is about; this in turn undermines both the sense of the belief and the description of it, rather than one of the connected beliefs, as false. Presumably Davidson's argument here assumes that we are, in general, able, because of our successful use of language in practical life, to think of our beliefs as having a definite sense and, sometimes, as false. Given, then, that we do successfully refer to objects and properties in the world, we must have large numbers of true beliefs.

The relativist might concede that any successful use of language in the world requires large numbers of true beliefs on the part of the language users, but still insist that there could be incommensurable, untranslatable languages. The difficulty with this suggestion is that, with the concession that both languages must be by and large true, it is hard to see how two largely true systems dealing with the same world could be incommensurable. Relativists usually claim that two rival systems could be equally good at coping with some set of phenomena and conclude from this that neither can be true in any absolute sense, but here we have an argument to show that any conceptual scheme that is embodied in a language that succeeds in dealing reasonably well with a world must be basically correct in its view as to what that world is like. Two competing systems dealing with the same subject matter that are both basically correct cannot be completely contradictory, nor can they be completely incommensurable: both these possibilities are ruled out by saying that they are dealing with the same subject matter. A relativism that rests on the fact that different theories are incommensurable because they are dealing with different subject matters is not only weak in its epistemological implications; it is implausible as applied to the basic level of description and observation embodied in two languages, which may be culturally diverse at the theoretical and ideological level, but which are still used by human beings living in the same world and having the same basic concerns. In any case, to take a further point made by Davidson, if we found some people apparently talking a language, but without being able to identify (in our terms) what they were talking about (which is what is implied in incommensurability of subject matter), what grounds would we have for thinking of the sounds they made as a theory, or of them having beliefs at all?

Of course, the shared truths of any sets of beliefs will generally be too dull, trite, or familiar to call for comment, as Davidson observes. Cultural and theoretical diversity is far more striking and interesting. But such diversity can exist only against the dull common background of shared and basically correct beliefs. How extensive does this background have to be? Arguing along lines similar to Davidson, Barry Stroud writes (1969, p. 92):

> We can give no content to the notion of a conceptual scheme
> or language which is a genuine alternative to our present one.
> No revision open to us can take us beyond the language we
> now use and understand – any 'alternative' is either something

we already understand and can make sense of, or it is no alternative at all. Any difference between ourselves and other tribes can therefore only be partial. . . .

To say that we *already* understand any future revision to our conceptual scheme is surely claiming too much. In what sense did Aristotle already understand or even have the conceptual equipment for understanding the theory of relativity? Nevertheless, Stroud is right to insist on the necessary continuity and common basis of alternative conceptual schemes which deal with a common subject matter. We have now arrived at a position according to which any conceptual scheme dealing with a given subject matter must be supported by a largely correct set of beliefs about the items it deals with, and that any competing schemes must have much common ground in the supporting sets of beliefs. This obviously rules out relativism in any strong sense, but it also conflicts with Popper's attitude to the justification of beliefs. We must now examine the implications of our opposition to relativism for Popper's view that all empirical statements are fallible and theoretical.

Popper claims that science can show us that 'the world is utterly different from what we ever imagined' (*LSD*, p. 431) and that it can change the world of appearances. If these remarks mean that beyond the observational level science teaches us that there are unexpected structures and entities, they are unexceptionable. If, however, they are taken in a stronger sense, to imply that our world of appearances is distorted and open to revision, they are more problematic. It is well known that Newton held that reality is not really coloured, while Eddington (1928, Introduction) held that our conception of the familiar table is an illusion because tables are really composed almost entirely of empty space. Against claims of this sort, Stebbing (1937, pp. 45–6) argued:

> the common use of language enables us to attribute a meaning
> to the phrase 'a solid plank'; but there is no common use of
> language that provides a meaning for the word 'solid' that
> would make sense to say that the plank on which I stand is not
> *solid*. . . . If the plank appears to be *solid*, but is really *non-solid*,
> what does solid mean?

An uncritical use of this sort of argument would, however, prove far too much, for the same sort of move might be made with a concept like that of 'witch'. Old women, it might be said, behaving in particular ways fulfil the criteria for picking out witches, and so just are witches.

We obviously want to avoid extending Stebbing's argument to concepts where powers beyond basically observable properties are involved. On the other hand, to deny that something is a solid table after we have eaten dinner from it is hardly intelligible. It will no doubt be objected here that theories about unperceived existence are involved in speaking of solid tables, but, as I argued in chapter V, any possible descriptive scheme must employ some concepts of stable and enduring objects. Given that 'table' is a concept which contains no more than that amount of theory, and given that it is normally successfully applied, there can be no harm in thinking of it as descriptive or observational rather than theoretical. It would certainly be perverse for someone in the presence of a table to ask whether anything can have the powers a table is supposed to have, while such talk would clearly be intelligible applied to witches, even in the presence of 'witches'.

Davidson's argument led us to see the necessity of many correct beliefs in order to identify the subject matter of incorrect beliefs. The correct beliefs will contain, as a large part, beliefs arising from the everyday use of the descriptive components of our language, where theory about underlying structures and invisible powers is not much in evidence. It is no accident that continuity in judgments on what things are red, solid, trees, stones, dogs, men and so on exists through great changes in theory. Homer and I would agree on most of these matters, despite having very different ideas on the nature of man, the world and gods. Because of the primarily descriptive function of such beliefs it is unintelligible to me to think of some future scientist telling me that what is outside my window is not a tree or that what I have just walked with is not a dog.

Popper has shown that the world may change; trees and dogs may cease to exist, and the stability required for any sort of physical description of states of affairs may leave the world. But this does not show that most of our present beliefs about what things are trees, dogs and so on, and what it is for something to be these things, are not true. What I have argued here is that, in view of our success in speaking about our world, they are true, that they form the foundations of our conceptual scheme and that because we live in a common world with common interests they, or similar beliefs, are likely to be held by other human beings who recognizably live like us and speak a language.

Given a common basis to any human conceptual scheme, a basis which is also true, the relativist incommensurability thesis fails, at least between human languages. There will be common epistemological foundations at the descriptive level, and even the most rarefied theoretical elements of a conceptual scheme will have to have some bearing on what is held true at the descriptive level. Even nuclear physics makes a difference to our lives. Given this, there will always be the possibility of comparison between competing theories, in terms of their predictive success at common descriptive levels (ultimately, if necessary, at the level of everyday behaviour). These comparisons will not always be conclusive, but the fact of disagreement could be due to a tension in the application of rational standards in theory choice between, for example, a demand for universality in a theory as opposed to the demand for precision of prediction, the very existence or applicability of which the relativist is out to deny, rather than to the non-existence of such standards. Where Popper is on weak ground in his anti-relativism is in his unwillingness to speak of empirical statements being justified, even at the level of description. His own account of theory choice remains, as we have seen, incomplete and unsatisfactory, resting on dogmatism (in the choice of descriptive statements) and illicitly (for him) inductive. Given that the successful speaking of a language requires both truth in many beliefs held by speakers and the assumption of a measure of continued stability in the world, and given that we are able to talk about the world, there can be no objection to basing opposition to relativism between competing conceptual schemes expressible in human languages on an epistemology which involves both a degree of inductivism and which accepts the justifiability of masses of our beliefs. Without these assumptions, however, it is unclear how Popper is able to provide any theoretical answer to relativism, for one dogmatism at the descriptive level is presumably as good as any other, while, for the future, too, any theory is as good as any other unless we are allowed a degree of inductivism.

VII

Probability and Indeterminism

Probability plays an important part in modern science. Many hypotheses are probabilistic; that is, they assign probabilities to events, instead of predicting them absolutely. There are considerable problems both in analysing just what this means and in seeing how a probabilistic prediction is to be falsified. In addition, there is the question of the assignment of degrees of probability to theories in the light of increasing evidence. We have already seen that Popper refuses to assign probabilities to theories or to interpret degree of corroboration as a measure of probability. Here we will briefly consider how he deals with the falsification of probability statements, before examining his account of the nature of probability itself. This will lead on to Popper's view that there is in fact objective randomness or indeterminism in the world, and to his further arguments showing that even if this were not so, and the laws of physics were deterministic, determinism in any empirically testable form would still be untenable.

1 The falsification of probability statements

Consider the statement that a given die has a 1 in 6 probability of landing on three. Assuming that we are treating this as asserting something empirical (and Popper does so treat it), we want to know how we would set about falsifying it. The problem is that any particular set of throws, whatever its characteristics, is compatible with the original probability statement, because any deviations between the ratio of threes to other throws in that set and the probability assigned to three by the original statement may be compensated for later on if we continue throwing long enough. Probability estimates, then, are not falsifiable.

Popper's response to this problem is to show how scientists can (and do) adopt methodological rules which enable them to treat logically unfalsifiable estimates of probability as falsifiable in practice. As Popper has proposed several different ways in which this might be done (and there is apparently yet another in the unpublished *Postscript*), I shall simply state here the basic intuition which underlies all his proposals. It is that, even though any actual outcome is logically compatible with any probability estimate, some actual outcomes would be very unlikely given the truth of the estimate and this can be mathematically computed. So we can know *a priori* what the likelihood of given outcomes would be, given the truth of a particular estimate; we can then treat highly unlikely outcomes as severe counter-evidence to the estimate (or as high negative corroboration). Estimates which receive high negative corroboration from samples of a large size, espe cially if other samples also yield high negative corroboration, will be ta ken to be refuted. The actual calculations of the *a priori* likelihoods and the initial decision as to what degree of negative corroboration to take as disastrous are presumably to be left to the statisticians and scientists involved, but Popper's general idea here seems to provide adequate support for his initial claim (*LSD*, p. 199) that physicists never use probability hypotheses as unfalsifiable, but rather as implying, within limits, the existence of reproducible regularities of a statistical sort. What Popper's falsificationism requires is that scientists stipulate in advance just how much deviation from the rule is to be allowed by a given probability estimate. Where this is done, statistical hypotheses can be seen in a deductive relationship to basic statements in the same way as other hypotheses.

2 *Subjective and frequency theories of probability*

What we want to say about probabilities assessed in mathematical terms, how such probabilities relate to one another and so on, has all been formalized in the probability calculus. However, a mathematical formalization does not tell us how its statements are to be interpreted. In particular, it does not specify what is meant by saying that the coin in my hand has a 1 in 2 probability of landing heads when I toss it. So, while not denying senses of probability not covered by the probability calculus, we can see a major part of the philosophical problem of probability as the problem of (semantically) interpreting the probability calculus. It is this that Popper is interested in, so that it can be no criticism of his theory of probability that it does not apply to situations where we speak about probability but where the probability calculus does not apply (for example, where no numerical degrees of probability are involved). As the details of the calculus are not in question and do not bear directly on the problem of its interpretation, we can confine ourselves here to giving an interpretation of formulae of the form

(1) $p(a, b) = r$

where $p(a, b)$ is the probability of a, given b, and r is some fraction between 0 and 1 (these limits included).

Popper considers at length both subjective and frequency interpretations of (1), but, before we turn to these, the logical interpretation should be mentioned. According to this, r represents the extent to which a logically follows from b. (In the logical and subjective interpretations a and b are read as referring to the statements asserting the existence of a and b respectively.) Thus, if $p(a, b) = 1$, b implies a, and, if $p(a, b) = 0$, a contradicts b. Problems immediately arise, however, when r lies between 0 and 1, for how is a logical relationship lying between entailment and contradiction to be thought of? Although there have been many versions of the logical interpretation, and many ways of quantifying r when it lies between 0 and 1, common to all is the view that r expresses the logical confirmation or support given to a by b. Thus, in the logical interpretation, a is usually seen as a hypothesis and b as some evidence. If b is a piece of evidence, then, r tells us what its logical proximity to our hypothesis, a, is. In one of Carnap's systems, for example, r is calculated as the ratio between the number of universes or state descriptions describable by our language in which both a and b occur and the state descriptions in which b alone occurs; r will then presumably express the chance of our b-universe being an a-universe as well. A problem with all of Carnap's systems appears to be that the resulting probability assessments vary with the language in which we are formulating our state descriptions, which is surely a drawback to an attempt to provide ourselves with guides to life. Indeed, we have no reason to suppose that any particular way of describing the world mirrors the distribution of properties within it, while if our choice of a language is made because it does mirror the empirical facts, the purely logical nature of our resulting probability estimates is surely only superficial. But it is in the attempt to analyse probability as a tautologous logical relationship between hypothesis and evidence that the logical interpretation has its greatest problem. For what we have in the logical interpretation is a combination of a synthetic statement (past evidence) with an analytic (language-dependent) assessment of the degree to which the evidence supports our hypothesis. But how, Popper (and all other critics of this view) will say, can any purely logical assessment of past evidence have any bearing on what we have not yet experienced, on which we propose to act? Whatever the sophistications of Carnap's various systems, this view of probability estimates as analytic assessments of evidence remains the basis of any purely logical interpretation of probability, and it fails to account for our interest in them as hypotheses to be tested. (The proximity of this criticism to our earlier criticism of Popper's own application of his tautologous degree of corroboration to rational action need not be underlined.)

The subjective interpretation of the probability calculus says that (1) is to be read as a measure of the belief or doubt raised in us by the assertion that a will follow, given b. Popper sees this interpretation as having much in common with the logical interpretation as it can also be seen as attempting to analyse probability in terms of the logical proximity which statements are believed to have to one another. Where it goes beyond the logical theory is that logical proximity is here cashed out in terms of the degree of (rational) belief we might have in a, given b, and so we can apply this interpretation to cases where we do not have to hand artificial languages with lists of primitive predicates in which we can define and relate various state descriptions.

Belief is (or should be) a factor of increasing evidence. The fact that opinions on probabilities among reasonable men tend to coincide with increasing evidence, despite initially large divergence of opinion, has been exploited in two ways by defenders of the subjective theory. In the first place they have been able to show that, by using Bayes's theorem, this convergence of opinion with increasing evidence can be systematically explained and predicted. Second, from this they argue that they do provide an account of the consensus on probabilities in the strict sciences which would otherwise be for them inexplicable. For the essence of the subjective theory is that a statement of probability does not reflect anything 'rational, positive or metaphysical' in the world (de Finetti, 1964, p. 152). It is a merely psychological device, used when we have ignorance of the full facts of a situation. In saying that the next toss of the coin has a 1 in 2 probability of being heads, we are simply expressing a subjective belief based on inadequate knowledge of the actual conditions of the next toss.

Even if it is true, as Ackermann (1976, p. 78) suggests, that Popper in his criticisms of the subjective theory has not taken sufficient account of the work of de Finetti and Savage in showing how increasing evidence does produce increasing consensus on probability (and hence that subjectivists can provide some account of the rationality of probability estimates), Popper's fundamental objection to the subjective theory remains unanswered (cf. *LSD*, pp. 150–1). It is that subjectivists provide at most an account of the consensus reached in probability estimates. They do not explain how what are understood by subjectivists as statements of ignorance, which have a merely psychological basis, are so brilliantly corroborated in the real world. Thus our estimates on, say, coin tossing appear to be telling us something objective about coin tossing, because of the way actual sequences of tosses confirm them. Against this, the subjectivist might argue that his account is intended to analyse the meaning of probability statements, rather than to speak of the grounds on which we come to accept them. But this analysis has to contend with what Popper calls the paradox of ideal evidence (*LSD*, pp. 407–8). Suppose we think that our statement that some arbitrary coin toss has a 1 in 2 probability of being heads is simply a statement of our ignorance ('I am ignorant about the outcome of the toss to degree 1 in 2'). We then observe a very large number of tosses, as a result of which we still hold that an arbitrary coin toss will have a 1 in 2 probability of being heads. If probability statements are only statements reflecting our ignorance of the conditions and out-comes of individual events, it seems that we are as ignorant as we were before our observations started, and that we have learned nothing at all. But against de Finetti, most people would feel that our coin-tossing probability statement does say something about how things (as opposed to beliefs) actually are, that what it says is a falsifiable hypo-thesis and that it has in fact been well confirmed; and, further, that a theory of probability should attempt to say something about the objective basis of such statements.

It is true that the logical and subjective theories, when spelled out in detail, do tell us how to make probability estimates. Thus the logical theory will provide an *a priori* means of measuring partial entailments between statements, and the subjective theory will tell us, also *a priori*, how far some evidence supports a partial belief. (It is because he sees the evidence–belief relationship in the subjective theory as ultimately resting on a notion of logical entailment that Popper holds that the subjective theory is based on the logical.) But the apparent strength of these theories is actually their greatest weakness, as we have already seen in the case of the logical theory. For these tautologous partial entailments are applied in the form of probability judgments to events in the real world that we have not experienced. Popper's hostility to the *a priori* inductive logic which the logical and subjective theories of probability involve has already been examined in chapter III, so rather than go over this again (or examine his somewhat inconclusive argu-ments against the subjective theory in 'PM'), we will turn to his own attempts to provide an objective basis for probability.

Popper was originally committed to the frequency theory of pro-bability. According to this, numerical probability statements are statements about the relative frequency with which an event of a certain kind occurs within a sequence of occurrences. Thus, in saying that there is a 1 in 2 probability of the next coin toss being heads, I am not really speaking about the next throw, but about the whole class of tosses, of which the next throw is only one element. My statement is properly to be understood as a statement about the relative frequency of heads within the whole class of tosses. This view of probability is objective because it bases probability in what is supposed to be a feature of the real world. It is obvious that in practice we often base our probability estimates on observations of relative frequencies and that we check them by such observations. Nevertheless, many objections have been raised against attempts formally to analyse probability judgments in terms of statements about relative frequencies.

In the first place, we apply probability estimates in areas where we feel that we are unable to apply rational methods of prediction to the individual events in question. Hence the attractiveness of subjectivistic approaches to probability, where probability estimates are analysed as statements of ignorance. But, as we have seen, we then get amazing empirical corroboration of our judgments supposedly based on ignorance. The frequency theory attempts to explain this by saying that there are cases where chance events can be shown to belong to sequences in which certain calculable probabilities are manifested (and to which the probability calculus can be applied). This raises the problem of showing how sequences of random events are to be defined in such a way that the individual members of the sequences remain significantly random or unpredictable while still obeying the calculus of probabilities.

Von Mises (the originator of the modern frequency theory) attempted to answer this question by saying that the probability calculus applies to certain potentially infinite sequences of events, which he called collectives. These are governed by the axioms of convergence and randomness. The axiom of convergence says roughly that if what we have is a collective, after observing a sufficient number of events in the collective, what we have observed of the relative frequency of the instances of the property we are interested in will approach the relative frequency of the property in the whole (infinite) collective. The axiom of randomness is intended to give mathematical expression to the chance-like character of the sequence. What von Mises wants is to ensure that there is no gambling system which can be successfully applied to a collective. A sequence would not be a collective if we noticed, for example, that, after a run of three heads, the chance of the next toss being tails was significantly higher.

Popper initially objects to this by saying that there is something paradoxical in combining the mathematical idea of a limit (axiom of convergence) with a demand that no mathematical rule or law is applicable (axiom of randomness). Apart from this, it has been shown by Church (1940) that there could be no sequences formally satisfying a sufficiently exact formulation of the randomness axiom as originally intended by von Mises. (For further details and problems involved in trying to repair the axiom, cf. Ackermann, 1976, pp. 71–7.) Popper points out (*LSD*, p. 360) that a collective in von Mises's sense could in its early segments have a high degree of order, to be offset by later randomness; to the early segments, then, a gambling system could be successfully applied. Popper, moreover, objects to the use sometimes made in practice of the axiom of convergence to justify probability estimates derived from large samples as being inductivist. We have no right to suppose in anything we observe that observed frequencies approach actual frequencies, nor can there be anything like empirical confirmation of such reasoning. What Popper attempts to do (*LSD*, ch. 8 and Appendices IV and *VI) is to repair von Mises's account of the frequency theory by introducing a concept of randomness sufficient for the purposes of probability theory, by showing how to construct sequences which are random on this basis, and by showing how, given segments of a chance-like sequence satisfying certain conditions, there follows logically a degree of statistical stability in the sequence as a whole. In other words, we do not need anything like an independent and quasi-empirical or inductive axiom of convergence, because the first law of great numbers (asserting that the chances of getting a fair sample from a random sequence approaches 1 if we make the segments we examine long enough) is a logical consequence of randomness. Popper's method here is to show how to construct sequences which have the greatest degree of randomness possible in the length of each initial segment we take, whether it is short or long. Sequences which are strongly random in this sense are shown by virtue of that alone to possess frequency limits – so a separate axiom of convergence is eliminated. We can then test whether actual empirical sequences are random by seeing whether they are statistically similar to an ideal sequence. Whether they will continue to be random and whether they will continue to have particular statistical characters remains a testable hypothesis, and it cannot be settled by any appeal to an axiom of convergence. Random empirical sequences will be free from predictable after-effects following specific occurrences within them, and thus entitle the frequency theorist to explain the probability relations obtaining within them in terms of objective properties of the sequences.

Popper, then, has indicated how specific problems relating to von Mises's axioms can be overcome. But there is still a major hurdle facing the frequency theorist. This concerns probabilities of single events. Even though the frequency theorist will deny that probabilities pertain to single events, he has to say something about the analysis of such statements. He will say that we are to regard a single event as belonging to a virtual sequence of events to which the probabilities properly belong but, even accepting the objectivity of virtual sequences, we still have a problem because one event can be seen as belonging to many different virtual sequences. Depending on which sequence we take as

providing the basis for our estimate, we will ascribe different probabilities to the outcome. If I describe my next coin toss as belonging to a
virtual sequence of non-biased coin tosses, the probability of heads
will presumably be 1 in 2, but if I describe it as belonging to a virtual
sequence of non-biased coin tosses in which heads is touching my
flicking finger, the probability of heads will be greater than 1 in 2. It is
beginning to look as if the probabilities we assign to single events are
strongly dependent on the amount of information we have about that
event, so that if we knew enough about the next coin toss we would
assign its chance of being heads as either 0 or 1. Indeed, Popper (*LSD*,
p. 212) allowed that he did not

> object to the subjective interpretation of probability statements
> about single events, i.e. to their interpretation as indefinite
> predictions – as confessions, so to speak, of our deficient
> knowledge about the particular event in question (concerning
> which, indeed, nothing follows from a frequency statement).

He went on to say that objective frequency statements are fundamental,
since they alone are testable, and that singular probability statements
are merely confessions of ignorance, on no account to be taken as
implying that some outcome is objectively undetermined or that
nature itself is indeterministic. We must now see why Popper has
come to hold exactly the view about singular probability statements
which he earlier condemned.

In fact it comes directly from reflection on the fact that there are
occasions when we decide on singular estimates of probability (and
on the type of virtual sequence in which to place the event in question)
by reference to the generating conditions of that event. In other words,
if we explain our probability estimate in terms of some virtual sequence,
our choice of the virtual sequence we consider to be relevant itself
requires justification by appeal to the conditions under which we
envisage the sequence being produced. To bring this point out,
Popper expounded the following argument in two articles ('PICP'
and 'PIP').

Consider a series of throws with a loaded die. We estimate after
observation that the frequency of a six being thrown is 1 in 4. Now
imagine a long series of throws with the loaded die, into which two or
three throws with a fair die are randomly inserted. Considered as
members of this new sequence, the fair-die throws will still have a
probability of 1 in 4 of landing on six. But we will want to say that the
fair die actually has a probability of 1 in 6. The frequency theorist will
analyse the situation by speaking of our complete actual sequence, in
which the probability of a six is 1 in 4, and of a second actual sequence,
the two or three throws with the fair die, in which six is taken to have

a probability of 1 in 6. But does it? For there are at most three throws here. In the actual sequence, six cannot appear 1 in 6 times. So we have to speak of a long virtual sequence of throws with the fair die. But this virtual sequence (whose members we may not even be able to identify in our actual series of throws) is characterized only by its generating conditions, whose repeated realization produces the elements of the sequence. We attribute the difference in the probability estimate for the fair die entirely to its different generating conditions, in such a way that probability is now being based ultimately there, and only secondarily in the sequences produced by the conditions:

> Now we can say that the singular event *a* possesses a probability *p* (*a, b*) owing to the fact that it is an event produced, or selected, in accordance with the generating conditions *b*, rather than owing to the fact that it is a member of a sequence *b*. In this way, a singular event may have a probability even though it may occur only once; for its probability is a property of its generating conditions. ('PIP', p. 34)

Although we still see probabilities as being displayed in frequencies in sequences, we now have to see what happens in the sequences as being dependent upon the propensities or tendencies of their generating conditions. In the next section, we will consider the implications of this view, both in terms of its own inherent plausibility and in its ability to deal with the problem presented for objective accounts of probability by the single case.

3 Popper's propensity theory of probability

What Popper's propensity theory says is that certain set-ups are random in their outcomes, in the sense that we cannot predict the actual outcome of any particular case where the set-up is instantiated, but that repeated experiments with or observations of the set-up will show statistical stability. The statistical stability is taken to be the result of the propensities inherent in the set-up. Put like this, Popper's propensity theory is an extension rather than a rejection of the frequency theory. Probabilities are still conjectured statistical frequencies of sequences, but are seen as being the manifestation of actually existing, but indeterministic, forces. These forces are taken to be properties of whole set-ups, relations between, say, dice and the circumstances in which they are thrown. Popper draws an analogy between propensities obtaining in experimental arrangements and Newtonian forces, which are also unobserved relational properties of particular arrangements of matter. Indeed, he sees propensities as an 'indeterministic generalization of an anti-Humean (i.e., realistic) view of causes, and more especially of forces (that is, causes of acceleration)' ('RC', p. 1130). At the limit, where we have propensities equal to 1, they are Newtonian forces. Popper insists that his belief in the physical reality of propensities is a physical hypothesis, on a level with Newton's postulation of forces. His hypothesis is that every experimental arrangement generates propensities, which are to be tested by observing actual frequencies. A difference between Popper and Newton here is that Newton's theory makes testable predictions about the forces, given that we know the relevant facts concerning masses, speeds, etc., in the experimental set-up. But we can guess at propensities only having observed how repeated instances of a given set-up behave. Popper's theory gives us no other way of postulating what propensities are obtaining. Nevertheless, he suggests ('PICP', 'PIP' and 'QM' that the two-slit experiment provides a crucial experiment between the propensity and frequency interpretations of probability. Looking at this claim will also show us why he finds it important to link propensities to experimental arrangements as a whole, rather than to objects taken in isolation.

We are asked to consider a case of a penny being tossed. The probability of its landing heads will be greatly affected if it is falling on a table with slots on it, in which the penny can be caught while still upright. The propensity it has for landing heads is then determined not solely by its own structure, but by the experimental arrangement taken as a whole. Similarly, the propensity a ball has to reach certain places on a pin-board will be affected and altered by changing the number and position of the pins on the board, even though in an individual case the ball may not actually hit any of the altered pins. The significant fact about the pin-board is that, if we are thinking of probabilities as propensities of individual experiments, they may change as a result of changes in the experimental arrangement as a whole, irrespective of what happens in any actual experiment. It is this feature of propensities that leads Popper to see his propensity theory as throwing light on anomalies of quantum physics, such as the two-slit experiment. The point about this is that the probabilities governing the distribution of particles such as photons which are fired through one slit of a screen alter depending on whether another slit elsewhere in the screen is open or shut, even though the photons go nowhere near the other slit. A common response to this phenomenon is to say that objects such as photons have peculiar properties in that, although they sometimes show particle-like behaviour, at other times they show wave-like behaviour, which is taken to explain why they are affected by the opening or closing of both slits. This view leads to further claims that it is meaningless to ask certain definite questions about the precise paths and momenta of individual photons, which would be answerable if they were classically determined particles. This un-answerability thesis connects with Heisenberg's view that quantum theory generally requires us to deny any sense to talk of precise positions and momenta of individual particles when they are scattered in particular circumstances because the quantum formulae allow no precise predictions in this area. Indeed, momenta scatter according to the degree of precision of the measurement of position, and vice versa. Popper's answer to the implicit instrumentalism in these interpretations of quantum phenomena is to say that they arise only if we misunderstand the fact that in quantum physics we are dealing with probabilistic theories.

Once we realize that, we will not be tempted to read a prediction that a particle with a certain precisely defined momentum will occupy a certain imprecisely stated area as implying that it will not have a precise position within that area, but rather as implying that our theory does not enable us to predict its position precisely. But our theory, being probabilistic, asserts that particles with similar momenta in similar circumstances will be probabilistically distributed within the position area predicted. Indeed, to test this theory, according to Popper, we have to calculate the positions of numbers of particles precisely. So quantum theory, far from ruling out talk of particles having at the same time precise positions and momenta, actually requires it. The two-slit experiment can be rescued from an instrumentalistic interpretation by pointing out that any change in an experimental arrangement (as on our pin-board) leads to a change in the propensities of that arrangement, and hence of the distribution of probabilities arising from them. What propensities and probabilities we find in experimental set-ups will depend intimately on the generating conditions of the set-up. This point enables Popper finally to dismiss Heisenberg's talk of the observer of a quantum experiment in some way actually bringing about the result he observes. Of course, says Popper, when someone actually observes the result of an experiment (whether it is a coin toss or something in quantum physics), the probability of a particular outcome can no longer be viewed as anything other than 1 or 0, whereas before the observation of the outcome we might have spoken of the outcome as having a probability of, say, 1 in 2. But this is not a case of the observer mysteriously causing a probability of 1 in 2 to collapse into one of 1 (or 0). What we have are two differently defined experimental arrangements, one in which the outcome is not given, and one in which it is. Both probability estimates remain true relative to the set-ups they are defined in terms of. There is no question of one probability suddenly changing into another as a result of the action of an observer or anything else. What we have are two different propensities relating to two different types of arrangement.

Although Popper's arguments hold water against the cruder sub-jectivistic positions of Heisenberg, it is unclear how far his analysis of the two-slit experiment provides the necessary support for the pro-pensity theory. What Popper argues is that in the two-slit experiment, as in a pin-board, change of experimental arrangement affects pro-bability distributions. However, as Feyerabend has argued (1964 and 1968–9), the kind of change involved in the two-slit experiment is very different from what happens on pin-boards. Balls on pin-boards move along well-defined paths, and their trajectories are influenced only by items in their immediate neighbourhood. From this it follows that the probabilities of particular events in global arrangements are the sums of the probabilities of the events in each of their mutually exclusive sectors, and that adding to an experimental arrangement will add possible trajectories but will not interfere with the trajectories already given, except where the addition is in the immediate neighbourhood of an old trajectory. None of this is true of the two-slit experiment, where probabilities are not additive and particles cease to behave as if nothing existed outside their own paths (which incidentally also goes counter to the energy-conservation laws). Opening the second slit appears actually to alter the paths of particles which go through the first slit, and does not merely affect the probabilities of their arriving at particular points beyond the slits. Talk of propensities hardly helps to clarify matters, because here we have propensities (or forces) of an apparently quite different sort from those encountered in pin-boards, dice games and so on. For this reason, it can hardly be claimed that the peculiar features of quantum physics decisively support the propensity theory against other theories of probability, or that the propensity theory really helps us to understand what is going on in quantum physics. Feyerabend concludes that the weakest point of Popper's discussions of quantum phenomena is that he unsuccessfully attempts to assign precise paths to electrons and photons as if they were like balls on a pin-board, influenced only by factors in their immediate environment. (He also argues that testing of the scatter relations does not, as Popper insists, require us to think of individual particles as having simultaneously precise positions and momenta: we can arrange our tests so that we take different groups of particles in similar initial conditions, measuring some for position and some for momenta.)

So quantum physics does not provide conclusive support for the propensity theory, because the quantum propensities must be forces of a unique and otherwise unknown variety. But what are we to make of the general point that experimental arrangements have propensities, which are manifested in statistical facts about sequences of experi-ments? Settle (1977, p. 179) says the probability of a red card being drawn 'is a propensity of the deck in the context of random or blind selection'. One's initial reaction to this is to say that whether there is a red on the top of the deck or not is objectively determined one way or the other and that a complete description would enable us to see which was the case. The reply is that while *that* is determined the probability estimate is based on a particular description of the generating conditions, where there is no complete description of actual arrangements. When the generating conditions are specified 'in the context of random or blind selection' we get from observation specific ratios of reds being drawn. While this reply is acceptable in itself, one wonders how what is being said differs from a frequency theory. Popper's objection to the frequency theory was that we were defining our virtual sequences in terms of their generating conditions. But I am not clear why a frequentist should be barred from doing this, or from investigating more precisely the nature of the generating conditions and what effect changes in them have on the resulting frequencies. It is true that seeing a particular event as being a member of one sequence rather than another will lead to different estimates of its outcome. This is not only also the case with the propensity theory, where the probabilities assigned will differ according to the type of set-up we see the event as being an example of, but it underlines the empirical nature of both theories, in that only empirical investigation and connections with other theories of matter can help us to decide which are the most useful ways of defining the sequences and set-ups we are actually to use in our calculations. As far as investigation of phenomena goes, the frequency theory can be just as realistic as the propensity theory, despite Settle's (1974) claim to the opposite. What the frequency theorist is not allowed to do and what Popper wants to do is to see the generating conditions producing real forces in individual cases.

But now we come to the decisive point against Popper's theory. Following Mellor (1971, p. 158), it is natural to ask what, in the individual set-up, are the forces involved? For these are forces which are not necessarily always manifested in an individual case, but only sometimes. In the individual case of a toss of a biased coin there might be a 1 in 3 chance of heads and a 2 in 3 chance of tails. Suppose it lands tails. What has become of the 1 in 3 propensity to be heads? Even worse, it lands heads. Yet there was supposed to be a 2 in 3 propensity to tails. If propensities were forces in the normal sense, the propensity to tails would always defeat the propensity to heads. In this respect, of course, propensities are not like forces as ordinarily conceived. What propensities are, are tendencies which do not manifest themselves directly in individual cases and which are not like forces in individual cases: they are features of sequences of events described in various ways. It is hard to see how, once it is realized that we cannot speak of propensities as if they were actual but intermittent causal links somehow, unobservably and at times ineffectively, present in single cases, the propensity theory differs from the frequency theory. The propensity theory was developed against the background of problems which the frequency theory had in dealing with single cases, but it makes no sense to speak in single cases of existing but unavailing forces (especially where the defeated force is said to have a higher numerical value than its conqueror). In order to make sense of such propensities, Popper surely has to refer to statistical features of sequences of events, and thus becomes a frequentist. Although other versions of the propensity interpretation have been proposed, which do not think of propensities as non-deterministic causes (and so avoid this problem), this 'new physical hypothesis' ('PIP', p. 38) is the central point of Popper's theory, and the one which he sees as making talk of probability fully realistic (because propensities are physically real features of individual situations). In order to see how this is so we must examine the connections between Popper's realism, the propensity theory and indeterminism.

4 *Realism, propensities and indeterminism*

For a determinist, asserting that a particular event will have a particular outcome with a certain degree of probability is tantamount to an admission of ignorance of either the laws governing the event or its initial conditions. For, where determinism is true, not only are outcomes fixed but they are fixed in accordance with physical laws. We may not know the relevant laws, or the number of factors operative in producing particular types of events may be vast so that in practice we have to make do with merely statistical laws, but this is very much a case of second-best, a reflection of ignorance or incompetence on our part. Popper, when writing *The Logic of Scientific Discovery*, was a determinist, and, as I have pointed out, was ready to interpret probabilistic singular predictions as confessions of ignorance. He was also emphatic that any argument from the existence of probabilistic theories to metaphysical indeterminism was mistaken. What was objective about such theories was their reference to sequences of events. It was not that the individual events themselves were hanging in the balance.

Popper sees the propensity theory as a conjecture about the structure of the world (cf. *LSD*, p. 252, fn*3), which gets empirical corroboration from the two-slit experiment, which is a crucial experiment between it and the frequency theory. As we have seen, this is doubtful, unless the forces involved are quite different from those operating elsewhere in physics. More fundamentally, it is unclear what might be meant by speaking of physically real propensities which are not always manifested. The frequency theory does not, of course, do this. What it asserts is that there are statistical regularities in some classes of events which either are not explicable in terms of deterministic laws or have not been brought under such laws. (This latter possibility may be either because of our lack of knowledge or because, like insurance companies, we are more interested in trends within classes of events than in the details of the individual members of the class.) If we are frequentists about probability and believe that in some cases pro-babilistic laws are basic (i.e., we are not determinists), then we will take a probabilistic law to be saying that within a given collective sometimes one thing happens and sometimes another, according to some statistically expressible pattern, but that there is nothing within each event which makes it necessary or predictable what the outcome will be. Popper would presumably not dissent from this. But he would add that within the situation there are real dispositions or forces which have an unpredictable and indeterministic effect on the individual out-come. But what work is talk of forces doing here, and why is an appeal to non-manifested forces more realistic than the frequentist's talk of sequences of events (which, after all, are not occult and which do give talk of probability a realistic non-subjective basis)? Popper compares his propensities to Newtonian forces, in that, just as Newton was the first to put relational properties into things (and led to talk of fields of forces), so his propensity theory speaks of indeterministic relational properties, but such talk can lead only to the puzzles we have considered about the existence of such properties. Puzzles of this sort do not, of course, arise in the case of Newtonian forces, which, though occult, are always manifested in that it can be predicted exactly what effect the presence of a given force will have in a given situation.

Talking of propensities more generally as dispositions (e.g., Popper, 'PICP', p. 70) seems once more only to take us back to the frequency theory. For an indeterministic disposition for a coin toss to fall heads is not something which can be said to have existed when tails has come down. In *that* case there was only a tendency or disposition for the coin to land tails. What might be said to have a disposition to produce sometimes heads and sometimes tails is a sequence of coin tosses. Of course, from the point of view of explaining events there is something unsatisfactory about a probabilistic theory. We feel that whatever happens does so because of some feature of the situation which brings it about that it does come about as it does. Popper's propensity theory may be seen as an attempt to see statistical theories as fully objective or realistic, and not as at some point an admission of ignorance. So he postulates really existing forces as underlying un-determined events. But in addition to leading to the problems we have considered earlier about the nature of such forces, this solution hardly satisfies our desire for a full explanation. For we will want to know, in a given case, why the forces have operated this way rather than that. All we can be told is that there is no answer. So how does this satisfy our desire for explanation any more than being told by a frequentist, who also believes that some fundamental laws are probabilistic, that within a collective there can be no reason for an event having one outcome or another? It becomes increasingly hard to see how Popper's propensity theory explains any more about undetermined events than the frequency theory does, or indeed how, in its uncontroversial elements, it differs from the frequency theory. This is ultimately because Popperian propensities (unlike Newtonian forces) do not lead to independently testable predictions about particular events, but only to predictions testable by reference to sets of events. Popper may want to say that his view of probability is more realistic than a frequentist's because he relates the statistical regularities with collectives to facts about the generating conditions of the collectives, but once again it is hard to see why a frequentist is forced to deny that the chance of a die falling on a certain number has something to do with the number of sides of the die, the surface it falls on and the way it is thrown. He would certainly expect a change in any of these factors to change the probability. What he would deny and what Popper wants to assert is that there are real dispositions within each throw which bring about the regularities observable within a sequence of throws, and it is precisely at this point that Popper's propensity theory needs clarification.

Although Popper's preference for the propensity theory of probability is due to his examination of quantum physics, and he does take some events to be governed at a fundamental level by propensities rather than by deterministic forces, his reasons for rejecting determinism as such do not derive merely or even primarily from the fact that much contemporary physics is probabilistic. (Indeed, he still holds that the success of probabilistic predictions does not in itself entail that the events covered by the predictions are themselves undetermined.) What convinced Popper of the truth of indeterminism, and what Popper thinks would still suffice for refuting determinism, even where the laws of physics were deterministic, is an argument which shows that in a world in which predictions and theories are possible, it would never be possible for any predictor to predict all its own future states or theories. What is taken to follow from this point is the conclusion that, as the future states of the predictor are part of the world in question and influence it, no predictor can ever successfully predict everything about its world. Therefore, for any predictor, there will always be unpredictable events, and, therefore, a determinism which requires that all the events in the world are predictable by some inhabitant of the world cannot be true of that world. The assumption here is that any determinism we were interested in as scientists would be one that entailed the actual predictability of events. Given this assumption, in pointing to the existence of necessarily unpredictable events, we seem to have shown that this scientifically interesting determinism cannot be held of our world by us as scientists. Certainly no predictor or set of predictors in the world will be able consistently to hold it, although of course he or they could continue to hold some purely speculative version of determinism that was not tied to pre-dictability. But even if this was done, it would still be true that the science that existed in that world would either be deterministic but fail to cover all possible types of event in the world or cover all types of event but be indeterministic.

The reason why a predictor cannot predict all its future states can be made clear by using the simple illustration of the point given by Popper ('RC', p. 1057). Imagine someone making a plan of the room in which he is sitting. This is going to be an uncompletable task be-cause his plan will never be able to include a representation of the strokes he is currently making. Even less will he be able now to represent all the moves he will make in the future. In a similar way physical science can never be completed because attempts to describe the present collections of descriptions in books and articles (let alone to predict future ones) can never include all the descriptions we have made; there will always be some that are not caught up with until after they have been made. If description of a world which includes descriptions in it can never be completed, *a fortiori*, says Popper, there can be no complete explanatory theory of that world. What Popper concentrates on in the argument is that the description and prediction of our scientific knowledge can never be total, and that we can there-fore not foresee all future scientific developments. So even in a world where the laws of physics are deterministic, in so far as our scientific theories affect the physical world, the future of the physical world itself will be open and unpredictable. What we must now do is to examine how the more detailed presentations of this and connected arguments in Popper ('IQP'), support the claim that the unpredictability of the whole of our future knowledge entails that there can be no complete explanatory theory of the world along deterministic lines.

The world considered by Popper ('IQP') is taken to be one in which the laws of physics are classical and in which there are predicting machines which are not subject to limitations through inadequate data storage capacity or mechanical malfunctioning. We imagine that the machines are supplied with all relevant laws and initial conditions and that the measurements involved are not subject to quantum mechanical uncertainty due to interaction between measurer and quantity measured.

Popper intends to show that, even in these circumstances, which are highly favourable to determinism, there will be prediction tasks which the machines cannot execute, and thus, even in this world, the deterministic principle that, for *any* specified finite prediction task, it is physically possible to construct a predictor capable of carrying out the task turns out to be untenable. The key assumption is that the predictors are part of the world, for the prediction tasks that are physically impossible are ones involving their own future states, either directly as self-predictions or indirectly through the effects of their future states on other predictors in the world or on the world generally. Popper concedes that, where the predictor is not part of the system to be predicted and where it does not interact in any way with the system, there may be no impossible prediction task, but our world is not of this sort. We are the predictors we are interested in, and our future knowledge is part of our world and does interact with it, so even if we were ideal predicting machines in the world of classical physics there would be things about our world which we could not predict. So determinism could not be for us a realizable possibility.

Popper provides ('IQP') three arguments to show that a complete prediction of future states of knowledge of the predictor is impossible. Two of these, the Tristram Shandy paradox and the Oedipus effect, have affinities with the map argument and may be taken together. In the Tristram Shandy paradox a machine C has complete information regarding its state at t, and knowledge of the relevant theories, on the basis of which it has to predict its state at t_5. As it is a physical system and as what is in question is a matter of deducing consequences, it will take time for the information it has, say until t_2, to do this. But its working from t_1 to t_2 will now be an additional element in its t_5 state, along with everything else in its history up to t_5, so it adds this to its prediction – but this, too, takes time, say until t_3. And now the t_2 to t_3 operation must be added, which takes us up to t_4. But then the t_3 to t_4 operation is to be added, and we are already up to t_5, but the t_4 to t_5 operation has not been included and cannot be until t_6. So only at t_6 can C produce a complete account of its t_5 state. Popper admits that this paradox can strictly be avoided if the print-out of an earlier state could be simultaneously read as a coded prediction of some future state, but this would be, as Ackermann remarks (1976, p. 136), a somewhat Pickwickian sense of prediction.

The Oedipus effect at first sight would appear to focus on the psychological effect that self-information has on a predictor. The point of the reference to Oedipus is that self-information about one's future interferes strongly in a psychological way with the knower and leads one to behave in such a way that one might defeat the prediction (even though, as in the myth, unbeknownst to the agent, he is thereby actually fulfilling the prediction). But it is not so much the psychological effects of knowledge of one's future that Popper is interested in as the regressive nature of any attempt to record or register the fact that one knows one's future. Given that such registering will take time, one will never be able to record the totality of what one will know at the future point until after it, so what we really have here is another version of the Tristram Shandy paradox (or the map example), which again can be avoided only by a coding which is a representation at the same time of a present and a future state.

A clearly distinct line of argument to the impossibility of self-prediction is given by Popper when he considers the existence of what he calls Gödelian sentences. As is well known, there are in any sufficiently rich deductive system formulae of that system which are true but which are not provable in the system, given that the system has only a finite number of axioms. So whatever is the highest deductive system within the scope of any mechanical predictor, there will always be formulae that it cannot decide. By exploiting this fact, together with the further fact that a formula's undecidability is not always recognizable in advance so long as we are restricted to the system within which it is undecidable, it is possible to formulate a question about an undecidable formula to our predicting machine which it will be unable to answer. We ask it at t_1 if at t_2 it will have decided whether a certain formula which is undecidable for it is decidable. Being unable to decide it now, it will not be able to answer that it will have decided it one way or the other, but this in itself will not show to the machine that by t_2 it might not have worked out some proof. As the machine cannot necessarily decide now that it is dealing with an undecidable formula, it will only be able to answer that it does not know where it will be at t_2, and it will not be able to give a definite answer (that it cannot answer it by t_2) until t_2 has already arrived. Even if we strengthen our machine by adding axioms to it to allow it to prove the true statements which were formerly undecidable for it, or by enabling it to recognize the numbers of the old Gödelian sentences and so to predict that it will not have decided them by t_2, new Gödelian sentences can be constructed which will be undecidable and unrecognizable for it in its new state. So Gödel's undecidability theorem can be taken to show that self-prediction in some instances is logically impossible even for highly sophisticated predicting machines. Popper concludes after his own detailed and highly sophisticated examination of the Tristram Shandy paradox, the Oedipus effect and Gödelian sentences that the existence of knowledge in the physical world creates a significant kind of indeterminism, for although our knowledge may conquer problems of determination, it will necessarily bring with it new predictive problems it cannot solve. So he sees his arguments as opening the way for creative and unforeseeable mental activity. Assuming the correctness of the arguments (and that we can, in the case of the Tristram Shandy paradox, at least for the purposes of considering human knowledge rule out the possibility of messages interpretable in two ways), do they in themselves open the way for any profound examples of imaginative creativity?

The point about Gödelian sentences, and application of this point by Ackermann (1976, pp. 137-8) to Turing machines, shows conclusively that there are sophisticated predictors which logically cannot predict all their future states, but conclusions about imaginative creativity can hardly be drawn from the existence of the undecidable formulae in mathematics and logic on which the unpredictability in question is based. Indeed, it is unclear whether the Gödelian sentences argument shows that there is any general unpredictability in self-knowledge, beyond our knowledge about our knowledge of the special formulae in question. The other arguments show a more general problem in representing our present and future knowledge to ourselves, but in these arguments this emerges entirely from the infinitely regressive character of any attempt to represent or speak about what we know. The arguments certainly say nothing about the impossibility of foreseeing or predicting our first-order knowledge about things other than our own future states.

Implausible as it may be to speak of myself foreseeing what I will later discover (for to foresee this in detail would be to know it now), this is neither the point Popper is making nor does it tell against any deterministic explanation of what I will come to know. For others, outside of myself, are not prevented by this or by Popper's arguments from predicting my future knowledge. Of course, Popper realizes and admits this, even in the case of Gödelian sentences, where computers at a 'higher' mathematical level can predict Gödelian outcomes of those on a 'lower' level. What he shows is that, within a certain framework (in which thinking or representing something I know takes time and in which the representing is done in a language with only one interpretation), it is logically impossible to execute a complete self-description or prediction. But why should such a logical impossibility, which is based purely on the self-referential character of the knowledge involved, be thought to tell against a scientifically significant determinism?

Popper has shown that there are specifiable finite prediction tasks which it is physically impossible to construct a predictor to undertake. But why should a determinist accept that his determinism entails that it is possible to construct a predictor to undertake any finite prediction task *however that task is described*? Surely, in view of the logical points made by Popper, it would be quite legitimate for him to say that although any state of any object ought to be predictable, determinism does not require (logically cannot require) that any state of any object is to be predicted when it is self-referentially described as a future state of the predicting machine itself. So long as the predictor does not interfere with the systems it is predicting, there is no reason why prediction of other systems should require that it can predict its own future states, and Popper's arguments provide no theoretical reason against his explaining whatever other systems he has theories for.

My conclusion is that, if there is creativity and unpredictability in human knowledge, Popper's analysis of indeterminism has not shown us where it is to be located, although, as we shall see later, Popper provides a much more substantial account of creativity in his three-world theory. The scientific determinist should not renounce his determinism on account of Popper's arguments, but only modify the requirement Popper lays down for determinism. In doing so, he will not be weakening the empiricism Popper requires of him, for he will still be committed to finding theories which will predict everything under suitably rich descriptions. All he will be avoiding is the commitment to a particular type of self-referential prediction, a commitment he should never have taken on in the first place, because, as Popper shows, it involves a logically impossible goal. Indeed, even accepting self-knowledge as part of the *explicandum* of a substantive deterministic theory in no way rules out the possibility of the determinist showing, after he has completed the description of his knowledge, that it could be retrospectively explained in terms of his deterministic theory (which he is applying predictively to the knowledge of others remote from him and so not interfered with by him). This surely suggests that the type of unpredictability of self-knowledge pointed to by Popper is a peculiarity of self-knowledge, rather than something in the way knowledge is brought about, for if our knowledge were unpredictable on grounds of some creative breaking with the past we could not, as Gallie shows (1957), be able even retrospectively to explain it under some generally applicable deterministic theory, but Popper's arguments ('IQP') do not rule out such explanation. I stress again that they involve not the substance of what one knows or how this knowledge comes about, but only second-order knowledge about knowledge. The grounds for creativity in knowledge and indeterminism in general cannot be found in the peculiar logical features of self-knowledge, nor is determinism even of a substantial sort necessarily refuted merely because we ourselves cannot predict all our future states of mind and the effects these states will have on the world. If we had good grounds for thinking that some other predictors, not closely interacting with us, could in the light of some theory successfully predict our states of mind (perhaps because we do the same in the case of others), determinism could still be in this area a tenable position.

Popper himself grants that the indeterminism shown by his 1950 arguments ('IQP') does not preclude that the world (and presumably our states of knowledge) are determined. They show that our knowledge will always be, in certain aspects, incomplete. Popper wants to argue in general for a universe in which genuine change and unpredictability have a part to play and in which our own futures, with respect to both our knowledge and the consequences of our actions, are unforeseeable. His arguments support this general thesis only in the special case of our own knowledge of our own knowledge. He does argue (OK, pp. 223–4) that there is something self-defeating about asserting that physical determinism is true, because this would be tantamount to an admission that our acceptance of determinism is not really based on our perception of the logical cogency of the arguments, but on the physical condition which makes us deceive ourselves into thinking that we are swayed by the truth. But the determinist could surely counter by saying that there is no reason why some people (or some machines) should not be determined in such a way that they accept only those positions which are reasonably argued, and he could perhaps materialistically analyse standards of truth and rationality of beliefs in terms of their contribution to the efficient behaviour of the believing organism. (Whether Popper succeeds in showing that there is any more to these standards will be examined in chapter IX.) What Popper considers only briefly (PH, p. 13) and what might well give more substantial support to his general theses is the effect that knowledge of some deterministic theory regarding knowledge and behaviour might have on the knowledge and behaviour of the theorists. In other words, a more general consideration of someone in the position of Oedipus, who is told that his future is closed in certain specific ways, might lead us to conclude that there could be something self-defeating about an attempt to apply a predictive explanatory theory to ourselves, because such self-prediction will interfere with the subject matter of the prediction. But Popper does not take this line, either in his 1950 article ('IQP') or in The Open Society and Its Enemies, where his remarks on sociological determinism tend to emphasize the empirical emptiness of such theories and their inability to explain creative development of the materials, social and psychological, that we are born with. Whether there is, or can be, such creative development, however, is just what the determinist will naturally wish to question, and it is far from clear that even the psychological applications of the Oedipus effect is any strong argument against this part of the determinist's thesis.

What remains true at the end of this rather inconclusive discussion of indeterminism is that, in the light of the widespread use of probabilistic theories in science and the possibility afforded by the frequency theory of regarding them as thoroughly objective, it can no longer be maintained that there is anything unscientific about regarding the physical world as open or undetermined. We then have a possible arena for creative activity on the part of human beings. Indeed, Popper has argued, following Peirce (1972, p. 213), that even in classical physics, as all physical bodies are subject to molecular heat motion, there must be room for indeterminacy and chance effects, without appealing to indeterminacy of the Heisenberg type. But, as he admits there, physical indeterminism alone does no more than create room for free and creative human action, which must be based in something more than mere chance. His solution to this problem is to appeal to the way our behaviour is guided non-deterministically by a world of abstract ideas and standards, so that what we do is neither purely random nor subject to deterministic control. But assessment of this claim must await our examination of World 3 in chapter IX.

VIII

Reason and Society

1 *Rationalism and irrationalism*

In considering the demarcation criterion, we saw that Popper's ultimate concern was not to distinguish between science and non-science, but to distinguish between criticizable and non-criticizable attitudes to theories of all types. Examples from science provided the initial clue to the importance of criticizability, but as we saw in detail in the preceding chapters a metaphysical thesis (such as determinism and particular philosophical accounts of probability and science), without being empirically falsifiable, can be submitted to critical examination with enlightening results. Popper (*OS*, vol. 2, p. 225) characterizes rationalism as 'an attitude of readiness to listen to critical arguments and to learn from experience'. Just as he thinks that rationalism in science (= falsifiability) can ultimately be advocated only through a judgment of value, so he argues that the adoption of rationalism as an approach to life generally is something that should be advocated (because it leads to a better society), but it can be advocated on grounds which are not only ethical, but ultimately irrational. This is not simply because we have no guarantee that rational methods will bring us to the truth either in science or elsewhere, but also because there is something paradoxical in the very attempt to produce a reasoned defence of reason itself. So, for Popper, rationalism, however desirable it may be, is ultimately a matter of irrational faith.

Thus we have the leading advocate of a humane and critical approach to problems in theory and practice basing his whole philosophy on a premise he admits to be indefensible when scrutinized in the way he insists that the foundations of the beliefs of others be examined. This is not only unsatisfactory in itself, but it lays him right open to what

Bartley (1962) calls the *tu quoque* of the irrationalist. The irrationalist is quite happy to say in his tiresome way that everyone, including the rationalist, makes some epistemological commitments which cannot be justified, and that on the level of ultimate commitment there is no difference between the man who says that we should be rational in our attitudes and only accept criticizable theories and the one who simply asserts that $2 + 2 = 5$ or that Jesus is the Son of God. But we may wonder whether it is so tiresome of him when we have Popper apparently agreeing with him (*OS*, vol. 2, p. 231):

> We may choose some form of irrationalism, even some radical or comprehensive form. But we are also free to choose a critical form of rationalism, one which frankly admits its origin in an irrational decision (and which, to that extent, admits a certain priority of irrationalism).

What Popper is saying here implies that even if there was some assured link between a critical methodology and truth the rationalist is hardly in a position to criticize the authoritarian dogmatist who advocates a society organized by a peace-keeping thought police, because he (the rationalist) cannot give in his own terms a defence of his preference for listening to argument and learning from experience. It is not that the rationalist has one irrational belief or commitment among many beliefs; it is that the body of his rationalism rests on the quicksands of an irrational commitment. Once he looks for something firmer, he begins to sink.

The reasoning behind this lies in the following argument. Rationalism is defined by Popper as a commitment to critical argument and experience. Any rational defence of a position is one that appeals to argument and experience. In the case of rationalism itself, then, a rational defence is viciously circular, and this would be the case even if we knew that adherence to rationalism guaranteed progress towards truth. To attempt to defend rationalism by claiming that assumptions not backed up by argument and experience frequently come unstuck may be to say something true, but it is to miss the point of the argument, which is to point to a fatal inconsistency in the very attempt to defend rationalism by rational means. A comprehensive or uncritical rationalism, which told us to hold no irrational beliefs, would, in Popper's view, assert its own falsity in much the same way as the liar paradox (*OS*, vol. 2, p. 230):

> It is easy to see that this principle of an uncritical rationalism is inconsistent; for since it cannot, in its turn, be supported by argument or by experience, it implies that it should itself be discarded.

The conclusion is that rationalism of this sort can be defeated by its chosen weapon (argument); as such it is untenable and should be rejected. Irrationalism is 'logically superior' to comprehensive rationalism. All we are left with to choose from are types of irrationalism, of which one is a critical (that is, a non-comprehensive, fundamentally irrational) rationalism.

That there is something spurious about this victory Popper is prepared to give irrationalism can best be illustrated by considering the (possibly hypothetical) case where it could be shown that a certain set of arguments and appeals to experience either guaranteed or very strongly supported the truth of the beliefs they spoke in favour of. Does Popper wish us to conclude that nothing can be said in favour of rationalism here? For irrationalism would surely now be tantamount to a declaration that one did not care about the truth of one's beliefs, and, as we have learned from Moore's paradox of the man who says that he believes p but does not think that p is true, to be in general indifferent to the truth of one's beliefs is to cast doubt on one's grasp of the concept of belief. This is precisely because to believe something is to think that it is true. So, not to care about the truth of one's beliefs, or to be indifferent as to whether one had good reasons for them or not, will result in one ceasing to see the propositions in question as beliefs, properly speaking.

Popper could deny that any of our arguments from experience, at least, are reliable, but his demonstration of the irrationality of rationalism, if it works at all, must work whether the arguments proffered can be shown to be reliable or not, because it says simply that any argumentative defence of arguments begs the question. Yet we feel that it would not be open to a man simply to ignore what has been said in the previous paragraph, as it is simply elucidating what would be involved in having a belief at all in certain circumstances. To ignore it would be for him to render his professions of belief unintelligible as such.

Popper's irrationalist is a man who is unprepared to be moved by argument in favour of rationalism, but by agreeing that this man is correct to argue that any argument against him begs the question, and that rationalists expose themselves to a beating 'in their own field and with their own weapon' whenever irrationalists take the trouble to turn it against them, Popper is surely conceding to the irrationalist far too much. For how can anything be discussed or argued about without using argumentation? In discussing the basis of logic ('LA', p. 288), Popper sees this perfectly well:

We cannot at the same time *use* a word, or a statement, or an argument, and *study* it . . . the study of words or statements presupposes the unhampered, although careful, use of some language in precisely the same way as the study of trees or of mental processes or of music . . . we should not attempt to analyse the arguments we are using while engaged in analysing the rules of argumentation. . . . Indeed, if this were not so, then *all* logical investigation would be impossible. *For if we wish to study something, we can, clearly, not begin by giving up the use of all' argumentation. . . .*

The irrationalist who is logically superior to the rationalist cannot, without self-contradiction, engage in argument, even so far as to point out the logical superiority of his position.

Nevertheless, if any defence of rationalism, however well the appeal to arguments and experience is defended, is going to involve argument, do we have to conclude with Popper that rationalism is based on an irrational faith in reason? In order to answer this question, it is necessary to establish with respect to what such a faith would be irrational. The mere fact that there is no non-argumentative demonstration of the rationality of the practices of rationality, especially the use of argument, is hardly surprising, given that a justification of a practice demonstrating the value of that practice can take place only within an argumentative context. Something (like immersing oneself in nature) can significantly be described as irrational or even non-rational only by contrast with rational ways of going on. But in the case of rational argument as such, as opposed to the use of arguments of certain types, there exists no further standard by which it might be called irrational, nor does its adoption involve an irrational faith. Irrational with regard to what? and in what sense a faith? are questions that would immediately arise.

The discussion of rationality by Popper and later by Bartley (1962, 1964) is based on so wide a characterization of rationality ('being ready to consider argument and experience') that no justification of rationality that will satisfy Popper is possible, given that argument or experience or both will be involved in any such justification. But the natural conclusion to draw from this is that the demand for justification of this sort is senseless. The very point which Popper takes to demonstrate the irrationality of rationality, and thereby to imply the existence of a gap in reasoning, actually shows that there is no gap to be filled. This last point could be put by saying that Popper fails to suggest any rational standard against which rationality, in his wide sense of the term, fails to be rational. It fails only to satisfy a demand which, for logical reasons, cannot be satisfied, and this could hardly be held against it or be taken to show its irrationality.

When someone is told to be rational about one of his beliefs, it is in the light of some standard which his belief apparently fails to meet. When Popper and Bartley speak concretely of irrationalism (Popper of the Hegelian tradition in German philosophy, Bartley of latter-day Protestant fideism), they speak of systems of argument or belief which, by other standards of argumentation, are unreasonable and which may, therefore, seem to rest on irrational commitments. In the case of rationality, however, there are no such standards. Bartley actually seems to see this (1962, p. 133) when he admits that the unjustifiable commitment to argument he and Popper speak of is not precisely parallel to the unjustifiable commitments 'existentialists, Protestant theologians, or Communists speak about' because

> whereas an argument on behalf of Communism presupposes in
> the listener a rationalist attitude in respect to itself, an argument
> on behalf of rationalism does *not* presuppose in the listener a
> Communist attitude in respect to itself.

His explanation of this 'trivial but interesting asymmetry' is that 'the rationalist position, characterised in a very broad sense as obedience to the result of argument, is logically more basic than the various other (irrational) positions and ideologies,' but he fails to see further that the sense of irrational (= not justifiable by argument) is one which Communist belief might well fail to fulfil, but one which argument as such cannot fulfil or fail to fulfil because such justifications are only to be found within argumentative contexts.

Bartley, in his discussion of the justification of rationalism, draws out more fully than Popper the implication of the conclusion that rationality itself rests on an irrational faith. Once the rationalist admits that his position rests on an irrational faith, he has no grounds on which to criticize the irrational commitments of others. All fundamental positions then become immune to criticism, a matter of arbitrary choice. The irrationalist, when challenged on the irrationality of his position, appears to be entitled to reply simply '*tu quoque*' to the rationalist. Much of Bartley's book is devoted to devising a way out of this for the rationalist, and much discussion of Bartley has been an attempt to assess the strength of his solution. With this we need not bother, because there is no reason why the rationalist should not simply reject the irrationalist's *tu quoque*: the irrationalist is accused of having a belief that ought to be justified, while the justification which the rationalist is supposed to lack is one which, as Popper has shown us, is logically unobtainable. Not only is there no real parallel between the two cases, but the rationalist's lack of justification can in the circumstances hardly be held against him, as we have a good argument to show why this has to be so.

There is a similarity and a contrast between what has been argued here about rationality as such and what Ayer says about induction. Ayer, it will be remembered, wrote (1956, p. 75) that induction

> could be irrational only if there were a standard of rationality which it failed to meet; whereas in fact it goes to set the standard: arguments are judged to be rational or irrational by reference to it . . . When it is understood that there logically could be no court of superior jurisdiction, it hardly seems troubling that inductive reasoning should be left, as it were, to act as judge in its own cause. The sceptic's merit is that he forces us to see that this must be so.

Bartley comments correctly on the question-begging nature of this appeal. What Ayer has to show is whether inductive standards do set the standards of rationality. Hume and Popper have attempted to show that there are standards of rationality which inductive arguments fail to meet, and, whether this is right or wrong, a defender of induction needs to show more than that inductive standards as a matter of fact characterize our notions of evidence. To take another of Bartley's examples, Karl Barth could well claim that submission to the Word of God in the New Testament goes to set the standards in theological argument and cannot be questioned. But surely, one will object, should there not be some argument to show that the Word of God is primarily manifested in *these* texts and traditions and not in others. In raising questions of this sort against Ayer and Barth, one is not questioning the idea of rational standards as such. As Bartley admits, the objections he raises against Ayer are not objections against rationality in the broader sense of a readiness to accept the results of argument wherever they might lead, but objections only to particular types of argument. These can be questioned in the light of the principles regarding the preservation and transmission of truth which govern the use of argument and language in general. In fact, of course, it is usually on the nature and success of particular types of argument that disputes between 'rationalists' and 'irrationalists' focus. It is in this context Ayer and Barth make their proposals. Neither is trying to defend or attack argument as such, but both are involved in a discussion of the nature and validity of particular types of argument. In contrast, nothing I have said here has been addressed to any particular type of argument, but only to showing, against Popper, that there is not necessarily anything irrational in being a comprehensive rationalist.

To maintain against Popper that a commitment to rationalism need not be based on an irrational faith is not, of course, to endorse the particular characterization Popper gives of rationality in his epistemology. Indeed, the distinction Popper continually draws between the well-corroborated and the true or the reliable led us to conclude in chapter III that for Popper there could really be no rational choice of a theory on which to act. So there is a sense in which for Popper rationally we might just as well consult oracles (irrational in our society) as scientists (rational in our society) when we want to build a bridge. When Popper accepts the full implication of his scepticism about induction, he is left with nothing to say about the rationality of embarking on the scientific adventure, beyond claiming that it will appeal to those who share certain value judgments and preferences with him. Does Popper really accept what is implicit in his rejection of induction? He claims also logical rigour and, significantly, practical applicability for his methods, but, I have argued, is unable to explain how their practical applications can be justified. So there could be for Popper a final advocacy of irrationalism at the heart of his defence of rationality in science: at the end of his *Logic of Scientific Discovery* (pp. 278–81) there is talk not of certainty, nor of final or even probable answers, but of a quest, an adventure, a recklessly critical proliferation of unjustified and unjustifiable theories. But this would be to argue that in empirical knowledge rationalism is impossible in practice, not that it is an inconsistent programme. There remains for Popper the moral defence of the critical approach in science: the preference for open discussion and freedom from dogmatism. If this was all there was to be said for it in science, it would be very much a question of personal preference. In the realm of public affairs, on the other hand, Popper is able to present a highly attractive application of rationality characterized as the readiness to listen to argument and to learn from experience, and to back this up with strong arguments in favour of an open, as against a totalitarian, society. We will now examine how Popper sees rationality operating in social and political life.

2 *The open society and social science*

We should take very seriously the dedication of *The Poverty of Historicism*:

> In memory of the countless men and women
> of all creeds or nations or races
> who fell victims to the fascist and communist belief in
> Inexorable Laws of Historical Destiny.

What Popper is attacking in *The Poverty of Historicism* and *The Open Society and its Enemies* is totalitarianism and its intellectual supports: the attempt to impose large-scale planning on the lives of individuals in the light of holistic and historicist considerations. Holism is the idea that some collection of people (such as a race, a state, or a class) is somehow greater than the sum of the individuals that compose it, that it acts on them and is subject to its own autonomous laws of development. Historicism is more difficult to define succinctly, but it involves the negative claim that in social life there are no significant laws which are equally applicable in different periods, and the positive claim that the student of history may be able by some intuition to discern through different periods an inexorable trend in history (towards the classless society, for example). The link between these claims is to appeal to the holistic view of society as an organism; it has a memory (its history and traditions) and it never experiences genuine repetitions of events. Even if a situation arises which is similar to an earlier one, the social 'memory' of the previous event will affect and alter the new outcome, so genuine novelty is a constant feature of human society and each important event is in a significant sense unique. More generally, holism entails that individuals (the atoms of history) are essentially formed by the social organisms of which they are a part, while historicism argues that we have to understand a social organism by intuitively grasping its spirit. Against this somewhat heterogenous body of doctrine, Popper proposes a view according to which society is no more than the sum of the individuals that compose it, that what happens in history and society is the result of the actions of individuals and that it must be measured against its effects on individuals, that successful large-scale planning to a pre-ordained blueprint is impossible because many of our actions have consequences we cannot in the nature of things foresee, that human behaviour and the laws that govern it are much the same from one place and time to another despite great differences of conditions and that the notion of a historical trend is based on a logical fallacy. What we should attempt to bring about is an open society in which governmental policies can be criticized and amended in the light of experience and in which the right of anyone to criticize and be listened to is safeguarded. Undesirable policies and policies with undesirable consequences will be weeded out in the same way as inadequate scientific theories are in science. Differences between individuals on policy will be resolved by discussion and argument, rather than by force, just as they are in science. Fallibilism, then, provides for Popper the epistemological background to both science and society.

What we shall do in this section is to consider in order the argument against a law of historical trends, the idea of an open society and its connection with piecemeal social engineering, and finally Popper's anti-holistic account of social science.

Popper's argument against someone who claims to discover a law of historical development according to which large-scale forecasts can be made is basically that he fails to understand the nature of an explanatory law. A causal explanation of an event is a deduction of that event from one or more universal laws together with a statement of the initial conditions. It will be argued by the historicist that in history there are spectacular differences between different periods so that we will never find universal laws operating in all periods. Against this, Popper argues there are also spectacular differences between natural environments, but this does not stop us looking for (and finding) universal laws applying throughout the physical world. Physical atoms change with their environment 'not in defiance of the laws of physics, but in accordance with these laws' (*PH*, p. 102). In social science, as in physical science, what we want are laws that explain change, not laws which are subject to change (which would then be unexplained). Laws which explain change are laws which predict differences of effect in differences of condition.

The historicist attempts to explain change by discovering a trend going through evolution or history as a whole, or through the history of each civilization. Popper's objection to this is that there is a sharp logical distinction between a trend and a law. A statement asserting the existence of a trend in given circumstances is a singular existential statement, whereas a law is a universal statement. This is crucial because predictions can safely be based on laws, whereas they cannot be based on trends, which may suddenly be reversed if the conditions obtaining suddenly change. There is little doubt, Popper says (*PH*, p. 116), that

> the habit of confusing trends with laws, together with the
> intuitive observation of trends (such as technical progress),
> inspired the central doctrines of evolutionism and historicism –
> the doctrines of the inexorable laws of biological evolution and
> of the irreversible laws of motion of society.

Yet, trends are not laws. Historicists discern trends in history and propose that they are unalterable laws. Forgetting that a trend (e.g., something getting hotter) depends on the continuance of given conditions (e.g., its being near a fire), they forget that a change in those conditions may well reverse the trend. At bottom, then, the poverty of historicism is a poverty of imagination, an inability to imagine a change in the conditions which produce an observed trend.

Trends exist in nature and (perhaps) in society. Popper does not deny that it is possible to explain trends by showing that the presence of specific initial conditions would lead to developments of predictable sorts in physical systems. He concedes that evolution itself may provide us with an example of an explained trend. What this means is that biological laws may be able to explain how it is that in an increasing range of environmental conditions the number and variety of biological forms will increase in the ways they do. Certainly, to take another of Popper's examples, if our solar system became filled with some new resisting matter (e.g., a certain gas), Newton's laws of motion and gravitation would lead us to expect the planets progressively to approach the sun. We could then predict the existence of this trend, so long as the new condition obtained.

Admitting that there can be explained trends (and indeed that it is part of the task of science to explain them) weakens Popper's case against a historicist who argued, not for absolute or unconditional trends in history, but for conditional or explained trends. Donagan (1974) suggests that Popper's distinction between laws and trends would provide Popper with no logical case against a sophisticated follower of Toynbee, say, who argued that, if a human society satisfied the conditions for being a Toynbeean civilization, it would pass through certain phases of growth and decay, however unlikely it might be that any such laws of social life cycles could be discovered. Presumably this historicist would turn his attention to evaluating the conditions in which his trend would disappear, but might he not conclude that in a given society and period these conditions are unlikely to occur? However, as Donagan points out, a very important part of the conditions prevailing in any society is the knowledge available in that society. Popper's arguments against a complete self-prediction could be invoked here to show that these conditions could never be fully known. More important, we could point both to the likelihood of unpredictable advances in knowledge and to the fact that the knowledge of the laws and conditions on which the historicist bases his predictions would itself show us how we would have to change the conditions to reverse the trend.

Popper's arguments against the large-scale prediction of history (through the establishment of a trend in history) are basically theoretical. His arguments against large-scale planning in society connect with the arguments against historicist prediction both because such planning is often devised in the light of the 'laws' (i.e., trends) of history and because of the relevance of the Oedipus effect to any attempt to execute any social policy. This provides us with theoretical reasons against thinking that we can totally plan for the future in so far as our future knowledge is part of what we are planning for. Once again, we will be unable to plan for unexpected advances in our knowledge or for the effect knowing our plans will have on our future knowledge and behaviour. Nevertheless, most of the specific arguments against total planning in society and in favour of piecemeal social engineering are of a more practical nature.

Popper (OS, vol. 1, p. 162) sees our knowledge of social life and social life itself in terms of experiments being made by the agents:

The introduction of a new kind of life-insurance, of a new kind of taxation, of a new penal reform, are all social experiments which have their repercussions through the whole of society without remodelling society as a whole. Even a man who opens a new shop, or who reserves a ticket for the theatre, is carrying out a social experiment on a small scale; and all our knowledge of social conditions is based on experience gained by making experiments of this kind.

This is, I think, the basic insight from which his advocacy of piece-meal social engineering against Utopian or wholesale revolutionary planning follows, as well as more general conclusions about the nature of the most desirable type of society. For if social action is a matter of an experiment based on some theory, we shall expect the theory to be tested against its effects. Someone who wishes to impose a Utopian blueprint on society will tend to overlook the initial effects of his revolutionary actions, which may well be unpopular and undesirable, because of his belief in the ultimate correctness of his theory about the ideal state. Indeed, he has to become dictatorial, if he is not to modify his blueprint against experience in such a way as to destroy its integrity. He has, in other words, to treat his blueprint as unfalsifiable, to treat human beings and their reactions as being tested by it, rather than vice versa. This will mean, characteristically, the suppression of criticism and the imposition of his policies by violent means, particularly if there is little chance of general agreement on the desirability of a revolutionary blueprint. Just because imposing an overall blueprint for society as a whole involves so much reconstruction of society, it is impossible to foresee all its consequences. Even though the recon-struction may claim to be based on rational insight, we lack the knowledge necessary to foresee what will happen if it is imposed. Even now we cannot foresee all the consequences of a new policy which stays within our current framework of institutions, so we will be even less able to foresee the effects of a policy which involves sweeping away the very background against which what knowledge we do have of social life operates.

The knowledge gained by social experimentation is gained through human effort and suffering. Because we cannot foresee in any case all the effects of such experimentation, we should confine our activity to areas where, if things go wrong, we can correct and readjust. In addition, by confining reforms to single institutions at a time (e.g., health insurance), we are more likely to reach agreement on what counts as a success. This perspective encourages us to seek to right agreed and manifest shortcomings in the workings of our society, rather than to attempt to impose a particular idea of the good life on everyone else, for there we are likely to find far less consensus. So piecemeal social engineering in an open society for Popper goes hand in hand with a commitment to negative utilitarianism.

There is, of course, a contrast between the advocacy of bold and revolutionary theories in science and their rejection in social policy-making. This is clearly because of Popper's belief that unforeseeable error is part of any theory. It is just not reasonable to suppose that a complete reworking of a social system would lead immediately to a workable system. Because human beings are the materials involved it is quite wrong to think in terms of starting anew with a clean canvas. (This type of image, like Lenin's notorious omelette, is redolent of totalitarian thinking.) But, while Popper's humanitarianism is to be respected, it is not clear that an open society, in which criticism is welcome from any quarter and in which learning from trial and error is accepted by all as a working premise, need be one that eschews large-scale reform or has to be committed to negative rather than to positive utilitarianism.

In the first place, the idea of piecemeal social engineering seems to presuppose that the general aims of a society and its institutions are both broadly agreed on by the members of that society and are already embryonically embodied in its institutions. At least, if such engineering is going to be able to correct large-scale injustice or tyranny in a society, we require that there exist in that society means of removing abuses which do not require the revolutionary overthrow of the status quo. In other words, for piecemeal social engineering to be effective and to perform the improvements Popper expects it to, we presuppose a society in which what is generally agreed to be an abuse can be peacefully corrected. Perhaps this is only a way of saying that piecemeal engineering presupposes an open society. While this may not be an objection to Popper, it is certainly true that there can be situations in which a society's rulers and institutions are so inflexible and unjust as to preclude all but revolutionary change. But revolutionary change need not in itself be Utopian or totalitarian. There is nothing paradoxical about a revolutionary transition to an open society (even if, as a rule, the agents of revolution are Utopians dogmatically sticking to a blueprint). Although Popper never explicitly rules out the possibility of a need for a revolution in an extreme circumstance, the tenor of his writing is always to emphasize the chaos and unpredictability a revolution will bring in its wake. He does not consider the possibility that there could be cases where the suffering implicit in a revolution might be preferable to present misery, or suggest how we might cope with such a dilemma. Nor need an open society, in being committed to trial-and-error methods and reason rather than violence, necessarily avoid seeking to promote positive goods. Of course, it may be difficult to reach consensus on social ideals and the means to their realization, but, as we shall see, Popper underestimates the degree to which agreement may be reached on the nature and eradication of suffering.

In weakening the links between the open society and a piecemeal and negative attitude to social policy, I do not want to imply that in some sorts of society revolutionary change towards some distant Utopia will not very properly be resisted; Popper's delineation of the unforeseeable and uncontrollable effects of revolution makes it highly unlikely that a revolution could ever be desirable in a Western democracy. But this is because these societies already have the institutions of an open society and (up to a point) the will to preserve them. One of the most valuable elements in Popper's account of the open society is his insistence on the need for vigilance and strong measures to safeguard it. He distinguishes between societies in which governments can be controlled and got rid of by the ruled (democracies) and those in which they cannot (tyrannies). Now, it is, of course, possible that a democracy could decide by popular vote to become a tyranny, so we need to found our adherence to democracy on something more than acceptance of the principle of majority rule. Indeed, Popper shows that the principle of majority rule (like any other principle of sovereignty which asserts the need for a certain type of ruler) leads to the following paradox: if the majority say that a tyrant should rule, the principle of majority rule says that we should both obey the tyrant (because the majority want him) and disobey him (because he is not the majority). What the open society should be based on is the non-paradoxical proposal to avoid and resist tyranny. Our institutions should be developed to this end (though that in itself will not guarantee openness unless those manning them are democrats in Popper's sense), not because a benevolent tyrant might not produce better policies, but because it is in an open society that we have the best hope of a social life rationally and humanely organized through listening to and taking account of the views of all (OS, vol. i, pp. 265–6):

> We demand a government that rules according to the principles of equalitarianism and protectionism; that tolerates all who are prepared to reciprocate, i.e. who are tolerant; that is controlled by, and accountable to, the public. And we may add that some form of majority vote, together with institutions for keeping the public well informed, is the best, though not infallible, means of controlling such a government. (No infallible means exist.)

Popper is emphatic that the liberation and tolerance he advocates need protecting against those who would subvert them. In other words, we need not extend freedom or tolerance to those who seek to destroy them. He thus avoids what he calls the paradoxes of freedom and tolerance (that unlimited tolerance or freedom allowed to bullies and tyrants will lead to the disappearance of tolerance and freedom for the less powerful). When extremism and terrorism are issues, Popper's insistence (OS, vol. 1, p. 265) on the right, in certain instances, to suppress the intolerant in the name of tolerance is extremely important:

> [The intolerant] may forbid their followers to listen to rational argument, because it is deceptive, and teach them to answer arguments by the use of their fists or pistols. We should there-fore claim, in the name of tolerance, the right not to tolerate the intolerant. We should claim that any movement preaching intolerance places itself outside the law, and we should consider incitement to intolerance and persecution as criminal.

If social action is to be regarded as a technological experiment and to be subjected to the analyses and criticisms we make of experiments in technology, the main task of the theoretical social sciences 'is to trace the unintended social repercussions of intentional human actions' (CR, p. 342). Popper is fond of quoting the example of a man who wants to buy a house, who thus inadvertently pushes up the price of houses. He thinks that by analysing the unintended consequences of actions we can explain how things in history come about that no one wants or foresees, without having to invoke holistic accounts of society or the state somehow manipulating its members.

His actual argument against holism of this sort amounts to asserting (PH, p. 82) that any collection of objects, even three apples on a plate, has relations obtaining between those objects which are not reducible to the simple existence of the individual objects. In this sense, a human society will be just as much greater than the sum of its parts as our three apples – and just as little. (I shall have more to say about the possibly intentional weakness of this example of the principle that the whole is greater than the sum of its parts later, in analysing possible senses of methodological individualism.) So, although Popper admits that a society is a system, in the sense that relations exist in it which are not analysable purely by reference to the individuals which compose it, what he admits gives us no grounds for thinking that the behaviour of the individuals is causally affected by their belonging to the system. Popper then *proposes* that we should be methodological individualists and attempt to explain all social phenomena in terms of the actions of individuals and their consequences, intended and unintended. By seeing social behaviour at differing times and places in terms of ex-periments conducted by roughly similar individuals in differing circumstances, he thinks he is able to explain and understand the different-looking behaviour of the agents involved without having to get inside their heads in some intuitive way. The historicist believes that people's actions and desires (and human nature itself) differ according to the spirit of their particular point in the development of history, and that we can understand them only by grasping the spirit of the age in question. Popper is particularly hostile to such talk, not only because of its holistic overtones, but also because it leads easily to proposals to remove those not in conformity with the spirit. Far from having our aims given to us by the spirit of the age, Popper's view is that we are responsible for them, even if holistic and historicist thinking encourages us to avoid this responsibility. He sees people, like atoms, as by and large similar; the differences between them are due to the different conditions in which they execute their piecemeal social experiments. What the historian or social scientist has to do with alien people is to reconstruct in his imagination the experiments undertaken naturally and largely successfully by his subjects. He, in other words, applies the method of trial and error to predicting the experiments of others. Although intuition and imagination about the states of minds of his subjects may help him to formulate his hypotheses, the criterion of success is always whether he is able to predict correctly the behaviour of his subjects, just as, if he was actually in another culture, his understanding of its customs would be manifested by the success or otherwise of the social experiments he undertook (i.e., whether his actions had the effects he expected).

In asserting that there is a basic unity of method between the natural and the social sciences, Popper is saying that the logic of explanation is the same in both. In both, what we seek are deductive causal explanations. We have seen at length what this amounts to in the natural sciences. In the social sciences, although what constitutes an explanation is the same (deduction of an effect from a universal law and initial conditions), the emphasis on the various elements in the explanation is rather different. A fairly obvious difference between the more theoretical natural sciences and history (to take the least theoretical of the social sciences) is that the latter is most interested in explaining unique events. To this extent, part of a historical account will be to show how a particular unique event was the result of the accidental concurrence of causally unrelated events. The historian is not, then committed to putting every effect directly into a deductive framework (any more, indeed, than a chemist who is accounting for an accident involving human error in a chemical works). In accounting for unique events, however, the historian, if he is like a practical chemist, will have to appeal to the laws governing the behaviour of the various accidentally concurring elements in the situation. These elements, of course, are human beings. Popper considers that even great historical events can be analysed in terms of the consequences, intended and unintended, of the behaviour of individual human beings. The explanation of individual human behaviour is to be given by showing how often rather trivial and obvious psychological laws lead to people behaving in particular ways in particular situations. But in explaining, for example, why Caesar crossed the Rubicon, the point of interest will be not underlying generalizations about ambition and energy but the reasons why this was (or was not) the logical choice for him at that moment. The historian or sociologist, then, will not make no use of universal laws, but he will tend to concentrate first on what Popper calls the logic of situations, showing how people's motives and actions are partially determined by the institutions and traditions in which they are living and the situations confronting them, and second on framing laws which capture the way in which so much of what actually happens is due to the unintended consequences of the actions of individuals in particular situations. (An example of such a law would be that you cannot make a revolution without causing a reaction.) Popper can thus justifiably claim that although his analysis of society will be based on individual behaviour, it is not psychologistic, because the behaviour of individuals is governed by their social situation as much as by their individual motives (which, in any case, are in part socially formed). Indeed, a purely psychologistic account of human behaviour may well be historicist, because of its need to explain in psychological terms. The psychologist will ultimately have to show how these are based in some pre-social 'human nature' and may so be led into speculating about the development of human nature. Popper, on the other hand, can explain both institutions and changing motivations in terms of social environments and unintended consequences of actions. Finally, Popperian social science, in stressing the unintended consequences of actions, will illustrate the poverty of conspiracy theories of history and society. For, although there doubtless are conspiracies, if so much of history is unintended by any individuals, little can be explained by appealing to the aims of conspirators.

Popper's social science is an attempt to avoid various extremes. It is individualistic without being psychologistic. It admits the autonomy of sociology, in saying that men are formed by traditions and institutions, but attempts to avoid holism by explaining events as the consequences of individual actions. It attempts to unify the methods of natural science and social science, and so to avoid the incursion of the mystical into social science, but admits the agent's perception of his situation as an essential part of any explanation. It is here, though, that the unity of method begins to break down. Examination of this point will lead us to suggest that the difference between Popper's methodological individualism and some form of holism is rather less than it seems at first sight and, finally, to question the adequacy of Popper's criterion for explanation in the social sciences.

How and why does Popper introduce the agent's perception of his situation into historical explanation? He does so because he is clear that 'in most social situations there is an element of rationality' (*PH*, p. 140). This can mean only that part of what is involved in an action is an agent acting for a reason. But the unity of method requires, for example, that insight into the insides of atoms is neither necessary nor sufficient for an explanation of their behaviour. In other words, the account of the agent's rationality is not to be given in psychological terms. What Popper proposes is a method of logical or rational construction of action, called the zero method (*PH*, p. 141):

> By this I mean the method of constructing a model on the assumption of complete rationality (and perhaps also on the assumption of the possession of complete information) on the part of all the individuals concerned, and of estimating the deviation of the actual behaviour of people from the model behaviour, using the latter as a kind of zero co-ordinate.

So the basis of our explanation and prediction of behaviour is an understanding of the rational thing to do in any situation. Once we see this, we will understand why people act as they do, except when they deviate from the rational. Here (and only here) psychological considerations will be paramount.

What Popper is saying here is that human beings faced with decisions are problem-solvers or experimenters. When we realize that action is a response to a problem and we understand the problem, we will have at least a basis for understanding the response to it. The analogy between human action generally and scientific activity is clear. In both cases, the response is intelligible in terms of the problem set, and we understand the actual response in terms of its approximation to the ideal response demanded by the problem.

However, if a zero method can work in the history of science, this is because in science the overall aims and criteria with respect to which rationality can be judged are preordained. But this is not the case with human activity generally. The rational thing to do in a given situation is not fixed independently of the agent's perception of it, and ultimately of his form of life, as can be seen from an example which might seem at first sight favourable to Popper.

It will be remembered that Popper, in his outline of the types of policy an open society should concentrate on, instanced the relief of suffering. This was at least partly because in this area agreement is most likely to be generally reached and moral relativism least likely to raise its head. So, assume that a young man finds a starving child abandoned on a river bank. Popper, I and many people would say that the rational and humanitarian thing to do is to save the child. But the hero of Edward Bond's play *The Bundle* decides that this is highly irrational if what one wants is a revolution, after which starvation will be altogether eliminated. By palliating suffering now, you are preventing a complete and genuine cure of present ills, which can come about only when the full horror of injustice is apparent to all. Popper would reply to this that the living have rights as much as the yet unborn; while this is a reasonable reply to Bond's hero, it hardly shows his attitude to be irrational. Relative to his aims, it remains rational, however contemptible we might find it. I do not know how to continue this example, but it is possible to think of other cases where people from certain religious backgrounds would not regard the removal of suffering as a particularly urgent aim and cases where what counts as suffering is defined only in terms of the form of life adopted. Both these points are exemplified in the *Bhagavadgita*, where physical suffering is played down and where it is stressed that shame, for example, is only felt in certain social strata.

It may be that Popper does not intend the zero method to be employed in abstraction from the agent's general background of attitudes and beliefs. Indeed, he speaks (*CR*, pp. 130–1) of one of the functions of social traditions as being to provide a background against which the consequences of and responses to their actions can be predicted by agents. Without such a background, it would hardly be possible to act rationally. In this case, the zero method would have to be relativized to the tradition in which the agent would be likely to locate the rationality of his action; in other words, we should understand someone's action when we understood what someone from his background would count as rational in that situation. Although this is perfectly reasonable in itself, it does put some strain on the unity of method, because we now seem to be admitting that there are differences between agents from different backgrounds which are crucial to the explanation and interpretation of their behaviour. The action which for Popper and me would be a piece of gross inhumanitarianism may be nothing of the sort for Bond's hero or a Buddhist priest, even if we from our point of view characterize it as inhumane. This difference in the description of the behaviour is not merely verbal. It characterizes the dependence of an action for its very sense on the background and attitudes of the agents involved.

Popper would presumably analyse differences of this sort not so much in terms of the individual psychology of the agent as in the tradition within which he confronts particular situations, and he will see this in terms of a variation in experimental conditions. But while this may help us to avoid psychologizing our explanations of action, it does not rescue the unity of method. For if social traditions are to be thought of as experimental conditions, they are experimental conditions of an unusual sort. As my example shows, without knowing something about these conditions, we are not in a position to know what the action is that has to be explained. Traditions are internally related to the descriptions of the data of the social scientist. It is not only that there is no absolutely rational course of action independent of a general set of aims or form of life; forms of life also determine what the actions are that agents do. It would, therefore, be wrong to consider them merely as different experimental conditions in which the same effects can indiscriminately appear.

That Popper does conceive the relationship between the social traditions within which we act and our actions themselves as an essentially external one is underlined by a passage (*PH*, pp. 135–6) in which he speaks of notions like 'war', 'army' and so on as abstract objects or theoretical constructions which, in the natural sciences, we use in order to construct theories for the interpretation and prediction of what happens to the concrete entities involved: the killing of many, the donning of uniform, etc. This thesis is a combination of the claim that social traditions (within which wars, armies and so on get their existence) have the function of bringing order and predictability into the social world with the view that what really exist in society are its individual members. But, as Winch has argued (1963, pp. 127–8), concepts like war do not bear a purely external or explanatory relationship to the actions of individuals. They make those actions the actions they are:

> The idea of war . . . was not simply invented by people who wanted to *explain* what happens when societies come into armed conflict. It is an idea which provides the criteria of what is appropriate in the behaviour of members of the conflicting societies. Because my country is at war there are certain things which I must and certain things which I must not do. My behaviour is governed, one could say, by my concept of myself as a member of a belligerent country. The concept of war belongs *essentially* to my behaviour.

This is where the unity of method finally breaks down. The social traditions within which people live have an internal relationship to their actions and cannot be thought of as either the experimental conditions of an independently describable action or explanatory models or backgrounds of an external sort. Elaborating a point of Winch's, we could say that a falling apple does not fall because it has the concept of gravity, but the possession of the concept of war by a soldier makes all the difference in the world between what he does in killing a man in battle and what he does in killing a man in a drunken brawl.

The internal relationship which exists between one's actions and the concepts which determine the nature of those actions also brings Popper's methodological individualism into question. For many of the concepts involved clearly depend on the individual seeing himself as a member of a social group and cannot be explained individualistically. As well as the examples of war and army already considered, we can think here of the concepts of promising, contracting, belonging to a team, being paid a salary, lecturing in a university, marrying and so on. It would be pointless to deny that much of any individual's behaviour is governed by concepts such as these and idle, as we have already seen, to suggest that these concepts simply provide individuals with explanatory models for their behaviour. Indeed, as Schutz (1970, p. 12) points out, those who are interested in explaining social behaviour (i.e., social scientists) will introduce theoretical constructs for this purpose, but their constructs, unlike those of natural scientists, will have to be based on the concepts under which the agents involved conceive their activity. What is done in social life is done because people see themselves as a member of a team, a university, a business, an army, a society; it would not otherwise be done and makes sense only given a self-perception of this sort. Because the institutions presupposed by many of the concepts in question make it possible for us to have many of our aims, it is not possible to see institutions in a purely instrumental way, as serving these aims. As Winch suggests (1974), Popper has a tendency to adopt an instrumentalist account of institutions; this would certainly be in line with his treating traditions as explanatory models and with his implicit assumption that humanitarianism can be presupposed as a general aim of society.

Popper's methodological individualism has a positive aspect: that the task of social theory is to explain social events in terms of the attitudes, expectations, actions and relations of individuals; and a negative aspect: the denial that collectives (states, nations, classes) do anything. To assert that individual actions are often the actions they are because the individual agent conceives himself to be a member of a collective is not, of course, to suggest that the collective causes his action in the sense that the agent was forced to act as he did because of his membership of the collective. On the other hand, it is rather more than an idea being transmitted through a social institution and 'captivating' an individual, as Popper puts it (*PH*, p.149). It is not that the individual is persuaded to act patriotically because of social influences, but that the possibility of his acting patriotically or unpatriotically is given to him by being a member of a nation. Because of this, some of what an agent does will be recognizable as the action it is in terms of his group membership. Into any description and explanation of many of his actions, terms referring to collectives rather than individuals will play an essential part, because the data to be explained can be identified for what they are when they are seen in terms of social concepts.

In order to see precisely what Popper is committed to by his methodological individualism, it will be useful to follow Lukes's (1968) contrast between Popperian methodological individualism and five distinct theses with which it can be confused. To take the contrasting theses first, we first have what Lukes calls truistic social atomism. This says simply that collectives consist of people. This is trivial, because it tells us nothing about whether or how the behaviour of people is affected by their membership of a group. Even an extreme holist could accept this. Second we have a thesis to the effect that every meaningful statement about a group or relations existing in a group either is or is reducible to a statement about individuals. Popper would appear to deny this, as he thinks that even plates of apples have relations which do not follow from their individual existences. Admittedly appeal to this type of external relationship would not convince all defenders of the second thesis, who would include statements about such external relationships in the class of statements about individuals. I am not clear whether, in his individualistic days, Popper would have conceded that there are cases of statements about groups which are not reducible to talk of individuals or their external relationships. I want to argue that these are not so reducible, and that this counts against what Popper clearly does hold – namely, that facts about individuals alone are explanatory. Third, there is an ontological thesis to the effect that in the social world only individuals are real. Popper may have had some affinity with this, when he spoke of collective terms such as 'army' as referring to theoretical constructions, as opposed to the concrete individuals who fight. In fact, as we shall see when we consider evolutionary epistemology and World 3, Popper would no longer incline to deny the existence of collectives, even if he once did. In any case, methodological individualism does not require ontological individualism of this sort. What it says is that facts about individuals are alone truly explanatory. This need not entail the prima facie absurd view that forests and armies do not exist while trees and soldiers do. (In the case of a soldier, if it is true to say that armies exist because of soldiers, it is equally true to say that soldiers exist because of armies.) Fourth, there is the view that sociological laws are impossible. Popper is clearly not committed to this, since he gives (*PH*, pp. 62–3) as an example of the sorts of sociological laws he is interested in such statements of unintended consequences as 'You cannot have full employment without inflation' and 'You cannot have a centrally planned society with a price system that fulfils the main functions of competitive prices'. It remains an open question as to whether, on his view of the general unpredictability of human behaviour, Popper ought to see any sociological statements as having the status of laws, and it is even more doubtful whether the examples he actually gives of such laws are either true or of universal applicability. Indeed, in favour of the historicist attitude to sociological laws, if there are any, following a suggestion of Professor A. G. N. Flew, I am tempted to question whether the second example quoted even makes sense, except as applied to certain historically conditioned societies, while the first example is plainly false if we consider it as ranging over tribal societies without money. The difficulty here is that Popper's account of the sociological laws he approves of is so nugatory as to make further discussion of it rather futile. Finally, there is the view that the end of society and social institutions is (or ought to be) the good of individuals. Popper clearly accepts this, and it is the point at which he sees his moral and methodological individualism coming together. But does the moral individualism depend on methodological individualism?

Methodological individualism is intended to deny the holist view that superhuman factors are operative in history. Presumably the holist who holds this view supposes that these factors use social institutions and the human beings in them to promote their own ends. Such an idea is clearly antithetical to Popper's idea of an open society. What Popper's methodological individualism asserts is that 'the functioning of all social institutions should always be understood as resulting from the decisions, actions, attitudes, etc., of human individuals' (OS, vol. 2, p. 98). If this is taken to mean that the individual attitudes in question have to be individualistic rather than social, the thesis is false. As we have seen, many of a man's attitudes are what they are only because he sees himself as a member of a society. But I do not think that Popper ever meant to be so restrictive in his account, particularly as he always denied that psychology could be the basis of social science, asserting instead that men and their motives and aspirations are the product of life in society. So we can take the attitudes of individuals here to include attitudes of an essentially societal sort. If this is the case, it would seem that the dispute between this methodological individualism and a moderate methodological holism, whereby reference to social wholes was taken to be an essential ingredient of any sociological theory, is a purely verbal one. Clearly no morally objectionable holism about nations seeking to preserve themselves and so on would follow from this, and we would be able to do justice to the place of societal concepts in the creation of an agent's attitudes. But it seems that Popper does want more from his individualism, for he says (PH, pp. 157-8) that

we must try to understand all collective phenomena as due to
the actions, interactions, aims, hopes, and thoughts of
individual men, and as due to traditions created and preserved
by individual men.

To this, it has to be insisted yet again that many of the aims, hopes
and thoughts of individuals are in turn due logically to the existence
of collective phenomena, by which it is not meant merely that social
traditions influence the minds of individuals, but that the very existence
of motives like patriotism or treachery, one way or the other, depend
for their sense on the individual's existence in a collective. Holism to
this extent is unavoidable.

In fact, in his later philosophy, Popper appears to abandon methodological individualism, arguing not only that sometimes groups can
affect the actions of individuals, but also that institutions develop in
part autonomously. He says (OK, p. 209) that his original anti-holistic
position was only directed against the superficiality of most holistic
theories and not against the existence (and presumably causal power)
of wholes in some cases, but the statement of methodological individualism just quoted seems rather stronger than that.

A further point about methodological individualism is that its
conception of the individual as the primitive term in which explanations of human behaviour are to be given appears to be rather uncritical in view of the many theories asserting that individual behaviour
has to be explained in terms of different or even competing phases or
aspects of the self. (Freudian theories and theories of roles are two
examples.) It seems likely that, if individual behaviour requires partial
explanation in terms of factors less than the whole self, some of the
natural antipathy to seeing the individual as requiring explanation in
terms of entities larger than the self will disappear. A grasp of the
form of life of an agent is necessary before we can identify what it is
that he is doing.

I want to conclude this section by suggesting that this fact points
to a crucial ambiguity in Popper's account of the explanation of action.
Much has been made (e.g., by Musgrave, 1974, pp. 570-1) of the fact
that Popper's criterion of explanation in history, as in science, is totally
objective and does not rely on relieving the puzzlement of the historian
or the scientist. We explain an event if, and to the extent that, we
succeed in deducing it from universal laws and initial conditions. This
makes it look as if we will understand the action of, say, a samurai
killing himself if we are able to predict this as the likely outcome of a
certain situation. Against this it will be felt by many that we might be
able to make such a prediction without in any sense understanding

what was going on. The behaviour of the samurai could remain completely foreign to us, even if we were able to predict something about his actions.

What I want to suggest is that there is something right and something wrong about both positions here. The opponent of the Popperian model of explanation is insisting that the actions of people in an alien culture will be understood by us only to the extent that we grasp the form of life of that culture and that, when we understand this, the feelings of puzzlement which now accompany our observation of the alien behaviour will be relieved. Musgrave and Popper object to the apparent subjectivism of this and insist on hard objective prediction of data. But what is hidden here is that the data involved are the actions of human beings and their perceptions of situations. A man disembowelling himself looks a fairly neutral datum, but how do we know that it is also a ritual suicide and how do we know that it is a response to a situation calling for such a thing? In predicting (or retrodicting) a disembowelment on the grounds that it is a samurai's ritual suicide, we will have to know a great deal about his form of life, about what, in other words, leads him to see certain situations as suicidal. So the description and explanation of action will require a degree of insight into the agent's form of life. Here Popper's model hides something important, particularly if it is seen as analogous to a scientific explanation. Of course, we might doubt that we understand an alien form of life if no predictions can be made. Here Popper is undoubtedly right. But before we can even begin to grasp the data to be explained (the individual actions), an understanding of a form of life is required. Such an understanding will, in all probability, relieve the puzzlement that initially worries us when we are confronted with an alien society.

IX

Evolution and World Three

1 *Evolution*

In *The Poverty of Historicism*, Popper had argued that there could be no law of evolution showing something like the necessity of the development from the amoeba to human beings. This is because any such 'law' would be a statement of a trend, and not a law at all. Darwinism itself, in postulating the survival of the fittest and adaptation for survival, appears to be a testable theory. On inspection, however, it turns out to be virtually tautologous, because modern evolutionists define adaptation and fitness in terms of survival value (cf. 'IA', p. 137; *UQ*, p. 172). Nevertheless, Darwinian evolutionary theory has become progressively more important to Popper, first as a metaphysical research programme, suggesting testable theories both in biology and psychology. It can do this partly because of its opposition to a Lamarckian point of view in which changes in both genetic structure and learning would be expected to arise in conformity to environmental conditions, whereas Popper sees such changes as stemming initially from the organism itself and then being modified by the environment. Also, Darwinism throws up problems of its own in biology, some of which Popper himself has attempted to solve. Thus, in order to explain the apparent goal-directedness of the evolution of complex organisms and the infrequency of accidental changes in species, which is a problem for traditional Darwinism, Popper (*OK*, ch. 7; 'IA', pp. 137–43; *UQ*, pp. 172–9) has distinguished between two levels of genes, one level controlling the preferences, aims and skills of organisms, and the other the shape and character of their organs. Although all genetic changes are still random on this view, the preference and skill level controls the selection of the changes at the anatomical level, so we can see why such changes as appear tend to serve the aims of organisms. But perhaps more important for Popper's philosophy as a whole than these aspects of Darwinism is the fact that, although in one sense evolution is very weak as an explanation, as the steps from one evolutionary level to another are all highly improbable, in it Popper has found a general framework in which to locate and develop many of the apparently diverse concerns which have occupied him through the years.

Popper sees Darwinism as an application of what he called (*PH*, pp. 149–50) the logic of situations. According to this, if we want to understand why someone did something or why some theory was proposed, we should see the action or the theory as a response to the problem being confronted. Problem-solving is to be seen in Darwinian terms. That is to say, the response to the problem is thrown up as a hypothesis and then subjected to environmental pressures, which lead to its complete rejection, its modification or its acceptance. But it will be accepted only so long as it is not confronted by a new problem it cannot solve. In all probability the new problem will be thrown up by the old solution itself. We are presented with the schema in Figure 1 in which P is a problem, TS a tentative solution and EE the work of error elimination.

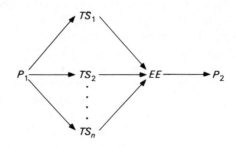

Figure 1

This is a Darwinian rather than a Lamarckian picture, because the competing tentative solutions do not arise through inductive instruction from the environment, but from the imagination of the problem-solver. Nor is it supposed that error elimination will lead to a final solution, but only to another problem.

Popper sees all life in terms of the schema. Organisms and species of organism are continually involved in problem-solving. The main difference between their problems and ours is that theirs are almost all directly and immediately concerned with survival: their solutions, some of which are anatomical rather than behavioural, are therefore likely to be punished by the death of the theorist. Our solutions even to survival problems, on the other hand, are often, because of their linguistic formulation, criticizable and modifiable before we ourselves die, unless we stick to them dogmatically. Although, through the critical method, we can let our theories die instead of us (*OK*, p. 261):

> from the amoeba to Einstein, the growth of knowledge is always the same; we try to solve our problems, and to obtain, by a process of elimination, something approaching adequacy in our tentative solutions.

Knowledge and theories are given a rather wide extension in Popper's new Darwinism, as they include behavioural and anatomical modifications in animals. Sense organs themselves are said to embody or even to be theories. The reason for this is Popper's concern to place human knowledge in an evolutionary context; to see it as obeying the same laws as evolutionary change itself. This is why, as we have seen, he says ('RC', p. 1061) that 'the main task of the theory of human knowledge is to understand it as continuous with animal knowledge; and to understand also its discontinuity – if any – from animal knowledge'. Darwinism provides parallels in its analysis of the evolution of species with the rejection of induction and of a theory-free observation language. For change is not directly due to environmental pressures but partly due to the activity of the organism, while anatomical developments (including those of sense organs) are, as controlled by natural selection, to be seen as solutions to problems. But the differences between human knowledge and the rest of nature are important too, and are an example of discontinuity in nature.

Although for Popper problems and problem-solving, and hence natural selection, are more or less synonymous with life, he sees ('SR', p. 272) a slight foreshadowing of natural selection even in the inorganic world, for example, in the selection of the more stable elements owing to the radioactive destruction of the less stable ones. But he is at pains to insist that nothing like atomic nuclei or even crystals can be seen as having survival problems. Living organisms – things having problems of survival and reproduction – are the only problem-solvers in the universe; there is radical discontinuity between the living and the non-living. There are also radically new developments within living things. Two of the most important are the emergence of consciousness (an amoeba or a tree can hardly be said to be conscious) and the emergence of human language (which, in its description and critical abilities, is a step beyond any animal communication system). So Popper's naturalism involves a belief in radical novelty or emergence, and hence of the non-reducibility to the physical or the chemical of sciences concerned with life in various aspects. This in turn implies a rejection of determinism in the physical sciences, for biology must work within the framework provided by physics and chemistry, but this framework must permit the emergence of new law-like properties. So indeterminism and Popper's evolutionism go hand in hand, even though his main philosophical arguments against determinism do not apply to the inorganic. (He does emphasize, however, that quantum mechanics, in insisting on microscopic indeterminacy, has broken the grip on us of the old deterministic picture of the physical world.)

The main argument Popper has for the existence of emergence and against such reductions as those from biology to physics or psychology to biology or sociology to psychology is that at each higher level there are developments which could not have been foreseen at the lower levels. Although reductionism (like determinism) is an important research programme, with some major success in showing how properties at one level can be explained at a lower level, most of its successes have been only partial in terms of a complete reduction of levels. For example, it has not been possible completely to reduce mathematics to logic or geometry to arithmetic, or even chemistry to physics. But the main objection to it is not so much its actual failures as its inherent unlikeliness. The reduction of all science to physics implies that mind and conscious experience are somehow potentially present in physical particles or structures: sufficient knowledge of these potentialities would have allowed us to predict the evolution of life and consciousness beforehand. Against this, however, is the fact that consciousness involves memory and, according to modern physics, two atoms of the same isotope are physically identical whatever their past history, so memory is not even foreshadowed at the level of physics.

Although man is seen as a product of evolution and human culture and development is subjected to a Darwinian analysis, the emergence Popper is most interested in is that of human self-consciousness. This he sees as fundamentally irreducible to any lower level of existence; indeed, he sees it as fundamentally immaterial. He argues ingeniously against epiphenomenalism and the identity theory by suggesting that, if human consciousness is only a reflection of physical processes and not really effective on those processes or if it is actually those processes themselves under another aspect, then natural selection can give us no reason for the evolutionary appearance and maintenance of human consciousness, whether it is seen as a reflection of material processes or an aspect of them. It must, according to Darwinian principles, have some real function, which would be denied by saying either that it was merely a reflection of physical processes, which would take place even if they were not so reflected, or that it was simply an aspect of physical processes, the laws governing which could be given entirely in terms of their physical or biochemical aspect and needed no invocation of predicates referring to consciousness. But his main argument in favour of what he sees as an emergent Cartesian self in human beings is to appeal to the fact that we understand and are influenced by abstract objects such as theories, standards and values. These Popper sees platonically, as having a real existence outside our minds and as being irreducible to physical objects. A theory, such as a mathematical system, is brought into existence by us, by means of language. (The discontinuity Popper sees between human language and animal communication systems consists primarily in the way we can, by means of language, lay out our thoughts objectively in symbolic form and then develop and criticize them.) But once a theory is expressed by us, it has a content and implications which are independent of us, about which we can make discoveries. The abstract world of theories is one we grasp through our mental processes and through them influence the material world, but its reality, and our interaction with it, is what takes us radically beyond the material world.

This transcendence of the material world is not merely a matter of understanding. The abstract world of ideas (what Popper calls World 3) allows us access to preferences and aims which are not merely instinctive but which can be chosen (and rationally criticized) in the light of ideas from ethics, aesthetics, science and so on. Indeed, Popper sees our being anchored in World 3 as enabling us to form for ourselves a plan of life (SB, pp. 145–6), something we create and choose for ourselves, against the background of World 3 ideas. This leads him to stress the value of individual creativity in life and to argue for limitations on state planning, which is in line with both his earlier individualism and his stress on mental indeterminism. Of course, the ability to choose effectively in the light of immaterial ideas presupposes that we are not totally determined at the physical level.

Popper's argument in favour of radical novelty (and immateriality) in human beings is his appeal to World 3. A full assessment of this claim must depend on our examination of World 3, but before we undertake this, some more should be said in detail about the connections and analogies Popper draws between evolutionary processes in general and human knowledge.

2 *Evolution and epistemology*

Popper's Darwinian account of epistemology applies particularly to two sets of epistemological problems, one concerned with the discovery of theories, the other with the nature of perception.

On the discovery of theories, we have seen how Popper compares our tentative solutions to the problems we are confronted with to genetic mutations made in animal species in response to environmental problems. According to Darwinian theory, mutations are thrown up

randomly, and only those which serve the ends of the species in particular environments are preserved. For Popper, theories, like genetic
mutations, are thrown up by creative intuition irrationally, as he says
(*LSD*, p. 32). The rational part of science consists in the critical testing
and modification of the work of irrational imagination or intuition.

But are theories really like irrational, unpredictable mutations?
Popper has to qualify the analogy by saying that we should think of
the theorist's imagination as blind rather than as random. The point
of making this distinction is that the theorist always begins from a
problem. Like a blind man, he searches actively and purposefully for
something he believes to be there ('RC', p. 1061):

> The searcher has a problem to solve, and this means that he has
> some knowledge, however fuzzy, previously acquired by
> essentially the same trial-and-error method: this knowledge
> serves as a guide, and eliminates complete randomness.

Once it is admitted that our tentative theories can be guided in their
formulation by past knowledge, however, we seem to be admitting
a degree of Lamarckian instruction in their discovery, a guiding of
our imaginations from without and the possibility of guessing in a
more or less informed way. Certainly there is more to be said now
about the evolution of hypotheses than there is in Darwinian theory
about the purely random appearance of mutations in genetic material.

Popper's justified hostility to any mechanical or inductive model
of theory discovery has all through his philosophy brought him to
the point where he claims that nothing can be said on the discovery
of theories. It is obvious why an analogy here with Darwinian genetics
appealed to him, but not only does the analogy make it impossible to
say anything about the rationality of the processes of discovery, it
also has ultimately to be qualified by Popper himself. In qualifying it,
he appears to be opening the way for talk of rationality at the stage of
theory formulation as well as at the stage of error elimination, but he
gives no clue as to what type of guidance from background knowledge
a theorist should look to in his formulation of theories. Surely a
logician of discovery, however, should be able to give help of just
this sort to a theorist, showing him how background knowledge might
be used to eliminate complete randomness in our trials, and how, even
where we are going beyond background knowledge (and so operating
blindly), past experience can help us bring some sort of order into our
trials.

Living things, for Popper, are above all else problem-solving
organisms. Practical problems arise when an organism is confronted
by some event it is unprepared for, when it has been let down by some
expectation or when it is organically unable to cope with some new

situation. But its previous expectations and structure are seen by Popper as being the solutions to earlier problems. So new problems are essentially bound up with old theories or solutions ('IA', p. 106; *UQ*, p. 133):

> since any practical problem arises relative to some adjustment of this kind, practical problems are, essentially, imbued with theories ... *Organic structures and problems arise together*. Or in other words, *organic structures are theory-incorporating as well as problem-solving structures*.

The theories organisms incorporate determine above all the way in which they perceive their environment. The view is clearly an extension of the view considered in chapter V that all observation is theory-laden and is elaborated in a theory of perception contained in *Objective Knowledge* and other later writings. We will now examine this theory both because of its own interest and because of the light it throws on Popper's earlier theories about observation.

Popper's view is that the brain and sense organs of an organism, for example, ourselves, constitute a decoding apparatus by which we are able to interpret states of our environment, including anticipating changes in the environment. In thinking of perception as a decoding process, Popper is intending to deny that we have access to any untheoretical data or that perception is pure and unproblematic. On the contrary, 'sense organs incorporate the equivalent of primitive and uncritically accepted theories, which are less widely tested than scientific theories' (*OK*, p. 146), a fact we should bear in mind before relying uncritically on perception. We should remember the fallibility of perception, thinking of our observations as '*highly complex and not always reliable though astonishingly excellent decodings* of the signals which reach us from the environment' (*OK*, p. 73). Perception, then, depends on our inborn (genetically inherited) or acquired theories of how to decode the signals which reach us from outside. It is neither immediate nor direct. Popper ('RC', p. 1062) quotes Donald Campbell (1974, p. 424) saying that 'from the point of view of an evolutionary epistemology, vision is just as indirect as radar' and adds

> This shows that nothing is 'given' to us by our senses; everything is interpreted, decoded; everything is the result of active experiments, under the control of an exploratory drive.

This is an evolutionary view of perception because it sees perception itself as being based in the process by which an organism adapts itself to its environment, in which suggestions are thrown out to cope with the environment which are then reinforced or extinguished under the control of the environment. A consequence of this view is that, with a change of environment, our perceptual apparatus may well let us down in the sense of failing to provide us with the information we need for survival.

We can begin our analysis of Popper's evolutionary theory of perception from this last point, because it is closely connected with the way in which Popper argues that perception is theoretical. As noted in chapter V, Popper uses the term 'theoretical' in diverse ways, without always carefully distinguishing them. Popper shows some recognition that this might be the case in the first sentence of the following passage (*OK*, pp. 71–2), in which he argues that our sense organs are theory-laden:

> Because all our dispositions are in some sense adjustments to invariant or slowly changing environmental conditions, they can be described as *theory-impregnated*, assuming a sufficiently wide sense of the term 'theory'. What I have in mind is, that there is no observation which is not related to a set of typical situations – regularities – between which it tries to find a decision. And I think we can assert even more: *there is no sense organ in which anticipatory theories are not genetically incorporated.* The eye of a cat reacts in distinct ways to a number of typical situations for which there are mechanisms prepared and built into its structure: these correspond to the biologically most important situations between which it has to distinguish. Thus the disposition to distinguish between these situations is built into the sense organ, and with it the *theory that these, and only these, are the relevant situations for whose distinction the eye is to be used.*

The conclusion is that what we perceive are not 'pure' data, but are interpretations of our environment themselves based on theories, a consequence of which is the failure of any inductive model of higher level theory-building by mechanical operations on an unadulterated observational input.

In so far as our observations lead us to have expectations about the future behaviour or regularity of what we currently observe, they might indeed be described as involving theories. But there are plenty of observations which are only of instantaneous states of things (like states of clouds and ball games); it is always possible to distinguish in principle between what is currently being perceived and what is expected of the objects of current perception. In order to show that observation is theoretical, Popper has to show that theories are involved at the level of current perception. What he does show is that we do not react to every potential sensory stimulus, but only to those that are biologically or culturally important. This is the familiar point about Eskimos and South Sea Islanders being able to distinguish shades of colour which we cannot. No doubt, if we were put into an environment where it was important to make such distinctions, our senses would let us down. There is something to be said for the view that theories are involved in deciding which sensory cues are likely to be important. But none of this shows that our observations are theoretical in the sense in which theoretical is contrasted with observational at the level of the observations themselves. It does not by itself show that our observations are unverifiable or transcend the given. Nor does the fact that they are selective show that they lack directness or immediacy, or that they come about through decoding signals we receive from the environment.

It is possible to distinguish in Popper's picture of perception elements which are plausible from those which are not. That perception requires a frame of reference, a sense of what types of discrimination to look for, is very plausible. That some frames of reference are inborn and others learned is also plausible. That in perceiving objects we make use of things we have learned about objects and their appearances is certainly true. So is the fact that until we learn certain empirical facts about the appearances of things (for example, that sticks look bent when half-submerged in water, that parallel lines seem gradually to come together as they recede from us, that a feverish man finds cold things hot), we are liable to be deceived by our senses. What is not so plausible is the view that facts such as these make all observations theoretical in the sense of being irreducibly uncertain or forever open to doubt. We saw at sufficient length in chapter V that this aspect of Popper's views on observations would lead us to raise doubts where doubting is not fully intelligible. What I shall now try to do is to show that Popper's thesis that perception is in some sense indirect and to be analysed in terms of decoding signals from objects we are presumably not in direct contact with also raises more problems than it solves.

At first sight, we have no clear idea of what it is to perceive something indirectly. To take the case of vision as an example, it is possible to distinguish various ways of seeing things other than seeing them normally; seeing a planet through a telescope, or a microbe down a microscope, seeing one's reflection in a mirror or a friend through a distorting lens, seeing the prime minister on television and so on. It is not obvious that it would be correct to describe any of these cases as *seeing* things indirectly, even though in some cases unusual or artificial means have been used to bring about my seeing them. (This may be because 'to see', like other verbs of perception, is, as Ryle (1949) points out, an achievement verb, not to be qualified by adverbs which apply properly to the tasks which may be undertaken in order to put us in the position where we are able to perceive what it is we are interested in.) Radar – the analogy Popper borrows from Campbell to explain the indirectness of perception – is certainly a case of seeing signals caused by some object, but it is not a case of seeing the object itself at all, directly *or* indirectly, any more than Robinson Crusoe saw Man Friday when he saw his footprints in the sand.

According to Popper (*OK*, p. 65) when a man sees a stone 'he decodes some of the signals that reach him from the stone'. This is perhaps more satisfactory than saying ('RC', p. 1065) that the *senses* themselves theorize – do my eyes theorize, or my hands? – but it still leads to several curious results. Unlike the man before the radar screen, in perceiving something we are conscious neither of a distinction between the signals and what they are signals of, nor, more importantly, of any process of decoding the signals or of relating them to what they are about. It is true that a radar observer may have become very quick and expert at decoding, so that he does it without noticing. Nevertheless, he had to learn how to do it and would, if asked, be able to retrace his steps, telling us how the lights on his screen were related to the things causing them. Although an archaeologist might well be able to tell us what it was about the square of earth in front of him that led him to see it as a post-hole, we would be completely at a loss if asked to give any such account of the majority of our everyday perceptual achievements.

The reason for this may well be not that we have become so quick and good at decoding the signals that come to us from sticks and stones, chairs and tables that we never catch ourselves doing it (as Popper claims (*OK*, pp. 63–4)), but because no such process takes place. In order to see the cylinder in front of me as a torch battery, I have to know what torch batteries look like. This is what is right in Popper's story. But we are asked to think of what happens when I see the battery in terms of a quasi-physiological process of decoding signals from the battery. Physiological processes undoubtedly do take place which result in my perceiving what I perceive, but to attempt to explain perception through interpreting these processes in terms of decoding raises a dilemma. In decoding signals (whether on a radar screen or from traffic lights) we must be able to perceive them. Indeed it is the logical possibility of distinguishing the perceiving of the signal from the decoding of it that gives talk of decoding its point. There must be *something* in undecoded form which is then decoded into something else. But this would seem to make it impossible to explain *all* perception as decoding. Either there is an infinite regress of signals, each of which is the result of decoding an earlier signal, or some signals must be directly perceived without being themselves the outcome of some decoding process. That Popper does have something like this in mind is apparent from the radar analogy, in which the signals are presumably directly perceived. But perception is not like radar in that

I am not as a rule aware of perceiving signals, nor can I become aware of perceiving anything more basic or direct than the common or garden objects that I am supposed to see as the result of decoding signals. Rather than saying that I directly perceive signals I am never conscious of perceiving, Popper would surely be better off without the decoding model, which in any case seems to involve him in direct perception at the level of the perception of the signals (or an unlikely infinite regress of decodings), when the point of introducing the model was precisely to rule out direct perception altogether.

If the decoding analogies are dropped from the evolutionary theory of perception, we are left with the familiar claim that all observation presupposes a point of view, together with an interpretation of the points of view as reflecting solutions to survival problems. My argument is not against this, but against seeing it in terms of decoding signals. In some ways dropping talk of decoding might be more satisfactory even to Popper. The signals emitted by stones before decoding bear an uncanny resemblance to the old sense data which Popper emphatically rejects. Moreover, the thesis of the indirectness of perception seems to make the objects of the world which can only signal to us as cut off from us as ever Kant's things-in-themselves were. At all events, there seems to be nothing here that on analysis gives any new support to the denial of any basic distinction between theory and observation, nor does an evolutionary analysis of sense organs appear to require us to consider perception to be indirect or radar-like.

3 *World Three*: *Popper's Platonism*

We have seen that Popper's situational logic combined with evolutionism leads him to think that theories are best analysed in terms of the problems that they are framed in response to and of the problems they bring in their turn. This is developed (principally in *OK*, 'IA', 'RC' and *SB*) into a fully fledged theory of the autonomous existence and development of theories and problems – autonomous, that is, of the psychology of the individuals who work on them. Popper's hostility to psychologism here receives its final form, while his hostility to relativism here receives a far stronger vindication than it gets from the fact of intersubjective discussion emphasized in Popper's earlier attacks on relativism: for if problems and theories (what Popper calls *knowledge*) are independent of human thought, the truth about them must also be non-subjective.

Popper begins by distinguishing three different worlds. World 1 is the world of physical objects and states, World 2 that of states of consciousness, mental states and behavioural dispositions to act, while

World 3 is the world of the objective contents of thought (including particularly scientific and artistic theories) and of institutions and values, considered abstractly. World 3 is separate from World 2 (the world of our actual thoughts and behaviour), because items from World 3 not only have an effect on World 2 (and through it on World 1 as well), but they contain within themselves the logic of their own development, which is irreducible to elements from Worlds 1 or 2. Popper's theory is Platonic in this respect, but unPlatonic in that he sees World 3 and its inhabitants as originating in human thought and activity. But once something is in World 2, in its development, it transcends its makers.

Like a book or a library, World 3 contains knowledge which no one is actually aware of (or has ever been aware of). But unlike books and libraries, what is in World 3 is there in an abstract form and, moreover, subject to its own autonomous development. So, for Popper, our theories, institutions and works of art are not just part of the natural history of man – his thoughts and behaviour – but rooted in another realm altogether. Knowledge in this objective sense, he says (OK, p. 109), is 'totally independent of anybody's claim to know; it is also independent of anybody's belief, or disposition to assent; or to assert, or to act'. The main reason for thinking this is that such products of our activity bring with themselves all sorts of consequences and further problems which are completely unexpected to us, their originators. These consequences and problems exist autonomously, awaiting discovery by us, just as the exosomatic products of animals, such as spiders' webs or beavers' dens, have an objective existence apart from spiders or beavers and bring with them new problems both for the animals concerned and for others. But the animal products provide only a partial analogy, for World 3 is above all a product of the human ability to express and criticize arguments in language. This is the point at which World 3 connects with Popper's evolutionism, for in its most interesting elements it arises from human linguistic and symbolic abilities. This is because it is in the objectively expressed products of our thought and art that we can most clearly see what the underlying theories and their consequences are and how they might be criticized, and it is primarily from language that we get the idea of logical consequence, on which World 3 so strongly rests.

Popper's picture, then, is of World 3, autonomous in its 'ontological status' (OK, p. 161), consisting of abstract contents of all kinds such as problems, theories and their unintended and unforeseen consequences. Although originating in human activities, especially linguistic ones, World 3 contains problems no one can solve and problems that are actually insoluble. So World 3 transcends us, challenges us and leads us on, and, through its influence on us, affects World 1 as well.

My criticism of Popper will be primarily to show that everything he wants to say about unintended and unforeseen consequences and the challenge of World 3 can be explained in World 2 terms, and that the idea of theories completely autonomous of human behaviour is misleading. (As the main interest here is in the supposed autonomy of World 3, the further question of the reducibility of World 2 to World 1 will not be pursued.) But before dealing with the autonomy of World 3, something must be said of Popper's claim that World 3 causally affects World 2, for this is part of his argument to the existence of World 3.

Popper appears to argue ('RC', p. 1052) that someone interested in a World 3 problem will be motivated to search for it, and that this is a type of World 3–World 2 interaction. As it stands, this gives no support to the existence of World 3, because it assumes that problems are in World 3, and this is what is at issue. But even if this is granted, and we accept that our minds are 'controlled by' World 3 products such as 'theories, systems of law and all that constitutes the "universe of meanings"' (OK, p. 251), we need to know how World 3–World 2 interaction is to be thought of. For Popper's view is not just that for some purposes (e.g., logical analysis) we can think of the content of a thought in isolation from anybody expressing it or thinking it, but that the content of the thought actually exists independently of any of its expressions and in this abstract form influences thinkers. His picture appears to be like this:

Stage A: the abstract thought that p (World 3)
Stage B: the thinker's grasping of the thought that p (World 2)
Stage C: the thinker's utterance or inscription: 'p' (World 1)

Each prior stage is the cause of its successor. The problem with this model is that it falls foul of Popper's own conditions for informative causal explanation in which the *explicans* must be identifiable independently of the *explicandum*. Given that the *explicandum* here is the utterance or inscription 'p', we have been given no independent way of identifying the elements in Stages A and B.

In any case, what utterances or inscriptions are being explained by this picture? An instructive contrast can be drawn between Popper's causal account of judgment (Stage B) and Descartes's in his *Fourth Meditation*. For Descartes, the mind naturally intuits what is true; it is designed to do so thanks to the goodness of God. How then do erroneous judgments arise? Through the influence of the will, says Descartes, which can cause the mind to pay insufficient attention to what it is looking at. Particular errors can then be generally attributed to our not having taken the necessary steps to secure sight of the requisite clear and distinct ideas. But what this theory explains is not our judgment that p, but the fact that we judged truly or falsely in a given case. Moreover, we can (within Descartes's psychology) identify independently a judgment and the act of will which brings it about.

Could it be that for Popper, World 3 has its impact on thinking in that a man who thinks correctly follows World 3 elements in the way that a Cartesian who reasons correctly allows himself to be moved by clear and distinct ideas and nothing else? World 3 is brought in here to explain not why someone thinks of p, but why, in thinking of p, he is reasoning correctly in the light of his problem. Some support for this interpretation might be found in Popper's assertion that World 3 contains all the consequences of the thoughts we actually have, including new theorems and proofs, which now exist awaiting discovery. But, as Popper goes on to say ('RC', p. 1051), World 3 contains not only true theorems, but also conjectures not known to be true or false, and

> with every truth . . . a falsehood (the negation of the truth),
> or even an infinite number of falsehoods. ($0 + 0 = 0$ brings in
> its wake the infinite procession of falsehoods $0 + 0 = 1$,
> $0 + 0 = 2, 0 + 0 = 3, \ldots$)

So World 3 is not invoked to explain how and why people reason correctly. As it apparently contains everything we can think with the concepts at our disposal (once they have been initially introduced by us into World 3), it is hardly surprising that it contributes little to any explanation of why we think as we do. Saying, as Popper does ('RC', p. 1071), that 'almost all the important things we can say about . . . our second world understanding . . . consist in pointing out its relation to third world objects' is not very helpful in this context. (This fully comprehensive aspect of World 3 does not, as we shall see, fit easily with Popper's central idea of World 3 controlling us when we argue and think correctly about problems.)

If Popper's account of the causal relationship between World 3 and World 2 is obscure, his account of the way in which World 3 elements get World 1 form as actual utterances or inscriptions is equally hard to follow. This, too, is involved in part of his reasoning to an abstract world of ideas, for he stresses heavily (*OK*, p. 230) the familiar argument from the existence of different physical expressions containing the same information to the abstract non-physical existence of that information. Of course, identity of information encoded in different forms gives no very powerful reason for thinking that the information can actually exist apart from some actual coding or other. Printers can be told what half-tone pictures they have to set up and print in a variety of ways (by being given a negative, a computer message, etc.), but this does not show that the information could exist or be understood non-physically. It merely shows that we can, if we wish, think of the information in abstraction from any actual encoding. So Popper's argument to the abstract meanings is weak. But having got there, he provides ('RC', p. 1052) the following account of the materializing of abstract meanings. The World 2 understanding grasps the World 3 problem or theory in one of its 'logically essential forms' and

> the liaison between World 2 and the brain (which presumably puts the problem in words) may play either no role at all in this action or – more probably – a role analogous to a recording machine which definitely encodes a sound *after* the sound has been produced.

What we have here is, in the context, a question-begging metaphor. A recording machine encodes a sound after it has been produced, but the sound is already something physical, ready to be encoded or recorded. The whole problem here is that the World 3 object is not in a physical form, so how can it activate the brain to encode it in language? An encoding machine needs an input, already in some physical form, which it then puts into some other form. What is unclear here is the nature of the input – how a problem or a theory which is not in one of its 'perhaps infinitely many physical codings' can be identified or even grasped, let alone encoded.

Underlying talk of the linguistic formulation of a thought being an encoding of that thought is the even more misleading metaphor of language itself as some sort of code. (Popper says ('IA', p. 147; *UQ*, p. 184) that when we read a book, we decode the abstract messages it contains.) In normal usage, codes are contrasted with natural languages in having to be deciphered in order that their messages can be understood. After deciphering, the message is intelligible because it is now in an ordinary language. When we understand an utterance or inscription of English we do not decode it, nor in using English do we encode what we want to say in the sort of way a spy might encode or decode his messages. Of course, in linguistics talk of decoding and encoding is fashionable, apparently as a way of explaining how it is we are able to understand what is said by others or to make them understand what we wish to communicate. There is no need to labour the disanalogies between a spy consciously decoding a message and an English speaker decoding an English utterance (*who* does the decoding? *Could* an English speaker ever be aware of decoding an English utterance in order to grasp its literal meaning?), because the decoding model completely fails to explain how a speaker understands his language.

The reason for this is very simple. A message that is decoded is put into another symbolic form so that it may then be understood. The problem of understanding language is to show how one gets from a message in any symbolic form to a grasp of the content of that message. If speaking and understanding an English sentence are thought of in terms of encoding and decoding, it is natural to ask *from* what and *into* what is that sentence encoded and decoded; it is clear that if the coding picture is meant to explain how we understand the sentence – how the sentence is related to what it is about, in other words – the encoding and decoding have to be from or to some other symbolic representation of what the sentence is about. The world itself (even World 3) is not located in my mind (or brain). But how is this new symbolism to be understood? How is it related to its extra-linguistic content? The problem of understanding simply reappears at the level of the new symbolism. Speaking of the English sentence as containing abstract messages or 'coded information' (as Popper does in 'RC', p. 1051) and suggesting that what exists before encoding and after decoding is some abstract message or information is no help in solving the problem of understanding. If 'information' *is* the relation of the message to its extra-linguistic content (i.e., its meaning), the problem is simply begged; while if 'information' is *another* symbolic representation of the meaning of the English statement, then the question of the relation of these symbols to what they refer to is simply pushed back another stage.

In short, talk of decoding and encoding processes or of semantic representations in the brain or elsewhere is irrelevant to the problem of understanding a language. This problem is addressed by showing how utterances and inscriptions of a language are related to what it is they are about: in laying bare their logical form. In comparison with what can be achieved at this level (in a Tarskian truth definition, for example) to insist on meanings as abstract and logically prior to symbolization is not only obscurantist, it is beside the point. For this reason, it is hard to see the force of Popper's claim (*OK*, p. 297) of the inadequacy of a view

> which sees language as consisting of physical objects – noises, or
> printed letters – and which sees ourselves as conditioned or
> dispositioned to react to these noises or letters with certain
> characteristic kinds of physical behaviour,

when the appeal to abstract meanings throws up such intractable problems of its own. It is by no means clear that a logical analysis which makes no appeal to abstract propositions, but which concentrates on the rules underlying the manipulation of the actual words we use, will fail to be satisfactory. It certainly promises more than the appeal to an immaterial sense underlying those words.

So the causal relations between the abstract World 3 and our thoughts (World 2) and our words (World 1) are highly problematic. But a more original and important aspect of World 3, and one which will take us deep into the central claims Popper wants to make for it, is his attempt to see it at once as a human creation and as something superhuman. When Popper says that World 3 has a history, he does not mean merely that there is a history of our treatment of World 3 problems. He means also that World 3 entities (such as numbers) and procedures (such as adding to integers) are initially invented by us. Once the invention had taken place, all sorts of theorems relating to the inventions came into existence, awaiting discovery. A problem with this from Popper's point of view is that it makes a complete break between the formulation of hypotheses which bear on already invented products, and which are to be explained by people grasping or discovering already existing World 3 entities, and the invention of new products or concepts, which is presumably not to be explained in World 3 terms. Aside from this, there is a destructive tension in the combined view that World 3 is partially constructed by us and partially autonomous.

Let us accept that the procedure of counting is invented at a certain time, say, by people who wish to regulate the exchange of goods. They do this by laying items to be bartered against marks scratched on a piece of wood. Suppose further that the laying process always began with the leftmost scratch and that, in a row of items, each item had to have a scratch corresponding to it. Exchange could be regulated by saying that, when items of one sort were being exchanged for items of another sort, the row of items of one sort had to reach a certain other specified scratch. It would be natural for the scratches to be given names. After a while a row of items could be counted without the physical scratches: the names of the scratches, starting with the leftmost and going in sequence, would be said for any set of items, one name per item, until there were no more items left. Once counting by means of reciting the names was established, the names could begin to be memorized and used on their own, independently of any particular set of scratches or items. They could be taken in a generalized sense as the names for counting rather than as names of particular scratches, having a mnemonic role in the calculation of quantities. (Sheep-counting rhymes would be a case in point.) Perhaps Popper has something like this in mind when (*OK*, p. 118) he speaks of the sequence of natural numbers as a human construction, though he never indicates precisely how he thinks the sequence was constructed. Numbers will enter World 3, presumably, when they are considered in abstraction from the calculating practices in which they originally had a use. Popper's picture now is of us being constrained and determined in unexpected ways as to what is right and wrong in all our future calculations with these numbers by World 3 realities. Once numbers get there, mathematics takes on a life completely of its own, independent of World 1 or 2. Now while *this* picture of mathematical autonomy is clearly appropriate for a full-blooded Platonist who wants to say that the whole of mathematics has a fully objective existence independent of us, it is not so obviously easy to maintain it if, like Popper, you want to hold that mathematics is initially a human creation.

Of course, the mathematical practices in which we engage have a certain stability and objectivity. We are taught to obey the calculating rules of our system and can be told when our calculations are right or wrong. In the context of the picture I gave earlier of numbers being introduced as a regulating tool in the matter of exchange, general observance of the rules is necessary for the effectiveness of the tool. But Popper needs to show more than objectivity and stability of this sort to establish the World 3 autonomy of mathematics; he needs to show that the stability involved can be explained only by appeal to a World 3, and that it is not simply a consequence of our having adopted certain practices which have certain consequences. World 3 autonomy presumably implies the existence of mathematical objects independent of our practices, which are simply mirrored by our practices. Yet, if mathematics is seen initially as a tool for regulating exchange (or as arising in some similar way within a practice of calculation), correctness cannot be seen as independent of the actual applications of the practice even though, once the practice is established, we will be able to distinguish between correct and incorrect calculations.

A famous example of Wittgenstein (1958, p. 75) is to the point here. A pupil is being taught how to construct series of numbers by adding a certain number (say 2) to the previous number in the series. So he starts 0, 2, 4, 6, 8, . . ., but when he gets to 1000 he goes 1004, 1008, 1012, . . .

> We say to him: 'Look what you've done!' – He doesn't understand. We say: 'You were meant to add *two*: look how you began the series!' – He answers: 'Yes, isn't it right? I thought that was how I was *meant* to do it.' – Or suppose he pointed to the series and said: 'But I went on in the same way.' – It would now be no use to say: 'But can't you see . . .?' – and repeat the old examples and explanations. – In such a case, we might say, perhaps: It comes natural to this person to understand our order with our explanations as *we* should understand the order: 'Add 2 up to 1000, 4 up to 2000, 6 up to 3000 and so on.'

There are difficulties in understanding this example because the move the pupil is making is not one that is possible for us. When he says that he is going on in the same way as he started, we are inclined to deny this. Yet it is not as if he has missed something discoverable or implicit in our instructions or in the intentions behind them. If we say that we 'meant' that he should go on with 1002, 1004, 1006, . . ., when he got to 1000, or that we 'knew' that 1002 was the next step after 1000, we cannot be saying that we were actually thinking of the step from 1000 to 1002. Of course, if we were asked what number should have been written after 1000, we should have replied 1002. We can be confident of this precisely because we are trained to recognize a certain way of going on in such cases as going on in the same way. *We* can then say that for us the steps are determined by the appropriate formula, but we should not think that they would necessarily be determined in the same way independently of our practice, because it is just what is to be taken as going on in the same way which is in question and which is only decided by an appeal to our already established practice.

If we return to the picture of mathematics as initially a tool, used in calculating and exchanging goods, we can imagine all sorts of different notions of what would count as going on in the same way, depending on the nature of the goods or the conventions for exchange. Suppose the world was such that every item placed on a heap of 1000 or more similar items immediately split into two or suppose collections of over 1000 items were specially valued, the tool might well have been developed so that people were trained to go 998, 1000, 1004, 1008, . . ., on the instruction 'add 2 to the last member of the series'. This example is no doubt outlandish but its outlandishness arises from the outlandishness of the imaginary world, not from the impossibility of the mathematics involved. As Popper himself points out (*CR*, pp. 211–2), our arithmetical laws are applicable only to certain types of thing. The laws of addition do not apply to drops of water or to rabbits of different sexes. It could be argued in line with our speculations about the invention of counting that we are trained to recognize certain ways of calculating as the correct ones (and hence as what is required by mathematical law) because of their general applicability to our world. The fact that we internalize these ways of going on and are able to do without scratches or counters does not show that the laws are processes which have an ontological status of their own, in-dependent of our practices or make-up. The reference to our make-up here is important, because Platonism in mathematics is sometimes supported by appeal to the fact that mathematical laws are not straight-forwardly discoverable by reference to objects in the physical world (World 1). But, as Feyerabend has argued (1974), this would support Platonism in general and Popper's World 3 in particular only if the mathematical laws in question could not be analysed in terms of regu-larities in the world taken together with the mental dispositions (or brain structures) of the calculating organisms. These, of course, would be World 2 (or even World 1) elements in Popper's sense, and what Popper has to show is that our mathematical laws and discoveries are due not to our 'proceeding actively in accordance with some slowly developing psycho-physical programme' (Feyerabend, 1974, p. 491) based in our interaction with our environment, but to passive observation of some non-physical and non-mental entities in a third world.

Here indeed we come to the crux of the matter. For Popper holds that, although we ourselves create World 3 objects, we have passively to discover their implications, which are not under our control. Naturally, a fully fledged Platonist who sees the whole of mathematics as a discovery will have no problem with the second part of Popper's picture, but it is not clear why someone who sees mathematics as initially our creation will need to explain its development as something completely outside our control. (Feyerabend comments pertinently on the intellectual passivity of Popper's new research programme compared with the activity of his older position; an analogous point will be made when we compare the new position on social institutions with methodological individualism.)

Popper's main argument for World 3 autonomy is that, although World 3 entities are created by us, they have consequences which are unexpected and unavoidable. The question is always whether the unexpected and unavoidable consequences which follow from our constructions are such as to require appeal to a World 3. So Popper's critics here will have to give some account of reasoning in mathematics and other World 3 areas which does not require us to go beyond Worlds 1 and 2. What I shall argue is that there are unavoidable mathematical implications, but that this fact alone does not require us to appeal to World 3, for Popper gives us no reason for not seeing mathematical development as being a study of *our* rules, our practices, rather than as a study of entities existing independently in a Platonic ideal world, and that, finally, even if Platonism of a Popperian or some other variety is plausible as an account of mathematics, it is not plausible as an account of the other areas which Popper's arguments would lead us to place in World 3.

Popper says (*OK*, p. 118):

> The sequence of natural numbers is a human construction. But although we create this sequence, it creates its own autonomous problems in its turn. The distinction between odd and even numbers is not created by us . . . Prime numbers are similarly unintended autonomous and objective facts; and in their case it is obvious that there are many facts here for us to *discover*: there are conjectures like Goldbach's . . . [which] refer directly to

problems and facts which have somehow emerged from our creation and which we cannot control or influence.

Elsewhere (*SB*, p. 80), Popper says very succinctly that the point at issue between someone who sees men as cued into World 3 (and hence as themselves spiritual – cf. my following section) and a physicalist opponent 'is precisely whether such things as logic (which is an abstract system) exist (over and above particular ways of linguistic behaviour)'. Calculating involves being able to recognize correct applications of the rules for calculation and proof. The rules establishing the definition of odd and even, and prime numbers, are clearly stated and involve no recognitional problems. Possibly, if a proof were found of Goldbach's theorem, it would consist of steps involving no unproblematic applications of well-established rules. In this sense it is true to speak of autonomous and objective facts in mathematics and logic, awaiting discovery. But this autonomy arises simply from the nature of mathematics as a rule-governed activity. In the same way, chess and football are autonomous; they, too, are rule-governed activities and presumably no one has foreseen every application of every rule. But it is not yet clear how the fact that a human activity is governed by rules shows that what counts as an application of a given rule is independent of the dispositions of us, the agents, to see our rules as determining correctness and incorrectness in particular ways. To talk of a rule-governed activity as having consequences unforeseen when the rules were first elaborated does not show that those consequences are laid up in heaven awaiting discovery independently of the dispositions of the agents to recognize how the rules are to be applied and their ability to recognize when they are being so applied. This is precisely the point at issue between intuitionists and Platonists when the one asserts and the other denies the application of the law of excluded middle in mathematics. Moreover, in calculation, as in any activity where there are rules, our day-to-day conclusions are determined by the steps we have initially taken, but, as the example from Wittgenstein quoted earlier suggests, it does not follow from this that the initial steps determine every future move we might make in calculating.

In order to see what is involved here, let us look at the position with regard to Platonism on mathematics and logic in a little more detail. World 3 autonomy here is proposed by Popper on the grounds that in mathematics and logic we discover facts and problems inherent in our constructions which are unsuspected by and beyond our control. There are at least three distinct ways of taking this: (1) we discover surprising and substantial truths about the systems we have created; (2) there are at least some facts about these systems which go beyond cases where what is at issue is the application of our rules in types of cases which our established practice has already rendered unproblematic and which may even transcend our ability to recognize these facts; (3) our practices are autonomous in the sense that they are beyond our control: they control us. Popper seems to want to hold all three of these positions. Position (1) is implicit in all he says about World 3, Position (2) appears to be implicit in what he says (*OK*, p. 161) about the existence in World 3 of autonomous problems we may never master and about the World 3 existence of infinite totalities ('RC', p. 1050), while Position (3) is implied by his talk of the rules of logic being 'exosomatic systems of control' (*OK*, p. 254). As I suggested earlier, when we saw that World 3 contains not only truths, but also vast numbers of falsehoods, and presumably all types of deviant logic, as well as non-deviant logic, it is hard to see how Popper can see World 3 as controlling thinkers. As Currie (1978) has pointed out, the all-inclusive nature of World 3 means that the connection between thinking a World 3 thought and thinking an objectively true or logically standard thought is by no means clear. Nevertheless, this connection does seem to be what Popper wants World 3 talk to give him. He intends it to provide him above all with an account of (correct) logical inference; I shall, therefore, assume in what follows that World 3 contains truth, rather than falsehood, and will direct my attention to the claim that talk of objective consequences in logic, mathematics and elsewhere requires the postulation of such a world developing autonomously and controlling our thoughts.

Position (1) is clearly true, but it is not necessary to be a Platonist in order to accept it. Constructivists and intuitionists would certainly accept that the determination of oddness or primeness for a given number is implicit in our original definitions of these notions, as well as other less obvious properties of the system of natural numbers. But what they would take themselves to be doing here would be to be examining consequences and applications of the rules we had adopted in mathematics, rather than to be using our rules to discover truths in a Platonic universe. Succinctly, for them our rules and the constructions deriving from them are the subject matter of mathematics, rather than merely the means of making discoveries about an independent subject matter with an existence autonomous of human imagination. For them, there can be no appeal to any existences other than what we can construct in our practices.

Position (2) is a typically Platonist position, which would be attacked by constructivists on the grounds that it makes no sense to speak of mathematical objects (such as transfinite sets or their power sets) which are beyond the ability of human beings to recognize or construct, because mathematics can never cease to be what it originally was – a human construction. Popper presumably thinks that there are such entities but he gives no convincing argument for maintaining this, as opposed to his weaker claim that there are mathematical truths and problems which we have not yet actually recognized, but which are within our competence to construct (which could be dealt with by constructivists under (1). Of course, there are well-known arguments in favour of (2) from the failure of constructivist attempts to provide a basis for set theory (where impredicative definitions are needed) or for a satisfactory study of the continuum. It seems that these branches of mathematics require us to speak of the existence of entities which are not humanly constructible or recognizable. Indeed, this fact led Bernays (1935) to suggest that, while constructivism may be adequate for the theory of natural numbers, a degree of Platonism, in the sense of Position (2), is required for mathematical analysis and set theory. It remains to be explained just how this Platonism is to be understood. Bernays himself sees it as an 'ideal projection of a domain of thought' (in which we think of the unthinkables on analogy with the thinkables), rather than what he calls absolute Platonism, 'the idea of the totality of all mathematical objects and the general concepts of set and function', for this would lead us straightaway to the paradoxes of set theory. It is unfortunately unclear where Popper stands on any of these issues, or just how he thinks of the existence of what we cannot construct being brought about inevitably by the existence of what we have constructed, because (for reasons we will come to) he does not base his Platonism in mathematics on any specifically mathematical considerations. His criticisms of intuitionism (*OK*, pp. 128–40) are largely directed against the idea that mathematical knowledge is a matter of intuitive perception and could be accepted by a constructivist without in any way weakening his interpretation of mathematical existence in terms of constructibility.

Position (3) is, I think, the main conclusion Popper wishes to draw from (1), and this goes for the logical and mathematical elements of World 3 as much as for any of the others. Consequences can be drawn from rules we have adopted, as a matter of logical consistency. The example quoted earlier from Wittgenstein can be interpreted as implying either that the rule for adding 2 was not spelt out enough to determine its application in cases where numbers above 1000 were involved, or (perhaps more plausibly in view of theses in Wittgenstein (1967)) as involving an extreme constructivism, according to which any rule requires at each point of application a new decision. This latter position appears to be quite implausible as an account of mathematical reasoning, as it rules out any place in an account of calculation for the idea of the calculators remaining faithful in terms of consistency to the original meanings they gave to their concepts. So let us assume, with Popper, that our concepts do have future implications, some of which may be surprising and even unwelcome. I have already argued that intuitionists and constructivists less extreme than Wittgenstein can account for this fact, without appeal to Platonic objects or worlds. What Popper's Platonism appears to come to here is an assertion that where some such unexpected consequence arises we are always to be governed by the rule system we have adopted. Otherwise, it is hard to see how the system leaves our control and begins to control us. This, however, is a conclusion which may be resisted, even in the case of logic and mathematics.

Consider, first, the classical truth-functional account of entailment, according to which any *modus ponens* inference will be a case of entailment. As is well known, it follows from this, and from the substitution of $- A \lor B$ for $A \supset B$, that any arbitrary proposition will follow from a contradiction. This reasoning is valid and inescapable, given that we do not alter any of the truth-functional meanings involved. But does it follow from this reasoning that the conclusion is part of our notion of entailment? Although Popper, along with many others, accepts that it is, Anderson and Belnap (1959) have criticized the classical employment of *modus ponens* in accounts of entailment, on the grounds that extension of the notion to accept that any proposition is entailed by a contradiction is highly dubious. This would be an example in which, on philosophical grounds, we might decline to be controlled by a logical system. In offering another logic for entailment, it is not clear that we are actually altering the original intention of the concept. Indeed, part of Anderson and Belnap's criticism of the truth-functional account is that it distorts what is involved in entailment. It might, most plausibly, be argued here that our concept of entailment is inherently vague and does not in itself determine any answer to the question of whether it would be correct to think of it truth-functionally or not. Such a conclusion would weaken the hold on us of any Platonism with regard to our practices. Analogous cases might be to question whether the liar paradox really throws any light on our notion of truth, or Gödel's theorem on our notion of proof. In all these examples, what is at issue is the question as to whether one should be controlled in one's philosophical conclusions about problematic concepts by particular logical formalizations, even though the logical conclusions are admitted to follow from the definitions used in the premises. In mathematics, too, Lakatos (1963-4) gives examples of how original definitions of concepts are altered to rule out unwelcome consequences they are discovered to have. Here, too, the World 3 picture of workers being controlled by the inevitable consequences of their premises has to be replaced by one in which they are able to control through manipulation the systems with which they are engaged, in the light of what they lead to.

In addition to the re-formation of logical and mathematical premises in the light of their logical and mathematical implications, it can also be argued that our choice of logic may be affected by empirical considerations concerning the subject matter to which the logic is to be applied. This would be in line with the account I gave earlier of the example from Wittgenstein and my suggestion that there is a general connection between correctness in calculation and empirical applications of calculation. Putnam (1969) argues that anomalies in quantum physics demand that we replace classical logic by a logic in which the classical laws of distribution do not hold. The reason for this is that, on a reading rejected by Popper, quantum physics makes it impossible to ascribe to a particle simultaneous position and momentum. So a statement, $P . M$, attempting to do this is ruled out as contradictory. But it is sometimes possible to ascribe to a particle a determinate position, together with a disjunction of momenta, i.e., $P . (M_1 \lor M_2 \lor \ldots \lor M_n)$. But this conjunction is not to be analysed truth-functionally in terms of the disjunction of quantum-theoretical contradictions: $(P . M_1) \lor (P . M_2) \lor \ldots \lor (P . M_n)$. Putnam's own attitude to the proposal is that failure of these laws should be accepted simply as a consequence of certain empirical facts, and that laws of logic are in principle empirical statements, though further from immediate experience than, say, the laws of physics. Against such views, Popper (*OK*, pp. 305-6) argues that (a) we should always use the strongest possible logic when we criticize a theory in order to make our criticism as strong as possible (and that any resulting 'anomalies' should be taken as counting against the theories or interpretations involved); and hence that (b) logic is not up for revision in the light of experience. On point (b), Haack (1974, pp. 37-8) has suggested that part of what may be behind Popper's position here is that, on the demarcation criterion, logic is not part of empirical science (because unfalsifiable) and should not be altered on the grounds suggested by Putnam, because to do so would be to impede the progress of science. But, of course, Putnam's point is just to question Popper's reason for demarcating logic from science in this way.

Nevertheless, against Putnam and in favour of Popper, Dummett (1973, pp. 603-7) has argued convincingly that the empirical significance of a theory requires that we distinguish between the content of a theory and logical principles under which consequences are to be derived from its content (p. 605):

If, now, when an antinomy appears to be derivable from some theory, it is to be licit to treat this as casting doubt, not on the theory, but on the principles under which consequences are to be derived, we can no longer feel that we know what significance any scientific theory has, or what accepting it as correct amounts to.

So, we must see a distinction between those parts of a theory which are directly empirical and those parts which are involved in elucidating the meanings and consequences of the terms of the theory. In rejecting the laws of distribution in quantum physics, Putnam must be understood to be using 'and' and 'or' in deviant (non-truth-functional) ways. Having said all this, however, it is far from obvious that there could not be empirical reasons for doing this, if, for example, we thought our subject matter had the peculiar properties of quantum phenomena. Provided that the quantum logician is prepared to specify the ways in which he now intends to derive consequences from the statements of this theory, its empirical content will be clearly defined, in the sense that we will know in advance what is to count against it. Because its empirical content is now clearly defined, it is hard to see why the theory is any less *criticizable* than a theory employing classical logic, although classical logic with its fully realistic implications regarding distribution and the law of excluded middle and so on may appeal on other grounds. Indeed, Popper's own espousal of classical logic does lead him to reject the interpretation of quantum physics that would rule out simultaneous ascriptions of position and momenta to particles, but, as I argued in chapter VII, the analysis of the experiments that he uses to back this up and his own interpretation of the phenomena remain, from a quantum-theoretical point of view, inconclusive.

The examples I have been considering here tell against the third interpretation of Platonism, because they suggest that choices in logic and mathematics can be made to fit our pre-systematic intuitions and even, in the case of quantum physics, World 1 realities. This is not to deny that a system may surprise us, but only to say that we are not bound to hold to particular systems in logic and mathematics, any more than we are prevented from altering the rules of games to cope with unwelcome developments. Although a game has rules, it does not thereby transcend and control the human beings who play it, because they can change the rules if they wish. What I want to suggest by these admittedly controversial examples is that the fact that systems in mathematics and logic can have surprising consequences is not enough to establish Popperian Platonism in the sense of (3), and that we do not need to adopt an extreme constructivist position to argue against Popper here. Platonism in mathematics and logic is better argued for along the lines suggested by Bernays, but this is not Popper's way, nor does it appeal to the mere existence of unexpected consequences in mathematics. So, in logic and mathematics, Popperian Platonism is far from conclusively established. But, even if it could be strengthened here, it by no means follows that he is justified in drawing World 3 conclusions from similar arguments applied to scientific theories, artistic styles, institutions or values.

Popper says that artistic aims and standards may 'like the rules of logic . . . become exosomatic systems of control' (*OK*, p. 254); that theoretical systems, problems and problem situations are inmates of World 3 (*OK*, p. 107); that values, in being criticized and discussed, belong to World 3 ('IA', p. 154; *UQ*, p. 194); and that institutions, too, though man-made, 'have a certain degree of autonomy' and 'belong to World 3' ('RC', p. 1116). This last point conflicts with his earlier methodological individualism and is more holistic than the position I put forward in chapter VIII. I argued there that membership of social groups made the possession of certain aims logically possible (and that therefore an individualistic psychology could not explain the aims of individuals). This seemed to go beyond Popper's individualism, in which the relationship of an individual to his society appeared to be one of external influence. Both Popper and I were agreed, however, that what happened in society was due to individual actions and their consequences (and hence that individuals were ultimately responsible for history), but now Popper apparently envisages that once we have created our institutions they have a degree of autonomous development.

In each of these cases of World 3 existence, the argument is the same: that the development of the entities involved is independent of the hopes, intentions and predictions of their creators. While it is true that we cannot always develop theories, art or institutions in ways we want or can foresee, this is not obviously because they have autonomy in a superhuman realm. Scientific theories and artistic styles are controlled in their development and in the ways they affect us by the facticity of their respective materials (nature and artistic media). Institutions, too, clash in various ways with the human beings who come into contact with them and with other institutions. Saying that they have unintended and unsuspected consequences need not in itself imply that they develop autonomously, but only, as Popper himself argued (*PH*), that the individuals who man them do not understand enough about the consequences of their actions. Our theories, styles and institutions do not take on a life beyond our control just because we cannot initially foresee where they will lead, any more than this would put any World I products with unforeseen consequences (such as motorways) in World 3. Their future development is still dependent on the conjunction of what we do with them and the materials involved, that is, on World 1 and World 2 factors.

Many of the results of human activity are unforeseen (and even unforeseeable). This includes the ways our theories, institutions and arts develop. Also these are characteristically collective products, not analysable in terms of the dispositions or activity of single individuals. Because of these facts, it is undeniably possible to think of them developing apart from the human thought and behaviour from which they spring and in which they live. But this thought is merely a possibility, for the facts on which it is based do not show that the development in question is independent of what human beings think or do and subject to its own laws and necessity. Moreover, this way of thinking – far distant from methodological individualism – may very well lead, as Marx said, to a situation in which people's 'own social action takes the form of the action of objects, which rule the producers instead of being ruled by them'.

The Marxist objection to seeing human institutions and processes as governed and controlled by inhuman laws is two-fold. On the one hand, such a perspective is misleading. What *we* have created is made to look like a purely natural or physical phenomenon, to be analysed in terms of natural necessities. On the other hand, this perspective leads to a passive attitude to what are, after all, our own creations. Lukács sums the situation up (1971, p. 131) as follows:

All human relations . . . assume increasingly the objective forms
of the abstract elements of the conceptual systems of natural
science and of the abstract substrata of the laws of nature. And
also, the subject of this 'action' likewise assumes increasingly
the attitude of the pure observer of these – artificially abstract –
processes, the attitude of the experimenter.

It is not necessary to accept the Marxist view that this type of false consciousness is peculiar to capitalist society or to decry social engineering in favour of historicistically inspired revolution to see the force of this objection to placing our social and artistic institutions in an inhuman realm. It is precisely when we see an institution as having to develop in its own way, beyond our control that the alienating quality of World 3 emerges. To quote Lukács again (1971, p. XXIV):

Only when the objectified forms in society acquire functions
that bring the essence of man into conflict with his existence,
only when man's nature is subjugated, deformed and crippled
can we speak of an objective societal condition of alienation
and, as an inexorable consequence, of all the subjective marks
of an internal alienation.

I take this to be saying that it is when we allow our institutions to take on lives of their own, seemingly independent of and possibly contrary to our wishes, desires or control (i.e., from Popper's point of view, flourishing in World 3), that we need to be reminded that they are ultimately only ours, based in our ways of thinking and behaving, and controllable by us if we have the will to take control of them.

One of Popper's underlying motivations for introducing a World 3 is undoubtedly to persuade us to look at human activity in all fields in terms of the problems and traditions in relation to which it is undertaken, rather than in terms of the states of mind of the agents. Against the view that art is a matter of self-expression, Popper will urge us to look at artistic works as the artist's attempt to grapple with his materials in a historically conditioned context, in terms of the schema:

Problem 1 $\rightarrow$ Tentative Solution $\rightarrow$ Error Elimination $\rightarrow$ Problem 2.

However, although this scheme asserts one totality (that of an action and its problem), Popper tends to use it to play down another: the totality of human beings together with their institutions. It is perhaps because he overlooks this that it is easy for him to think of World 3 autonomy of knowledge and institutions.

Certainly the thought experiments used by Popper (*OK*, pp. 107–8) to establish the independent existence of World 3 do not show that it is capable of autonomous development. In the first experiment, all our machines, tools and subjective knowledge of how to use them is destroyed, but not our libraries or our capacity to learn from them. In the second, our machines, tools and knowledge of how to use them is destroyed as before, and also our libraries. In the first case, civilization will re-emerge after some pain, but in the second, because the libraries are destroyed, any such re-emergence will take many millennia. The conclusion is that this shows the reality, significance and autonomy of the objective knowledge stored in the libraries. But it could equally well be argued that the experiments point to the uselessness of what is stored in libraries, independent of the ability people have to use them (which, significantly, is preserved in the first experiment). Outside the context of the specific human life and reactions in which it makes sense, all that libraries contain is a mass of undeciphered scripts. Be this as it may, the experiments singularly fail to show any degree of autonomy of human behaviour in the knowledge stored, for libraries do not develop on their own at all. Even if they were to contain computers endlessly printing out tables of logarithms (to take one of Popper s examples), there is no suggestion that any of the new facts appearing on the print-outs have emerged independently of the computer programmes, whose genesis, we have suggested, can be explained in World 1 and World 2 terms. Nor would someone not otherwise attracted to mathematical Platonism be convinced that World 3 transcends its own encodings ('RC', p. 1050), because it 'incorporates' an infinite series of natural numbers. For an intuitionist or constructivist, the theorem that every number has a successor (mentioned by

Popper in support of this claim) in no way demonstrates the actual existence of a completed infinity. The theorem itself, for the intuitionist, is a mental construction, something in World 2.

To sum up: the argument from the unintended consequences of ideas and institutions to their autonomous existence in World 3 is (even in the mathematical case) inconclusive. This is because it is not clear that the logical development of Popper's World 3 entities requires appeal to a Platonic realm, or that the control they exercise over us is independent of the ways they relate to the physical or human world, and the ways we actually develop them. The arguments involving the causal effects and the abstract nature of World 3 bring with them a host of unanswered problems. It is certainly possible and sometimes useful to think of our ideas abstractly, and to analyse their development in isolation from human behaviour, but to abstract them totally from their human context and to suggest that they rule us rather than vice versa is not only not required by the facts, but it can also have a deeply alienating effect.

4 *The self-conscious mind*

Popper sees the self-conscious mind as an evolutionary product of the human brain, but transcending it, so that we have to see it actively directing and assessing brain processes. In *The Self and Its Brain*, he takes this idea literally: it is the mind that decodes the coded information about the visual field received from the retina and on this basis forms expectations about the world and prepares to act in the world (pp. 476–7); the mind or the self controls the brain, particularly on those occasions when we see an optical illusion and are aware that what we are seeing is an illusion (p. 515); we can also switch at will the way we 'read' a particular illusory figure (p. 99). I have already criticized the decoding analysis of perception. While some of my criticisms are answered by saying that it is the mind that does the decoding, the idea of an immaterial mind interacting with the material brain brings up problems of its own, familiar enough since Cartesian days, some of which we have already encountered in considering the interaction between Worlds 1, 2 and 3. Apart from this, it is not clear that the facts about the perception of illusions which Popper appeals to here have to be explained by introducing the idea of an immaterial self controlling the brain. Popper considers and dismisses an explanation in terms of hierarchies of control within the brain itself (*SB*, p. 515), but it is unclear what his reasons are for this, especially as he later suggests that the achievements involved in re-reading an illusory figure correctly are eventually encoded in the brain (p. 523).

The hypothesis of an active, immaterial self interacting with the material world is the climax of Popper's insistence, against inductivists, on our active imposition of theoretical structures on the data of experience. But what now, above all, imposes on the material world and our frontier with it is a self which 'plays on the brain, as a pianist plays on a piano or as a driver plays on the controls of a car' (*SB*, p. 495). The remarks about illusion are perhaps best seen in this context, not as a less than conclusive proof of Popper's hypothesis about the self, but as an illustration of it, an illustration which indeed brings out some of the problematic aspects of his picture. For he is not simply pointing here to the fact of consciousness and to our ability to switch our attention so as to look at illusions in different ways; he is exploiting this fact to elaborate a full-blooded Cartesianism. (Indeed, there is even a Popperian equivalent of the pineal gland, when he speaks (*SB*, p. 495) of a liaison brain as both the result and the area of interaction between the brain and the self.) What is difficult, though challenging, about Popper's contribution to *The Self and Its Brain* is that in it Popper continually writes as though interactionist dualism were the only viable alternative to crude materialism.

He does indeed show how some familiar theses are either directly or covertly materialistic, and as such fail to do justice to the facts of consciousness. Thus materialistic attempts to analyse consciousness in purely physical or behavioural terms have problems with explaining the fact of actual feeling which we experience, and which underlies its behavioural manifestations. They also fail to account for the way ideas in our mind influence and control our behaviour. Panpsychism and epiphenomenalism, on the other hand, admit that there is such a thing as consciousness, but try to explain it away. The one does so by attributing mind, or the vestiges of mind, to the whole of matter, but this is brought into question, as we have seen, by the lack of any analogue of memory at the atomic level. The other maintains that conscious processes are only a reflection of material processes. In this it has some affinity to another familiar proposal, that of the identity theory, which maintains that conscious processes actually are material processes. Popper criticizes both epiphenomenalism and the identity theory for being able to give us no good Darwinian reason for consciousness. For, on both accounts, it is physical processes considered as such, subject to the normal all-encompassing physical laws, which provide us with the ultimate reason for the occurrence of conscious processes. The mental reflections or conscious aspects of the physical events thus have no genuine influence on what happens, and so no biological function.

So, assuming for the sake of argument that there is no materialist counter to these points, how are we to explain the existence and effectiveness of the mind? Popper opts for a fully Cartesian self, a 'ghost in the machine', as he admits, and is apparently prepared to dismiss problems involved with mental–physical interactionism as being based on long-superseded views of causation and physical determinism (cf. *CR*, p. 298). It is difficult to know how to deal with this aspect of Popper's thesis, as he spends no time at all considering the well-known philosophical objections to the 'ghost in the machine' canvassed by Ryle (1949), Wittgenstein (1958), Melden (1960), and so many others. The objections I have in mind are not against the idea that one is sometimes conscious of oneself, but against the driver in the car view of the self. One such objection (due directly to Melden, but analogous to points made earlier here about immaterial acts of judgment) arises because we can give no account of the alleged volitional activity of the self without reference to relevant bodily phenomena. As such, whatever role talk of doing something because one has willed it may play in our lives, it is not to assert a causal relationship between the action of an (immaterial) driver and his vehicle. A materialist, who held that volitions were events in the brain, could avoid this objection by saying that in principle they could be identified as such, rather than as mental acts characterizable only in terms of their physical effects, and that they were thus identifiable independently of the actions they caused, but this way out is clearly not open to Popper or anyone who holds that they are essentially immaterial. Here the connection between volition and act is a logical one, not due merely to the way we happen to describe the events. Another type of difficulty (due perhaps to Wittgenstein) would be the problem of knowing other essentially incorporeal selves and the weaknesses of any arguments from analogy, from my (single) case to that of others. Simply to point to the fact that we do assume that we speak to people rather than to machines (as Popper does in *CR*, p. 297) is not enough to show that we could get to this assumption only if we were all Cartesian selves. What these and other problems have led many to do is to argue that, however we are to look at human beings and their thoughts and their probable irreducibility to the laws of physics, seeing them as immaterial minds, causally operative in bodies, is bound to be unsatisfactory.

Rather than echoing familiar objections to Cartesian selves, it would be better to turn to the two positive reasons Popper gives for them, both of which come unsurprisingly from language, which Popper sees as biologically our highest function, giving us an entry to an immaterial World 3 of objectively criticizable theories. The first argument is based on what Popper takes to be the inadequacy of a materialistic account of language. He argues (*CR*, pp. 297–8) that naming is not merely a matter of a speaker or a hearer associating a sound with an object but that there must be some intention to use it, and more generally that when we listen to others we assume that they mean what they say. What Popper insists on is that the use of language is based on intentions in speakers and hearers. Even if this were correct, it has still to be shown that talk of intentions has to be explained in a mentalistic or Cartesian spirit, before it would provide any support for Popper's talk of selves. Wittgenstein (1958) gives powerful arguments against thinking of meaning as involving mentalistic intentions behind the words. Apart from this, however, against Popper's argument here, it would surely be enough to suggest that if, in all his linguistic behaviour, someone uses language properly, there is no room to ask if, over and above his behaviour, he is also intending to use his words with the correct senses.

Popper's second (and main) line of argument (*SB*, pp. 75–81) in favour of Cartesian selves is to appeal to the way our linguistic behaviour is directly based in World 3 and in so doing he gives a slightly different argument for World 3. The invocation of World 3 here is undoubtedly one powerful factor in Popper's advocacy of an immaterial self. He argues in effect that materialism is a self-defeating position, because any attempt to define it presupposes notions such as truth and validity of argument, which cannot be explained in materialistic terms. He concedes that a machine can operate in accordance with (say) the laws of logic, and even that we might be conditioned to reason and act intelligently; what he wants to deny is that logic and rationality can be explained in World 1 terms.

Against this, he envisages a materialistic opponent arguing that our adoption of logical rules was to be analysed in terms of their usefulness to us. The materialist admits that logical standards exist, but that they do so as states or dispositions of people's brains, and that the standards are particular ways of linking statements that have been found useful in the struggle for existence. Popper's reply here (which would tell equally against someone who also wanted to see logic as a tool, but in terms of World 2 as well as World 1) is to deny that all logical inferences are useful. Sometimes (often) valid inferences are trivial and uninformative (*SB*, p. 80):

> Thus a valid inference always transmits truth, but not always
> usefulness. It cannot therefore be shown that every valid
> inference is a useful instrument, or that the routine of drawing
> valid inferences is as such always useful.

The upshot of the supposed failure at this point of an instrumentalist account of logical inference (such as I supported earlier) is that we have to appeal to World 3 in order to explain our behaviour of argumentation, and that this means that we must ourselves be in our self-conscious minds linked to World 3. But it is unclear that an instrumentalist account of logic is committed to claiming the usefulness of each individual inference, so long as it can be shown that the adoption of the system of rules as a whole is highly useful. This might be done first by showing that it is useful to have a system of rules for general application and then, second, that some particular set is the simplest and most useful so far discovered. We can claim this without having to claim that each particular application of the tool is useful. Indeed, part of the training in its use might even be to understand this and to become proficient in distinguishing between its trivial and its substantial exploitation. (In teaching logic, we may ask students to distinguish between good and valid arguments.)

In so far as Popper's anti-instrumentalist account of logical inference fails to lead beyond practices we have found useful in our World 2 dealings with World 1 to an immaterial World 3, much of the motivation for postulating an immaterial self to communicate with World 3 also evaporates. Popper sees our self-consciousness and our transcendence of the narrowly material as due to our encounters with World 3. In this way we are anchored there; we are enabled to view our theories objectively and exosomatically and to criticize them (this is, in fact, taken to be the main biological function of World 3); we are able to propose to ourselves goals and to act in the light of objective standards and ideals. What is true about this is that the existence in human life of institutions and standards as a background to our actions and behaviour makes it possible for us to go beyond motivation in terms of the instinctive or the narrowly hedonistic, and also gives us a sense in which we may make ourselves responsible for the standards we adopt. Descriptive language with its dual possibilities of correspondence or lack of correspondence with the world makes it possible to draw a distinction in individual cases between the true and the useful. Our consideration here of the anti-materialistic arguments from language serve only to reinforce the conclusion of the last section, that none of these facts need World 3 explanation; in this way, what Popper says about the immaterial self serves only to underline our objections to World 3, and in so doing removes any need from that angle for talk of an immaterial self. The problem of giving an adequate account of human consciousness and institutions which avoids the pitfalls of a crude materialism or an obscure dualism remains, but it cannot be said that Popper has made dualism any clearer.

Conclusion: Popper's Scepticism

There is a good case for thinking of Popper as a systematic thinker. That is to say, his thought hangs together to form a coherent account of knowledge, life and society. Although he presents detailed arguments to support the various particular positions he wishes to defend, his overall attitude is largely determined and his individual theses are coloured by his initial characterization of theories as guesses to be weeded out by criticism from theorists or the environment. This characterization pushes in two ways. It pushes downwards into the world of natural selection and develops into an epistemological Darwinism in which even sense organs and their observations are analysed as embryonic scientific theories. It pushes upwards into the social world, in which society itself is viewed optimally as a community of scientist-like individuals engaged in falsifying their theories, and on into the abstract World 3 of objective knowledge. Rationality itself is seen as the critical approach to whatever subject matter one is involved in, while indeterminism at the level of both matter and knowledge provides the conditions for the imaginative invention and application of theories.

Yet, hovering over the picture and entering it at every point is Popper's deep scepticism. This is the other side of the rejection of justificationism. Theories are bold guesses, and what success they have cannot be underwritten. Everything, from the 'observations' of the amoeba to the theories on the basis of which we build bridges and send craft to the moon, is riddled with uncertainty (*LSD*, p. 280):

Bold ideas, unjustified anticipations, and speculative thought,
are our only means for interpreting nature: our only organon, our
only instrument, for grasping her. And we must hazard them
to win our prize. Those among us who are unwilling to expose

their ideas to the hazard of refutation do not take part in the scientific game.

Science is a game, like evolution itself. Perhaps science is the ultimate evolutionary game. All the security that Popper feels able to give us is the security of knowing that we are playing a well-entrenched game. We have no guarantee, from any level of our experience, that our games correspond to reality.

And yet, Popper remains an objectivist, an implacable opponent of relativism and irrationalism. Is he choosing the right targets for the weapons he has? We should not be blinded here by his talk of World 3 as a world of *objective* knowledge, nor by his appeals to Tarski's theory of truth, which Popper regards as having rehabilitated the correspondence theory of truth (from paradoxes involved in the notion of truth). He claims that, because we can now safely see truth in terms of correspondence, we may without hesitation speak of theories as being absolutely speaking true or false, and so view them realistically. It is far from clear that Tarski's definition of truth permits any such conclusion, for his definition is always of truth relativized to a particular language and not of truth as such. Aside from this, however, it is one thing to be told, formally, what it is for the sentences of a given language to be true, and quite another to be in a position to know whether the conditions for truth are ever fulfilled. It is just this, with his insistence on the theoreticality of all statements, that Popper denies us. So even if, through Tarski, and in World 3, theories are either true or false, this information is at most something leading us on. The unattainability of certainty and the provisional nature of all our appraisals of truth mean that Popper can hardly appeal in any effective way to the notion of truth in his grappling with relativists and irrationalists, as we saw in considering the demarcation criterion. If science and rationality are to be defended, it must be by appeal to their moral effects rather than to their truth. Of course, Popper sees this consequence of his views, and ultimately he does defend science on just those grounds, denying that it can claim to have attained truth or probability. But, at the same time, he speaks of it as more than a useful instrument with survival value, as a search for truth, characterizing its theories in terms of verisimilitude. It is as if he wants to soften the effects of his scepticism, and it is undeniable that, without some such softening, few would follow him far.

For Popper, we can never at any level get out of our theoretical structures to attain reality itself. All we have are successions of frameworks. Theory-less reality is a myth. In this, as in his speaking of science as a game, he shares a point of view with the later Wittgenstein. For Wittgenstein, too, there was no direct contact between language and the world, through observation or pointing or anything else, but unlike Popper, he was well aware that speaking of propositions as true or false tells us nothing in abstraction from the ways in which we set about verifying or falsifying them. Certainly it would give us no licence to argue in favour of an optimistic realism about science, itself perhaps the product of an uncritical acceptance of certain scientific ways of speaking and thinking.

Wittgenstein, then, did not attempt to forge an uneasy alliance between a view of language and thought as an enclosed system and talk of a metaphysically realistic search for truth. Instead, he saw part of the task of philosophy as being to outline the frameworks within which we organize our experience. One of my main criticisms of Popper has been his failure to see the extent to which justificationism at both observational and theoretical levels is part of our framework. Popper realizes that transcendent justifications of our practices of knowledge and behaviour are not possible, from the point of view of eternity, but he then proceeds to divide up our practices into those he does approve of (the critical elements) and those he does not (the justificatory elements). In so doing, he is able neither to defend transcendentally the critical elements nor to account for the role played by justification.

In fact, as Putnam has suggested (1974, p. 222), Popper fails to see the role science plays in human life generally:

> When a scientist accepts a law, he is recommending to other men
> that they rely on it – rely on it, often in practical contexts.
> Only by wrenching science altogether out of the context in which
> it really arises – the context of men trying to change and control
> the world – can Popper even put forward his peculiar view on
> induction. Ideas are not *just* ideas; they are guides to action . . .

This is a mistake Wittgenstein would never have made, and it is easy to see how, having torn ideas from their living context, Popper was led both to his radical scepticism and to his postulation of an abstract world of ideas, in which he perhaps finds a promise of the transcendent justification his scepticism is striving for. This is, finally, the root of the dissatisfaction I find with Popper's philosophy: that having failed to find a transcendent justification of our epistemological procedures, he abandons all attempt to distinguish between the relative justifications we are able to provide for our beliefs, or between the levels at which language and theory interact with the world. Nor is the failure of his attempt to reconstruct a system of knowledge in which justification plays no part in any sense rescued by appeal to a non-human realm of pure ideas, for this bold idea rests on extremely shaky foundations.

Bibliography

Note: This bibliography contains only works referred to in the text other than those by Popper. The abbreviation *BJPS* stands for the *British Journal for the Philosophy of Science*.

Ackermann, R. (1976), *The Philosophy of Karl Popper*, University of Massachusetts Press.

Agassi, J. (1975), *Science in Flux*, Reidel, Dordrecht.

Anderson, A. and Belnap, N. (1959), 'A Simple Treatment of Truth Functions', *Journal of Symbolic Logic*, 24, pp. 301–2.

Ayala, F. and Dobzhansky, T. (eds) (1974), *Studies in the Philosophy of Biology*, Macmillan, London.

Ayer, A. (1954), 'Can There be a Private Language?', *Proceedings of the Aristotelian Society*, Supplementary vol. 28, pp. 63–76.

Ayer, A. (1956), *The Problem of Knowledge*, Penguin Books, Harmondsworth.

Ayer, A. (1968), *The Origins of Pragmatism*, Macmillan, London.

Bar-Hillel, Y. (1955), 'Comments on "Degree of Confirmation" by Professor K. R. Popper', *BJPS*, 6, pp. 155–7.

Barker, S. (1965), 'Is There a Problem of Induction?', *American Philosophical Quarterly*, 2, pp. 271–3.

Bartley, W. (1962), *The Retreat to Commitment*, Knopf, New York.

Bartley, W. (1964), 'Rationality versus the Theory of Rationality', in Bunge (1964), pp. 3–31.

Bartley, W. (1968), 'Theories of Demarcation between Science and Metaphysics' and 'Reply' in Lakatos and Musgrave (1968), pp. 40–64, 102–19.

Benacerraf, P. and Putnam, H. (eds) (1964), *Philosophy of Mathematics: Selected Readings*, Prentice-Hall, Englewood Cliffs, N.J.

Bernays, P. (1935), 'On Platonism in Mathematics' (translation of 'Sur le Platonisme dans les mathématiques', in *l'Enseignement mathématique*, 34, pp. 52–69), in Benacerraf and Putnam (1964), pp. 274–86.

Blackburn, S. (1973), *Reason and Prediction*, Cambridge University Press.

Buck, R. and Cohen, R. (eds) (1971), *PSA 1970: In Memory of Rudolph Carnap*, Reidel, Dordrecht.

Bunge, M. (ed.) (1964), *The Critical Approach to Science and Philosophy*, Free Press, Chicago.

Bunge, M. (ed.) (1967), *Quantum Theory and Reality*, Springer, Berlin.

Campbell, D. (1974), 'Evolutionary Epistemology', in Schilpp (1974), pp. 413–63.

Carnap, R. (1962), *Logical Foundations of Probability* (2nd ed.), University of Chicago Press.

Carnap, R. (1963), 'Replies and Systematic Expositions', in Schilpp (1963).

Carnap, R. (1968), 'Inductive Logic and Inductive Intuitions' and reply to critics of the same, in Lakatos (1968b), pp. 258–67, 307–14.

Church, A. (1940), 'On the Concept of a Random Sequence', *Bulletin of the American Mathematical Society*, 46, pp. 130–5.

Cohen, R., Feyerabend, P. and Wartofsky, M. (eds) (1976), *Essays in Memory of Imre Lakatos*, Reidel, Dordrecht.

Cohen, R. and Wartofsky, M. (eds) (1969), Proceedings of the Boston Colloquium for the Philosophy of Science, *Boston Studies in the Philosophy of Science*, vol. 5, Reidel, Dordrecht.

Colodny, R. (ed.) (1965), *Beyond the Edge of Certainty*, Prentice-Hall, Englewood Cliffs, N.J.

Currie, G. (1978), 'Popper's Evolutionary Epistemology: a Critique', *Synthèse*, 37, pp. 413–31.

Davidson, D. (1973), 'Radical Interpretation', *Dialectica*, 27, pp. 313–28.

Davidson, D. (1974), 'Belief and the Basis of Meaning', *Synthèse*, 27, pp. 309–24.

Davidson, D. (1975), 'Thought and Talk', in Guttenplan (1975), pp. 7–23.

Davidson, D. (1977), 'The Method of Truth in Metaphysics', *Midwest Studies in Philosophy*, 2, pp. 244–54.

de Finetti, B. (1964), 'Foresight: Its Logical Laws, Its Subjective Sources', in Kyburg and Smokler (1964), pp. 97–158.

Donagan, A. (1974), 'Popper's Examination of Historicism', in Schillp (1974), pp. 905–24.

Dummett, M. (1973), *Frege, Philosophy of Language*, Duckworth, London.

Eddington, A. (1928), *The Nature of the Physical World*, Cambridge University Press.

Emmet, D. and MacIntyre, A. (eds) (1970), *Sociological Theory and Philosophical Analysis*, Macmillan, London.

Feyerabend, P. (1964), 'Realism and Instrumentalism: Comments on the Logic of Factual Support', in Bunge (1964), pp. 280–308.

Feyerabend, P. (1965), 'Problems of Empiricism', in Colodny (1965), pp. 145–260.

Feyerabend, P. (1968–9), 'On a Recent Critique of Complementarity', *Philosophy of Science*, 35, pp. 309–31 and 36, pp. 82–105.

Feyerabend, P. (1970a), 'Consolations for the Specialist', in Lakatos and Musgrave (1970), pp. 197–230.

Feyerabend, P. (1970b), 'Against Method', in Radner and Winokur (1970), pp. 17–130.

Feyerabend, P. (1974), Review of Popper's *Objective Knowledge* (1972), in *Inquiry*, 17, pp. 475–507.

Gallie, W. (1957), 'The Limits of Prediction', in Körner (1957), pp. 160–4.

Grünbaum, A. (1976a), 'Is Falsifiability the Touchstone of Scientific Rationality? Karl Popper versus Inductivism', in Cohen, Feyerabend and Wartofsky (1976), pp. 213–52.

Grünbaum, A. (1976b), 'Can a Theory Answer More Questions than One of Its Rivals?', *BJPS*, 27, pp. 1–23.

Grünbaum, A. (1976c), 'Is the Method of Bold Conjectures and Attempted Refutations Justifiably the Method of Science?', *BJPS*, 27, pp. 105–36.

Grünbaum, A. (1976d), 'Ad hoc Auxiliary Hypotheses and Falsificationism', *BJPS*, 27, pp. 329–62.

Grünbaum, A. (1979), 'Is Freudian Psycho-Analytic Theory Pseudo-Scientific by Karl Popper's Criterion of Demarcation?', *American Philosophical Quarterly*, 16, pp. 131–41.

Guttenplan, S. (ed.) (1975), *Mind and Language*, Clarendon Press, Oxford.

Haack, S. (1974), *Deviant Logic*, Cambridge University Press.

Harré, R. (ed.) (1975), *Problems of Scientific Revolution*, Clarendon Press, Oxford.

Harris, J. (1974), 'Popper's Definitions of "Verisimilitude"', *BJPS*, 25, pp. 160–6.

Horton, R. (1967), 'African Traditional Thought and Western Science', *Africa*, 37, pp. 50–71, 155–87 (reprinted in Young, 1971).

Howson, C. (1973), 'Must the Logical Probability of Laws be Zero?', *BJPS*, 24, pp. 153–63.

Hume, D. (1888), *A Treatise of Human Nature* (ed. L. Selby-Bigge), Clarendon Press, Oxford.

Katz, D. (1953), *Animals and Men*, Penguin Books, Harmondsworth.

Körner, S. (ed.) (1957), *Observation and Interpretation*, Butterworth Scientific, London.

Kuhn, T. (1962), *The Structure of Scientific Revolutions*, University of Chicago Press.

Kuhn, T. (1970a), 'Logic of Discovery or Psychology of Research?', in Lakatos and Musgrave (1970), pp. 1–23.

Kuhn, T. (1970b), 'Reflections on my Critics', in Lakatos and Musgrave (1970), pp. 231–78.

Kyburg, H. and Smokler, H. (eds) (1964), *Studies in Subjective Probability*, Wiley, New York.

Lakatos, I. (1963–4), 'Proofs and Refutations', *BJPS*, 14, pp. 1–25, 120–39, 221–43, 296–342.

Lakatos, I. (1968a), 'Changes in the Problem of Inductive Logic', in Lakatos (1968b), pp. 315–417.

Lakatos, I. (ed.) (1968b), *The Problem of Inductive Logic*, North Holland, Amsterdam.

Lakatos, I. (1970), 'Falsification and the Methodology of Scientific Research Programmes', in Lakatos and Musgrave (1970), pp. 91–195.

Lakatos, I. (1971), 'History of Science and Its Rational Reconstructions', in Buck and Cohen (1971), pp. 91–182.

Lakatos, I. (1974), 'Popper on Demarcation and Induction', in Schilpp (1974), pp. 241–73.

Lakatos, I. and Musgrave, A. (eds) (1968), *Problems in the Philosophy of Science*, North Holland, Amsterdam.

Lakatos, I. and Musgrave, A. (eds) (1970), *Criticism and the Growth of Knowledge*, Cambridge University Press.

Lukács, G. (1971), *History and Class Consciousness* (trans. by R. Livingstone of new ed.), Merlin Press, London.

Lukes, S. (1968), 'Methodological Individualism Reconsidered', *British Journal of Sociology*, 19, pp. 119–29.

Malcolm, N. (1963), *Knowledge and Certainty*, Cornell University Press.

Melden, A. (1960), 'Willing', *Philosophical Review*, 69, pp. 475–84.

Mellor, D. (1971), *The Matter of Chance*, Cambridge University Press.

Michalos, A. (1971), *The Popper–Carnap Controversy*, Martinus Nijhoff, The Hague.

Mill, J. S. (1887), *A System of Logic* (8th ed.), Harper, New York.

Miller, D. (1974), 'Popper's Qualitative Theory of Verisimilitude', *BJPS*, 25, pp. 166–77.

Miller, D. (1975), 'The Accuracy of Predictions', *Synthèse*, 30, pp. 159–91.

Miller, D. (1978), 'The Distance between Constituents', *Synthèse*, 38, pp. 197–212.

Mott, P. (1978), 'Verisimilitude by Means of Short Theorems', *Synthèse*, 38, pp. 247–73.

Musgrave, A. (1974), 'The Objectivism of Popper's Epistemology', in Schilpp (1974), pp. 560–96.

Musgrave, A. (1975), 'Popper and "Diminishing Returns from Repeated Tests"', *Australasian Journal of Philosophy*, 53, pp. 248–53.

Niiniluoto, I. (1978), 'Truthlikeness: Comments on Recent Discussions', *Synthèse*, 38, pp. 281–329.

O'Hear, A. (1975), 'Rationality of Action and Theory-Testing in Popper', *Mind*, 84, pp. 273–6.

Putnam, H. (1969), 'Is Logic Empirical?', in Cohen and Wartofsky (1969), pp. 216–41.

Putnam, H. (1974), 'The "Corroboration" of Theories', in Schilpp (1974), pp. 221–40.

Putnam, H. (1976), 'What is Realism?', *Proceedings of the Aristotelian Society*, 77, pp. 176–94.

Quine, W. V. O. (1960), *Word and Object*, MIT Press.

Radner, M. and Winokur, S. (eds) (1970), *Analyses of Theories and Methods of Physics and Psychology*, Minnesota Studies in the Philosophy of Science, vol. 4, University of Minnesota Press.

Rosenkrantz, R. (1975), 'Truthlikeness: Comments on David Miller', *Synthese*, 30, pp. 193–7.

Ryle, G. (1949), *The Concept of Mind*, Hutchinson, London.

Salmon, W. (1967), *The Foundations of Scientific Inference*, University of Pittsburgh Press.

Schilpp, P. (ed.) (1963), *The Philosophy of Rudolph Carnap*, Open Court, La Salle, Illinois.

Schilpp, P. (ed.) (1974), *The Philosophy of Karl Popper*, 2 vols, Open Court, La Salle, Illinois.

Schutz, A. (1970), 'Concept and Theory-Formation in the Social Sciences', in Emmet and MacIntyre (1970), pp. 1–19.

Settle, T. (1974), 'Induction and Probability Unfused', in Schilpp (1974), pp. 697–749.

Settle, T. (1977), 'Popper versus Peirce on the Probability of Single Cases', *BJPS*, 28, pp. 177–80.

Stebbing, S. (1937), *Philosophy and the Physicists*, Penguin Books, Harmondsworth.

Stroud, B. (1969), 'Conventionalism and Indeterminacy of Translation', *Synthèse*, 19, pp. 82–96.

Tichý, P. (1974), 'On Popper's Definitions of Verisimilitude', *BJPS*, 25, pp. 155–60.

Tichý, P. (1978), 'Verisimilitude Revisited', *Synthèse*, 38, pp. 175–96.

Watkins, J. (1968), 'Hume, Carnap and Popper', in Lakatos (1968b), pp. 271–82.

Watkins, J. (1974), 'The Unity of Popper's Thought', in Schilpp (1974), pp. 371–412.

Winch, P. (1963), *The Idea of a Social Science* (3rd imp.), Routledge & Kegan Paul, London.

Winch, P. (1974), 'Popper and Scientific Methods in the Social Sciences', in Schilpp (1974), pp. 889–904.

Wittgenstein, L. (1958), *Philosophical Investigations* (2nd ed.), Blackwell, Oxford.

Wittgenstein, L. (1967), *Remarks on the Foundations of Mathematics* (2nd ed.), Blackwell, Oxford.

Wittgenstein, L. (1968), 'Notes for Lectures on Private Experience and "Sense Data"', *Philosophical Review*, 77, pp. 271–320.

Wittgenstein, L. (1969), *The Blue and Brown Books* (2nd ed.), Blackwell, Oxford.

Young, M. (ed.) (1971), *Knowledge and Control*, Collier-Macmillan, London.

Index